NEUROLIBERALISM

Many governments in the developed world can now best be described as 'neuroliberal': having a combination of neoliberal principles with policy initiatives derived from insights in the behavioural sciences.

Neuroliberalism presents the results of the first critical global study of the impacts of the behavioural sciences on public policy and government actions, including behavioural economics, behavioural psychology and neuroeconomics. Drawing on interviews with leading behaviour change experts, organizations and policy-makers, and discussed in alignment with a series of international case studies, this volume provides a critical analysis of the ethical, economic, political and constitutional implications of behaviourally oriented government. It explores the impacts of the behavioural sciences on everyday life through a series of themes, including: understandings of the human subject; interpretations of freedom; the changing form and function of the state; the changing role of the corporation in society; and the design of everyday environments and technologies.

The research presented in this volume reveals a diverse set of neuroliberal approaches to government that offer policy-makers and behaviour change professionals a real choice in relation to the systems of behavioural government they can implement. This book also argues that the behavioural sciences have the potential to support much more effective systems of government, but also generate new ethical concerns that policy-makers should be aware of.

Mark Whitehead is Professor of Human Geography at Aberystwyth University, UK.

Rhys Jones is Professor and Head of Department (Geography) at Aberystwyth University, UK.

Rachel Lilley is a behaviour change and mindfulness consultant and PhD candidate at Aberystwyth University, UK.

Jessica Pykett is Senior Lecturer in Human Geography at the University of Birmingham, UK.

Rachel Howell is Lecturer in Sociology and Sustainable Development at the University of Edinburgh, UK.

Economics in the Real World

For a full more information on this series, please visit www.routledge.com/Economics-in-the-Real-World/book-series/ERW

1. Education Is Not an App
The Future of University Teaching in the Internet Age
Jonathan A. Poritz and Jonathan Rees

2. The Privileges of Wealth
Rising Inequality and the Growing Racial Divide
Robert B. Williams

3. Neuroliberalism
Behavioural Government in the Twenty-First Century
Mark Whitehead, Rhys Jones, Rachel Lilley, Jessica Pykett and Rachel Howell

NEUROLIBERALISM

Behavioural Government
in the Twenty-First Century

*Mark Whitehead, Rhys Jones, Rachel Lilley,
Jessica Pykett and Rachel Howell*

Routledge
Taylor & Francis Group

LONDON AND NEW YORK

First published 2018
by Routledge
2 Park Square, Milton Park, Abingdon, Oxon, OX14 4RN

and by Routledge
711 Third Avenue, New York, NY 10017

Routledge is an imprint of the Taylor & Francis Group, an informa business

© 2018 Mark Whitehead, Rhys Jones, Rachel Lilley, Jessica Pykett and
Rachel Howell

The right of Mark Whitehead, Rhys Jones, Rachel Lilley, Jessica Pykett,
and Rachel Howell to be identified as authors of this work has been
asserted by them in accordance with sections 77 and 78 of the Copyright,
Designs and Patents Act 1988.

British Library Cataloguing-in-Publication Data
A catalogue record for this book is available from the British Library

Library of Congress Cataloging-in-Publication Data
Names: Whitehead, Mark, 1975- editor.
Title: Neuroliberalism : behavioural government in the twenty first century
/ Mark Whitehead, [and four others].
Description: Abingdon, Oxon ; New York, NY : Routledge, 2017. |
Includes bibliographical references and index.
Identifiers: LCCN 2017014361 | ISBN 9781138923829 (hardback) |
ISBN 9781138923836 (pbk.) | ISBN 9781315684772 (ebook)
Subjects: LCSH: Economic policy--Psychological aspects. | Liberalism--
Psychological aspects. | Neoliberalism--Psychological aspects. | Political
psychology. | Economics--Psychological aspects.
Classification: LCC HD87 .N47 2017 | DDC 320.01/9--dc23
LC record available at https://lccn.loc.gov/2017014361

ISBN: 978-1-138-92382-9 (hbk)
ISBN: 978-1-138-92383-6 (pbk)
ISBN: 978-1-315-68477-2 (ebk)

Typeset in Bembo
by Saxon Graphics Ltd, Derby

CONTENTS

ILLUSTRATIONS

Figures

Tables

Box

ACKNOWLEDGEMENTS

This volume is not simply the product of the authors whose names are found on the front cover. This book is the outcome of a series of acts of support, generosity, inspiration, kindness and understanding that have been extended to us as researchers and writers over the last eight years. The research presented in this volume is the product of three interconnected projects that were generously funded by the Leverhulme Trust (*The Time Spaces of Soft Paternalism in the UK*: F/00 424/L) and the Economic and Social Research Council (UK) (*Negotiating Neuroliberalism: Changing Behaviours, Values and Beliefs*: ES/L003082/1; and *Mindfulness, Behaviour Change and Psychological Capital*). These projects enabled us to conduct over one hundred in-depth interviews and run a series of trials, which have informed and shaped the arguments that are presented in the pages that follow. While we cannot mention by name all of those whom we interviewed (for both practical and ethical reasons), we would like to thank them all for opening their doors (or Skype portals) to us. Without their invaluable insights and perspectives this volume would be much diminished.

We would like to particularly acknowledge the help and inspiration of five organizations: Corporate Culture; Global Action Plan; the Welsh Government; Ogilvy Change; and the Social Brain Centre. While we talk about the work of these organizations later in this volume, they supported our work in particularly important ways. At an individual level we would like to mention six individuals who offered particularly valuable forms of support to our work. John Drummond of Corporate Culture, Tom Veitch of Global Action Plan, Jez Groom, of Ogilvy Change, and Jonathan Rowson of the Social Brain Centre were invaluable 'industry insiders' who supported and trusted us when they really had no reason to do so. Diana Reynolds and Emma Small of the Welsh Government believed in our work when many wouldn't have, and facilitated the mindfulness and behavioural insights trials we recount in Chapter 9. Diana and Emma also served on a project steering committee that guided some of the research on which this volume is based. We would also like to acknowledge the support offered by other members of that steering committee: Alison Armstrong, Chris Baker, and Kayleigh van Oorschot. Your collective insights and advice were a great source of encouragement for us all.

This volume has also benefited greatly from the insights of fellow academics and writers. We would like to mention in particular Ben Anderson; David Berreby; Maria Fannin; Martin Burgess; Will Davies; J. D. Dewsbury; Kathryn Ecklestone; Osian Elias; Liz Gagen; Matt Hannah; Jesse Heley; Gareth Hoskins; Peter John; Rhys D. Jones; Peter Merriman; Will Leggett; Joe Painter; Steve Pile; Mitch Rose; Mike Woods; and Sophie Wynne-Jones. We have benefited greatly from being able to share our ideas with you, and from your perceptive insights into the work we have conducted. While writing this book we were also fortunate enough to co-host a series of five ESRC seminars on the theme of *Behaviour Change and Psychological Governance* (grant number: ES/L003082/1). We would like to thank the co-organizers of these seminars and the numerous presenters who inspired us with their ideas.

Finally we would like to thank the team at Routledge, and in particular Laura Johnson and Andy Humphries, for their great enthusiasm for this book and their support in the production process.

This book is dedicated to our friends and families.

ABBREVIATIONS

BIT	Behavioural Insights Team
CBT	Cognitive Behavioural Therapy
CSC	Civil Service College
ISM	Individual/Social/Material
MBCT	Mindfulness Based Cognitive Therapy
MBSR	Mindfulness Based Stress Relief
MDBI	Mindfulness, Decision Making, and Behaviour Change Intervention
NESTA	National Endowment for Science Technology and the Arts
NPM	New Public Management
NSMC	National Social Marketing Centre
OIRA	Office of Information and Regulatory Affairs
POP	Practice-oriented participatory (backcasting)
RCT	Randomized controlled trials
RMO	Dutch Council for Social Development
RSA	Royal Society for the Encouragement of Arts, Manufactures and Commerce
SBC	Social Brain Centre
SBST	Social and Behavioural Sciences Team
SRL	Self-Regulation Lab
WRR	Scientific Council for Government Policy, Netherlands

1

NEUROLIBERALISM

Introduction

It is normally advised that when choosing the title of a book you should adopt one of two strategies. Your first is to select something that is immediately arresting: *Discipline and Punish* perhaps, or even better, *The End of History and the Last Man*. These are titles that seem to compel a potential reader to pick up a book and find out what it is all about. The other option is to lace your book title with well-known terms and concepts: in the 1990s that may have been *globalization* or *social capital*, in the 2000s *climate change*, *resilience* and *security*. What you absolutely should not do is burden your book with a title that very few people have ever heard of, and that many may even have trouble pronouncing. So, neuroliberalism ...

Government and the behavioural sciences

The idea of neuroliberalism is the central focus of this volume and as with all neologisms it requires some provisional explanation. Most simply, we use neuroliberalism to refer to *the use of behavioural, psychological and neurological insights to deliberately shape and govern human conduct within free societies*. There are three aspects of neuroliberalism that we want to highlight at this point. First, neuroliberalism is, in part, based upon emerging insights into the role of the central nervous system (and in particular the brain) within the constitution of human decision making and social life (Damasio, 1996). Recent advances in the neurosciences now afford us opportunities to see the brain and its role in social and biological life in ways that were previously unimaginable (Rose and Abi-Rached, 2013). But, in keeping with much contemporary work within the behavioural sciences, we use the prefix neuro to refer to more than the brain, neuron, spinal cord and nervous system. For us the zone of the neuro spans the science of *neurology* and the psychology of *neurosis*: it is in effect the meeting place of brain, mind and behaviour. This volume is framed by recent developments within the neurological, psychological and broader behavioural sciences, which have demonstrated that actually existing human behaviour is conducted in ways that are very different from the popular assumptions we hold. While as humans we like to cling to the myth that our behaviour is the product of well informed, deliberative and well-balanced decision making (or rationality), the sciences of behaviour are telling us something quite different.

Neuroliberalism denotes the arrival of a more complex (and certainly more complicating) vision of the human within various schemes of government- and conduct-shaping activities. These schemes of human government can be seen everywhere: the voting booth and the supermarket, in the tax office and on Facebook, in job centres and the driving seat of your car. The vision of the human condition on which these schemes are based comprehends behaviour as more than individual acts of calculated self-interest and strategy, and recognizes the vital role of emotional responses (including joy, suspicion, love, anger, relief, anxiety) habits, intuition, social norms, behavioural heuristics, group mimicry inter alia, within human life. Furthermore, neuroliberalism is characterized by an appreciation of the role of the automatic, unconscious and involuntary within human action, and an ability to be able to predict, respond, regulate, enhance and exploit these behavioural vectors. On these terms, neuroliberalism seeks to govern in and through aspects of human behaviour that have previously been seen as either insignificant or unknowable aspects of social life.

Neuroliberalism and freedom

The second aspect of neuroliberalism that we wish to highlight in this brief introduction is its connections to liberal society and associated ideas of liberalism. The principles of liberalism find their origins in the European Enlightenment and stress the moral principles of autonomy and equity. In stressing the equality of each citizen and their right to a life of self-determination, liberalism was, in large part, a reaction against the hereditary power, political despotism and religious dogmas that had characterized the medieval world order (Foucault, 2007 [2004]). While liberalism has much in common with democracy, they are actually distinct categories. Alexis de Tocqueville emphasized this distinction in his classic book *Democracy in America* when he described the 'despotism of the majority' (2002 [1835]). De Tocqueville used the notion of collective forms of despotism to argue that even within democracies, the opinion of the majority does not provide a mandate for that majority to interfere in the details of liberal citizens' everyday life. Liberalism is thus characterized not only by equity and autonomy, but also by tolerance of views and behaviours that run against popular orthodoxy (Furedi, 2011). Despite its deployment of behavioural forms of power, which often operate at unconscious levels, neuroliberalism is firmly grounded in the principles of liberalism (see Sunstein, 2014).[1] As we will see later in this volume, in order to continue to wed the moral norms of liberal society with new insights into the human condition, neuroliberalism is characterized by a rethinking of the notions of autonomy, equity and tolerance and the broader role of the government in society.

John Stuart Mill famously outlined the limits of governmental power within liberal societies on the following terms:

> The only purpose for which power can be rightfully exercised over a member of a civilized community, against his will, is to prevent harm to others. His own good, either physical or moral, is not a sufficient warrant (sic).
>
> *(1985 [1859]: 68)*

The 'harm to others principle' has been something of leitmotif of liberalism and a test bed for those societies who claim to be liberal. We mention it here because it has become a touchstone of debate for neuroliberalism (see Sunstein, 2014, 2016). Through revised interpretations of human autonomy and equity, and the application of new styles of behavioural governance, neuroliberalism has sought to enable governmental influence within the personal affairs of individual citizens (particularly in relation to their health and financial practices). While these forms of intervention have not necessarily been 'against the will' of citizens, they have often been based on a circumscribed vision of human will. We will say more about the particular styles of behavioural government employed within neuroliberalism, and its implications for classical understandings of human autonomy later in this volume, but at this point it is important to assert that neuroliberalism seeks to combine new forms of behavioural power with liberal social norms.

From neo to neuroliberalism

The third of aspect of neuroliberalism to emphasize is that it is a direct play on the word neoliberalism. While providing a convenient linguistic echo of neoliberalism, it is our contention that neuroliberal forms of government are deeply interconnected with (if still distinct from) neoliberalism. Neoliberalism is a significant concept that is now used widely across the social sciences. Described by John Clarke as simultaneously omnipresent, omnipotent and promiscuous, the notion of neoliberalism is the subject of much debate and controversy (Clarke, 2008). Put simply, neoliberalism is a system of government that promotes the use of market-oriented styles of social and economic organization (Peck, 2010). According to Friedrich Von Hayek – one of the founding fathers of the neoliberal thought collective – neoliberalism finds its origins in the terminal decline of liberal Victorian values that began around 1870 (Hayek, 1944; Mirowski and Plehwe, 2009). In response to the associated rise of big government, state regulation, bureaucracy and coercion, a group of scholars, led by prominent thinkers such as Von Hayek, explored the ways in which market-based societies could provide bulwarks against the rise of socialism and fascism (ibid.; David, 2014; Mirowski and Plehwe, 2009). At its epistemological core, neoliberalism seeks to address the fundamental problem that faces liberal societies: how is it possible to harmonize the desire for freedom with the needs for socio-economic stability (Friedman, 2002 [1982]). According to neoliberal thinking, markets provide contexts within which freedom can thrive because they encourage the entrepreneurial spirit of individuals (which itself requires freedom), and produce inherently unpredictable outcomes (which are difficult to coercively shape to favour one social group above another) (Davies, 2014). At one and the same time, neoliberalism is seen to afford stability to a community through the profit motivation and rules of voluntary market exchange. While often equated with the reincarnation of Victorian laissez-faire capitalism, neoliberalism is a 'new' form of liberalism to the extent that it generally acknowledges the need for a broader role for the state within society than classical liberalism, albeit largely as an arbiter of market-based transactions (Davies, 2014; Hayek, 1944).

While the neoliberal thought collective first emerged in Europe during the 1930s and 1940s, it was not until the late 1970s that these ideas started to have a significant impact on public policy and governance. David Harvey identifies the years between 1978 and 1980 as a 'revolutionary turning point in the world's social and economic history' and the birth point of neoliberal government (2005: 1). This three-year period was witness to Deng Xiaoping's first moves towards economic liberalization in China, the election of Margaret Thatcher as British Prime Minister, and the coming to power of Ronald Reagan in the US (ibid.). These leaders were the first to attempt the systematic application of neoliberal ideas at a national level. Subsequently, neoliberal practices have spread around the world to the point at which only a very small number of states could now be considered not to be neoliberal to some extent. Over time, the connection between neoliberalism and personal freedom has become somewhat obscured. Where neoliberal economic policies have been adopted by politically repressive regimes such as China, Chile and Argentina in the 1970s, the link between economic and political freedom has become totally lost (Klein, 2004). Even in more liberal political states, neoliberalism has tended to become associated with supporting the freedoms of the corporate sector more than the general populace (Davies, 2014). Notwithstanding this, we claim that in societies with liberal political traditions, neoliberal governance continues to be founded upon an enduring belief in the ability of markets to maintain equity (particularly in relation to opportunities to participate in the marketplace) and liberty (in relation to the freedom to choose what you produce and consume).

The relation between *neuro-* and *neo*-liberalism can be understood in two general ways. First, neuroliberalism is a reaction to neoliberalism. In one context, neuroliberalism reacts to the neoliberal depiction of humans as rational market actors: instead claiming that human behaviour is composed of a much more varied set of rational and 'irrational' drivers. In another context, neuroliberalism reflects a response to some of the socio-economic problems that neoliberalism appears to have produced: particularly in relation to rising levels of personal and collective debt, climate change, unhealthy lifestyles and political disengagement. Neuroliberalism is in part predicated on the assertion that many of the problems of modern liberal societies derive from false assumptions about the ways in which people act in the free market, and the failure of free markets to consistently facilitate personal autonomy. Second, we claim that in many of its iterations, neuroliberalism continues to support the market-based orthodoxies of neoliberal government. To these ends, while neuroliberalism reveals flaws in the logics of neoliberalism – relating to both the nature of human behaviour within markets and the connections between markets and human autonomy – it utilizes these insights to provide governmental correctives that simultaneously recognize the limits of markets, and continue to support market-based values and modes of operation.

Neuroliberal developments

So far our discussion of neuroliberalism has been relatively abstract. However, within this volume we claim that neuroliberalism can be seen in a series of actually existing systems of, and experiments in, behavioural government. As a technique of government, neuroliberalism is most commonly associated with the rise of behavioural insights teams and so-called *nudge units* within a series of states including France, Germany, the Netherlands, New South Wales (Australia), the UK and the USA (Whitehead et al., 2014) (see Chapter 6 in this volume). Neuroliberalism is also evident in the programmes and policies of a series of international organizations such the World Bank, OECD, the World Economic Forum and USAID. And neuroliberal techniques are also providing the basis for a new sector of economic development, as a bewildering array of new start-ups (including The Behavioural Edge, MindLab, Behavioural Architects, Change Lab and Ogilvy Change) seek to commercialize the emerging insights of the behavioural sciences (see Chapter 7 in this volume). Neuroliberal insights are also evident in the operation of more established corporations such as Volkswagen, Nike, Facebook and Unilever. These companies are increasingly exhibiting the characteristics of neuroliberalism in the way that they seek to sell goods and in the development of novel corporate social responsibility initiatives.

Neuroliberalism is also evident within a series of emerging and experimental partnerships between academia, governments and corporations. There are now a series of academic centres including the Behavioural Insights Group at Harvard, The Centre for Behaviour Change at University College London, The Centre for Understanding Behaviour Change at Bristol University, iNudgeyou in Denmark and the Self-Regulation Lab in Utrecht, which are exploring how the behavioural, psychological and social sciences can inform new systems of behavioural government. Finally, the principles of neuroliberalism are shaping the work of third sector organizations such as Corporate Culture, Global Action Plan and Action for Happiness, as well as inspiring the development of a new breed of non-governmental organizations such as GreeNudge (Norway).

Having gained some degree of cross-sector acceptance the actual impact of neuroliberalism is being seen in a range of different contexts. These contexts include, but are not limited to: organ donation programmes, pension policies, low-carbon living strategies, corporate social responsibility schemes, urban planning and design initiatives, international aid policies, taxation systems, charitable giving and volunteering initiatives, fitness schemes, healthy eating initiatives, safe driving campaigns, patient care in hospitals and pro-voting schemes. Throughout these varied forms and iterations neuroliberalism has had a decidedly mixed response. While some laud neuroliberal systems of government as a new era of smart, cost-effective, 'what works' government, others claim that it raises significant ethical and constitutional issues (compare John et al., 2011 and Jones et al., 2013). In the UK, for example, the House of Lords has already held a full-scale inquiry into the forms of government policy that are associated with neuroliberalism (House of Lords, 2011). Within this volume we critically scrutinize different aspects of neuroliberalism, while trying to consistently avoid seeing it axiomatically in either celebratory or dystopian terms.

It is, perhaps, important at this point to recognize that the emergence of neuroliberalism is not the first, or necessarily most significant, coming together of government and the behavioural sciences. There is a long, complex and often controversial history of interaction between the behavioural sciences and government. This is a history that incorporates the impact of the psychological sciences on statehood in the nineteenth and twentieth centuries (see Rose 1998), the Iowa experiments in social climates and democracy (Lezaun and Calvillo, 2013) and the emergence of therapeutic state forms (Nolan, 1998). In this volume we claim that there is something about the extent and novelty of neuroliberalism that invites a renewed critical scrutiny of this broad field. In the remainder of this chapter we begin this process of critique by looking more closely at different examples of neuroliberalism in the world around us. The chapter then moves on to outline the particular set of interpretative perspectives that we hope to bring to this field of enquiry.

Neuroliberalism in the world around us

From invisible hands to animal spirits: (re)interpreting the credit crunch at Deutsche Bank

Any words that contain fifteen letters and end with an ism will inevitably have a somewhat abstract feel. It is therefore important to provisionally outline some of the varied, real-world situations where neuroliberalism is being discussed, implemented and contested. In this way, although we use the word neuroliberalism as a short-hand to signal the influence of behavioural and neurological sciences on the shaping of human conduct in free societies, our approach in this book is to analyse, in historically and geographically specific contexts, varied incarnations of neuroliberal *practice*. To these ends, we begin our journey at the offices of Deutsche Bank Research in the summer of 2010. Deutsche Bank Research provides independent advice and consultancy to Deutsche Bank on macroeconomic trends. In particular, Deutsche Bank Research applies the insights from social, behavioural and economic science to emerging issues confronting the banking group. In 2010, Deutsche Bank Research, as with many other financial consultancies, was trying to work out what had caused the credit crunch and financial crisis of 2008. In their report *Homo Economicus – or more like Homer Simpson* (2010), the consultancy drew attention to the underlying psychological assumptions of our economic system. The report observed:

> It clearly emerges that in real life people do not always make rational decisions based on established preferences and complete information. In many ways their behaviour thus contradicts the homo economicus model. Much of the behaviour observed is caused through people trying to cope with the complexity of the world around them by approximating, because collating and evaluating all the factors of relevance to a decision overtaxes their mental processing capacity. As a rule these approximation methods deliver serviceable results, but they often also lead to distorted perceptions and systematic flaws.
> *(Deutsche Bank Research, 2010: 1)*

We will reflect in greater detail on the figure of homo economicus (and, indeed, Homer Simpson) later in this volume (see Chapter 3). At this point, however, we want to draw attention to a key feature of neuroliberalism that is being expressed in the work of Deutsche Bank Research. In drawing attention to the relationship between macroeconomic crisis and the 'psychologically driven inadequacies' of individuals, Deutsche Bank Research echoes a key principle of certain strands of neuroliberal thought: that failures in neoliberal society can be traced back to the psychological shortcomings of human decision making. The report goes on to articulate the particular nature of humans' psychological inadequacies:

> Distortions [in investment decisions] arise due to information availability, errors of judgement about how representative such information is, loss aversion, the search for confirmation, isolation and endowment effects, status quo bias and – particularly on the financial markets – the misinterpretation of patterns.

> *(ibid.: 1)*

The psychological deficiencies outlined here are actually part of a much broader set of cognitive biases or heuristics. Approximately 150 cognitive biases have been identified and diagnosed by behavioural scientists. In general terms, these biases involve tendencies to follow the behaviours of those around us, a preference not to change existing forms of conduct and a proclivity to prioritize present desires ahead of the needs of our future selves (John et al., 2011). These heuristics are important because they make it easier for humans to make complex decisions (Kahneman, 2011). These forms of intuitive decision making appear to have evolved over very long periods of time, and have helped the human species survive. According to certain forms of emerging neuroliberal government, such behavioural patterns are, however, why people do not live in the rational (at least as determined within neoclassical economics) ways that help to secure stability within market-based societies.

Deutsche Bank Research is not alone in making connections between the financial crisis and the psychologies of human behaviour. The economists George Akerlof and Robert Shiller have drawn attention to the psychological origins of economic disruptions (Akerlof and Shiller, 2009). Drawing on the reflections of John Maynard Keynes, they utilize the notion of *animal spirits* to interpret the behaviours that contributed to the credit crunch. Unlike cognitive biases, the notion of animal spirits speaks more broadly of the non-economic motives that drive human behaviour and contribute to observed fluctuations in the economy. While acknowledging the biases that humans routinely use to address uncertainty, the idea of an enduring animal spirit running through society speaks of the role of 'changing confidence, temptations, envy, resentment, and illusions' in human action (ibid.: 4). Unlike the disembodied 'invisible hand' that Adam Smith claimed helped to rationally shape a market-based society, Keynes' animal spirits speaks of a more disruptive and deeply corporeal force within society, which resides in emotional responses to the situations we encounter. According to Akerlof and Shiller '[t]hese intangibles were the reason why people paid small fortunes for houses in cornfields; why others financed those purchases; why the Dow Jones average peaked above 14,000 and a little more than a year later fell below 7,500' (ibid.: 4).

If neuroliberalism is in part characterized by a recognition of the often overlooked human traits that contribute to broader patterns of socio-economic change and fluctuation, the financial crisis of 2008 could also be seen as a key harbinger of neuroliberal forms of government. As we will discuss at greater length in Chapter 2, the intellectual and practical history of neuroliberalism is actually much longer and more complicated than this. The history of ideas that have informed neuroliberalism can, in part, be traced back to the great depression and Keynes' invocation of animal spirits in his 1936 volume *The General Theory of Employment, Interest and Money* (Keynes, 1936). But neuroliberaism is also part of the much longer history of entanglements between the practices of governing and insights of psychology that goes back as least as far as the nineteenth century (Rose, 1998). More specifically, however, we claim that neuroliberalism finds it origins in the complex fusions between economics and psychology that began in late 1940s, but did not come to fruition until the 1970s and 1980s (Jones et al., 2013). More will be said about these overlapping genealogies of neuroliberalism in Chapter 2.

Facebook, big data and the 'guinea pig economy'

Our next journey into the realms of neuroliberalism takes us to the offices of Facebook's Data Science Team. It is Tuesday, 6 November 2012 and people across America are waking up to Election Day. Facebook's Data Science Team decided to use this day to test out an evolving feature of its social network site, the so-called Voter Megaphone. The basic idea behind the Voter Megaphone project was to try and enhance voter turnout. In any democracy the levels of voter turnout are often interpreted as an important sign of the relative health of a democracy, and as evidence of citizen engagement in the political process. In many democracies around the world there has been a general decline in the numbers of people who are voting in both provincial and national polls. Increasing participation within the electoral process represents an interesting problem for behavioural government. Some countries, such as Australia, see voting as so important that authorities have made it legally compulsory for citizens to complete a ballot paper for state and federal elections. Other democracies appear to recognize the right not to vote as an important value within a free society, and thus use the more conventional methods of mass marketing to promote voting. Facebook's Voter Megaphone reflects an innovative intervention within the field of voting behaviours. First introduced in the US elections in 2010, the initiative enabled Facebook users to display a simple 'I Voted' button, which then appeared in their news feed and was visible to their friends on social media. This simple scheme reflects the behavioural insight that people do not always act because it is the morally right thing to do. Neither do they reliably respond to generic marketing campaigns that promote virtuous behaviour. The Voter Magaphone project responded to the fact that a key motivational factor within human behaviour are the observed behaviours of those around us. As human beings we have evolved patterns of conduct that routinely rely on an awareness of what others are doing. This herd mentality is practically important because when faced with complex decisions it helps us draw on the collective wisdom of crowds and also facilitates our acceptance in the communities on which we rely. This mentality is strongest when the behavioural crowd is composed of individuals whom we like and deliberately align ourselves with, as is (often) the case with our Facebook friends. The power of social influence on human decision making was evidenced in the Voter Megaphone programme by the fact that in 2010 it was linked to a boost in voter turnout of at least 340,000 votes (Sifry, 2014).

The 2012 iteration of the Voter Megaphone was, however, different. Many Facebook users reported not having the option to use the 'I voted' button, while others reported not seeing evidence of the button in their news feed. On further investigation it transpired that the Facebook Data Science Team were using the 2012 election to run a series of randomized controlled trials to test out the effectiveness of its Voter Megaphone initiative. These controlled trials resulted in some Facebook members being subjected to the Voter Megaphone utilities, while others were held in control groups and did not have the opportunity to either use the 'I Voted' button and/or see whom among their friends had signalled that they had voted. While no one suggested that the Voter Megaphone project had a significant impact on US election results in 2012, concerns were obviously raised over Facebook's non-consensual use of a trial in which participants did not even realize they were involved, and the fact that such trials had the potential to change real world political events (Tufekci, 2014). It has subsequently emerged that in January 2012 Facebook was also responsible for deliberately modifying the news feed being received by 689,003 of its users to see if exposure to more positive or negative comments could affect the emotional content of the posts sent out by people in the trial group (see Sifry, 2014b). Facebook's emotional contagion experiment (as it was officially known) generated significant controversy and again led to questions about the manipulative behavioural capacities of large corporations such as Facebook.

It is our contention that Facebook's Voter Megaphone initiative and emotional contagion study reflect key aspects of emerging forms of neuroliberal government. In one respect these initiatives are indicative of the growing role of corporations within the fields of public behaviour change that were traditionally the reserve of the state (see Chapter 7 in this volume). In another respect these initiatives reflect an emerging shift in behavioural government that places increasing emphasis on the development of real world experimentation at large scales (John et al., 2011). The particular use of randomized controlled trials within the practice of governing reflects the transfer of a preferred methodological practice of the behavioural sciences into the realms of social government (see Chapter 6 in this volume). Finally, these initiatives embody the practices of neuroliberalism to the extent that they are able to exploit the behavioural potentials of digital technology and social media. We will discuss the relationship between technology and behavioural government later in the book (see Chapter 10). At this point we want to simply note that the emergence of digital technology and smart devices is enabling neuroliberal styles of behavioural government to proliferate. Parmy Olson goes as far as to suggest that '[t]he proliferation of connected devices – smartphones, wearables, thermostats, autos – combined with powerful and integrated software spells a golden age of behavioural science. Data will no longer reflect who we are – it will help determine it' (Olson, 2015). Indeed, a range of new start-ups are fusing the insights of internet optimizing experiments with those of the behavioural sciences. It is now possible for energy companies, supermarkets, fitness firms and financial groups to continuously test their latest application of behavioural insights on their clients' consumption and behavioural habits. As household technologies (such as smart energy metres, smart TVs and mobile health monitoring wrist bands) become ever more interconnected, the potential for behavioural modification and experimentation becomes ever greater. Olson suggests that we are now seeing the emergence of a whole new form of economic development: the *guinea pig economy* (ibid.). Within the guinea pig economy big profits can be made from the real-time, personalized experiments to which we are all continuously and unwittingly subjected. As we will explore in this volume, the guinea pig economy, with its attendant experimental citizens, is a key facet of the neuroliberal era.

The World Bank and the automatic brain: rethinking international development

Ahead of the publication of its prestigious 2015 *World Development Report*, the World Bank carried out a series of survey-based tests with its employees. Staff at the Bank's headquarters in Washington DC as well as the 950 country offices it runs were invited to take part in the tests (World Bank, 2015: 190). The purpose of the survey was to explore the extent to which development professionals employed by the World Bank exhibited the decision-making flaws that behavioural scientists have identified within our routine decision making. In general terms, the World Bank was keen to explore the application of new insights into human behaviour within the field of international development. The World Bank was particularly interested in the ways in which the behavioural sciences could help us better understand how poverty generates bad decision making. Studies have consistently shown that poverty places a form of cognitive tax on those who are subjected to it, which erodes people's decision-making resources and often leads to poor long-term decision making (Mullainathan and Shafir, 2013). The behavioural survey of its staff was, however, designed to investigate the extent to which behavioural biases are actually a universal aspect of the human condition and not merely a product of extreme decision-making situations such as poverty.

One of the behavioural tests conducted on World Bank staff investigated the impact of context on human decision making. In particular, this test sought to compare the ways in which World Bank staff valued time relative to money, when compared to those living in poverty. Significantly, the test revealed that the bank's staff thought of the relationship between time and money very differently to those subject to poverty (with staff at the bank favouring time savings over money savings much more than those in poverty) (World Bank 2015: 186–7). The test was actually designed to explore the operation of a well-documented cognitive bias: the scarcity heuristic. The scarcity heuristic is a behavioural shortcut that is commonly used to assess the value of a thing (such as time, money, or a specific product) in relation to how easy it is obtain, and how easily it could be lost. The scarcity heuristic itself, and the divergence in decision making observed between the two groups in the World Bank trial, cannot be easily explained by theories of pure economic rationality. The scarcity heuristic often (but not always) results in systematic errors emerging in behaviour, as in the rush to make decisions we quickly calculate what best to do on the basis of the apparent shortage or abundance of a given resource. The divergence in group behaviour observed within the trial is a product of socio-economic context, and the fact that for many relatively affluent World Bank staff it makes sense to trade money for time (and a hoped-for improvement in quality of life); while for those on the poverty line saving money is what matters most. The broader significance of this finding for the World Bank is that it indicates that while its staff are subject to the same forms of cognitive bias as the communities they serve, they do not share the same mental models. The cogitative dissonance that is likely to emerge in such situations may lead to the design and development of policies that are not well suited to the needs and motivations of the communities they are meant to support.

Related behavioural tests carried out by the World Bank on its staff revealed the presence of other cognitive biases including *confirmation bias* (the selective prioritization of data that supports an existing belief, and rejection of evidence that does not support that viewpoint), and *sunk-cost bias* (the tendency of people to continue with particular courses of action, no matter how damaging or pointless they prove to be, once an initial investment of time and/or resources has been made into that action) (ibid.: 182–6). The insights of these behavioural trials ultimately fed into the production of the World Bank's 2015 World Development Report: *Mind, Society and Behaviour.* This report argues for nothing less than a fundamental redesign of international development policy so that it reflects the emerging insights of the behavioural and natural sciences into the automatic and socially conditioned nature of human decision making. As with Deutsche Bank's assessment of the financial crisis, the World Bank argues that the failings of international development policy are in part a product of an inaccurate understanding of human decision making. As we have previously discussed, this inaccurate, neoclassical economic model of decision making assumes independent deliberation and the existence of consistent self-interested preferences as frameworks for long-term patterns of human action. According to the World Bank, the rethinking of development economics should be based upon recognition that human decision making is often automatic in nature, based upon social norms, and dependent upon the mental models that help people navigate the complexities of everyday life (ibid.: 5).

It is easy to overlook the significance of the World Bank's *Mind, Society and Behaviour* report. As a prominent advocate of neoliberal government and policy throughout the world, the World Bank has been synonymous with the global promotion of the Washington Consensus and the neoclassical insights into human behaviour and the economy on which it is based. By embracing a distinctively neuroliberal view of international development, the World Bank is essentially sanctioning the emergence of new kinds of policy experimentation that rejects many of the assumptions that have been the cornerstone of its strategies over the last thirty years. Ultimately, the Report emphasizes that new behavourial insights are likely to play an important part in tackling a range of international development priorities including poverty alleviation, early childhood development, household finance, productivity, health, and climate change (ibid.: 4).

For the purposes of this book, the World Bank's behavioural reorientation is important on a series of levels. First, it indicates that neuroliberalim is likely to be a prominent feature of international development in the coming decade. It is, however, important to note that many of the insights associated with neuroliberalism are already widely used within international development programmes (see Whitehead el al 2014). Nevertheless, it is clear that with the backing of the World Bank, the geographical spread of neuroliberalism is likely to accelerate. Second, the Report is significant because it illustrates how neuroliberal policy seems to say something universal about the human condition, but also emphasizes the significance of local social and environmental context in the shaping of human behaviour. On these terms, it is noteworthy that the World Bank does not simply identify cognitive biases within the behavioural constraints that poverty places on decision making in less economically developed countries; it also identifies these error-prone heuristics within its own staff. The World Bank report does, however, also recognize that certain forms of human behaviour can be properly understood only when positioned within the local socio-cultural and economic circumstances in question. Third, the World Bank report indicates not only what neuroliberalism may involve when it is applied to the development of public policy, but also what it may mean for the internal operational dynamics of global institutions such as the World Bank. The World Bank claims that in order to be able to address behavioural biases within its own staff, a series of working practices should be employed. These practices include the routine exposure of individuals to ideas that oppose their own (so-called *red-teaming*); developing new relations with policy failure (essentially being more comfortable to acknowledge and learn from policy failure); and facilitating situations in and through which staff are able to experience at first hand the policy programmes they are delivering (a process known in the commercial world as *dog-fooding*). In these contexts it is clear that neuroliberalism has implications for the lives of those working within the institutions of global governance as well as those that are the subjects of behaviourally oriented government (see Chapter 6 in this volume).

Rethinking irrationality at the Max Planck Institute

Our final stop on this introductory tour of some of the places where neuroliberalism is being discussed, implemented and contested takes us to south west Berlin and the Dahlem Science Park. The Dahlem Science Park is home to the renowned Max Planck Institute of Human Development. The Max Planck Institute of Human Development is an interdisciplinary academic centre that focuses on questions of human advancement and education. Drawing on the insights of psychology, education, medicine, history, economics, computer science and mathematics inter alia, the Institute has been a prominent contributor to emerging debates within the behavioural sciences over the last twenty years. The Max Planck Institute houses the Center for Adaptive Behaviour and Cognition, which is home to the German psychologist Gerd Gigerenzer. For several decades Gigerenzer and his colleagues have been studying various aspects of human behaviour and decision making. His team's research starts from the same basic insight that lies at the heart of the broader neuroliberal project: namely that there are significant limits to the human capacity to make information-rich and deliberative decisions. In their studies of the behavioural shortcuts, biases, emotions and social influences that fill the voids that are defined by our bounded rationality, the Center for Adaptive Behaviour and Cognition interpret the human reliance on automatic, unconscious and involuntary acts in novel and challenging ways.

One of the most famous insights of Gigerenzer and his team into human decision making emerged out of a failed experiment. While teaching at the University of Saltzburg, Gigerenzer was studying the so-called hard–easy effect (the hard–easy effect relates to people's tendency to be overconfident about their ability to answer a difficult question correctly, but not of their chance of providing the correct answer to an easier question) (Gigerenzer, 2000). In order to test aspects of this effect Gigerenzer and his team (he worked on this project with Ulrich

Hoffrage and Heinz Kleinbölting) asked their German-speaking students (studying in Austria) to compare pairs of German and American cities and decide which they thought had the largest population. The premise behind this test was that the German city pairs would provide the students with the easy questions (as they were cities that they would be most familiar with), while the American city pairs (with which the students were less familiar) would offer the hard questions (ibid.: 127). While their experiment did not provide the insight into the hard–easy effect the team had been hoping for it did throw up a peculiar result. As it turned out the German-speaking students proved to be better at guessing the relative size of American cities than German cities (with a 76 per cent success rate for American cities and only a 75.6 per cent success rate for the German urban centres) (ibid.). While this may not look a big difference in relative levels of performance, given the fact that the German students would generally know much more about German than US cities, it did offer an important insight into human decision making.

While Gigerenzer and his team were initially disappointed with the results of their experiment, with time they came to realize that they had unexpectedly uncovered something important. Gigerenzer came to realize that the reason that the students were better at comparing the relative size of US cities than German ones was not, as classical economic theory would dictate, because they knew more about American cities, but precisely because they knew less about cities in the US. What Gigerenzer had discovered was the so-called recognition heuristic. The recognition heuristic relates to the way in which we use our relative levels of recognition of a thing or situation as a basis for making assumptions about it. In the case of Gigerenzer's experiment, the students were able to use the fact that they did not recognize certain American cities as a basis for assuming the city with which it was paired (and of which they had heard) was larger. The Austrian students could not use the recognition heuristic as much with German cities, with which they were generally more familiar.

The recognition heuristic clearly has much in common with the other behavioural insights that are associated with neuroliberal government. It emphasizes the ways in which human behaviour is often based upon intuitive shortcuts that rely on only limited information. Where it is different from the cognitive biases so far discussed is that rather than seeing heuristics as a flawed and compromised form of decision making that requires correction, the recognition heuristic demonstrates that intuitive decision making can actually be more *accurate* than knowledge-heavy systems. Ultimately, the recognition heuristic reveals the wisdom that sometime resides in a lack of knowledge (ibid.: 127). Drawing on this insight, the Center for Adaptive Behaviour and Cognition has been testing and exploring various aspects of intelligent intuition, knowledge and time-limited decision making. In summarizing the work being carried out in the Max Planck Institute, Gigerenzer observed:

> I view the mind in relation to its environment rather than in opposition to the laws of logic or probability. In a complex and uncertain world, psychology is indispensable for sound reasoning, it is rationality's fuel rather than its brake.
>
> *(Gigerenzer, 2000: viii)*

In exploring the relationship between the mind and the environment within which it happens to be operating, the Center for Adaptive Behaviour and Cognition has sought to understand the 'ecology' of intuitive decision making. By understanding human decision making in relation to how it adapts to cope with the constraints and opportunities that environments present, Gigerenzer and his team present a challenge to the very notion of rationality. Ultimately they argue that rationality is not a measure of how closely a given action conforms to the expected super-charged psychologies of homo economicus, but how well adapted a decision is to the situation in which it is being made.

The work of Gigerenzer is important to the broader analysis of neuroliberal government developed in this volume. It is important because it raises fundamental questions about what the target and purpose of neuroliberalism should be. A significant portion of what we would identify as neuroliberalism is based upon the assumption that the human dependency on heuristics, emotion and intuition leads to bad decision making and requires some form of correction (see Jones et al., 2013). Related systems of government also assume that problematic forms of intuitive decision making are so baked into the human condition that little can be done to empower individuals to improve their decision making in the long term. The work of Center for Adaptive Behaviour and Cognition challenges these assumptions to the extent of suggesting that not only may heuristics be a positive aspect of human behaviour that should be celebrated, but there is evidence to suggest that humans can actually become more effective intuitive decision-makers. Whether the notional figure at the centre of neuroliberal systems of government is a flawed decision-maker or smart adapter to environmental circumstances has significant implications for the styles and intent of behavioural government that are likely to emerge (see Chapter 4 in this volume). It also has crucial implications for how notions of freedom are approached, secured and consolidated within systems of behavioural government (see Chapter 5 in this volume).

Our exploration of emerging manifestations of neuroliberalism raises important themes that will run through this volume. Crucially it has revealed the contested nature of neuroliberalism. While broadly based upon a common set of insights into the more-than-rational nature of human decision making, emerging forms of neuroliberal government have exhibited many contradictory traits. In relation to understandings of the human subject, some branches of neuroliberalism pursue correctional strategies for the flawed psychologies that people routinely exhibit, while others explore the potential for enhancing the emotional intelligence and intuitive decision-making capacities of citizens. Neuroliberalism is also characterized by tensions between the promotion of universal views of human behaviour and decision making (which emphasizes the cross-cultural prevalence of cognitive biases), and a concern with the role of local socio-cultural context and everyday circumstances within the shaping of decision making. Finally, neuroliberalism is associated with very different forms of governance techniques. At times it involves the development of fairly conventional forms of behaviourally intelligent, but generic policies, which are implemented by national governments and international organizations. In other circumstances, neuroliberalism is synonymous with new vectors of government power that are orchestrated from corporations and digital platforms and are characterized by highly personalized systems of behavioural experimentation. Perhaps the most important insight to emerge from such evident diversity is that neuroliberalism is far from a finished or coherent project of government. As with neoliberalism, it appears that neuroliberalism is marked by a distinctively contradictory process of evolution that is characterized by forms of creative *adaptation* and *differentiation* (Peck, 2010: 6–10). While this adaptation and differentiation are perhaps to be expected, it is surprising how much they are overlooked within meta-narratives of the spread of new systems of behavioural government. As we move through this volume we consistently attend to these moments of differentiated development in order to consider the alternative paths that neuroliberal government could take.

Exploring and analysing neuroliberalism

Between conformity and critique

In this volume we develop what we believe to be an original analysis of neuroliberalism. At present analyses of neuroliberal forms of government take two broad forms. First there is the perspective of what we call the *behaviouralists*. The behaviouralists are comprised of academics, policy-makers, politicians, corporate strategists and project practitioners who believe that there is much to be learned, and gained, from a sustained dialogue between those involved in the business of behaviour change and the behavioural sciences. The academics in this group are generally drawn from the psychological and economic sciences. The policy-makers, politicians and practitioners in this group are usually concerned with addressing emerging problems associated with personal finance, health, environment and allied public policy priorities, and generally work in national and local government, and in third sector organizations. The corporate contingent include those who are using the behavioural sciences to support the conventional sales activities of their companies, and those who are now concerned with broader questions of corporate social responsibility and the potential role of corporations within the promotion of positive lifestyle changes in their customer base (see Chapter 7). What unifies this group is the common belief that emerging neuroliberal practices reflect effective, pragmatic responses to behavioural problems, and that they do not present significant ethical or constitutional issues (see Thaler and Sunstein, 2008; Sunstein, 2013).

Perhaps the most prominent figure in the behaviouralist group is the legal scholar Cass Sunstein. In 2008, Sunstein published, alongside behavioural economist Richard Thaler, what many would identify as the most influential book in the neuroliberal cannon, *Nudge: Improving Decisions about Health Wealth and Happiness* (Thaler and Sunstein, 2008). Having met Barack Obama at the University of

Chicago, Sunstein served as a campaign advisor (and door-to-door campaigner) for the future president (Sunstein, 2013: 17). Following Obama's election to the Presidency in 2008, Sunstein was appointed Administrator of the White House Office of Information and Regulatory Affairs (hereafter OIRA) (see Chapter 2 for a more detailed discussion of Sunstein's tenure at OIRA). Sunstein used his position in the OIRA to develop a series of neuroliberal style policy interventions that were applied across the Federal Government in the US (these initiatives ranged from reforms to the federal student aid application process to fuel economy labelling).

The intellectual and practical positions that Sunstein has adopted in relation to the neuroliberal policies he has promoted are emblematic of the behaviourist group. First, Sunstein has suggested that related policies offer effective and relatively low-cost ways of changing public behaviours in socially and economically beneficial directions. Second, he has argued that related policies do not raise significant ethical challenges with regard to the role of the state within society, or human freedom and autonomy (although he does recognize that related policies challenge Mill's aforementioned 'harm to others' principle (see Sunstein, 2014) (although also see Sunstein, 2016)). Ultimately, and as is common in the behaviourist camp, Sunstein suggests that neuroliberal policies do not reflect a fundamental shift in behavioural government. According to Sunstein, these policies embody the development of a more behaviourally pragmatic style of government. As such, they draw on the empirical insights of the psychological sciences and principles of cost–benefit analysis in order to counteract the behavioural guesswork of previous policy regimes (Sunstein, 2013).

A group we refer to as the *ethicists* offer the second set of analytical perspectives on neuroliberalism. This group is also comprised of academics, politicians and policy practitioners. The academics in this analytical community are drawn largely from the social, political and philosophical sciences. The politicians and policy-makers in this group are often working alongside the policy executives in the first analytical group, but tend to take a different view on neuroliberalism. This group is unified by three general arguments concerning neuroliberalism. First, that despite the relatively high profile of many of its contemporary manifestations, neuroliberal policies remain relatively marginal to the broader policy-making process. Second, they argue that despite the marginal nature of neuroliberal policy, many of its iterations raise significant ethical and constitutional issues concerning the nature of human autonomy and the broader role of government within society. Third, they claim that behavioural policies are based upon flawed understandings of the nature of human behaviour, which tend to reduce human conduct to the isolated and momentary actions of individuals that can be measured in laboratory and field experiments.

One of the most prominent and insightful voices in the ethicist camp has been Frank Furedi. A British sociologist and commentator, Furedi has developed an ongoing critique of emerging manifestations of neuroliberalism (see Furedi, 2011). At the centre of Furedi's analysis is an assertion that neuroliberal styles of government reflect a significant threat to the freedom of those who are subject to its practices. Furedi's critique of neuroliberal government operates on two levels: one is epistemological, the other moral. Epistemologically Furedi's work implies that human autonomy cannot be easily equated to the automatic, unconscious responses that have been revealed within the behavioural sciences (see also Tallis, 2011). Morally, Furedi claims that behaviour-changing policies reflect a reorientation of tolerance within society. Furedi asserts that under neuroliberal styles of government people's right to be wrong (or unhealthy and financially irresponsible, for example) is significantly eroded. For ethicists, then, the intolerance displayed by neuroliberals towards purportedly irrational behaviour essentially transforms private preferences into objects of government regulation (ibid.: 137). There is more to the ethicists' critiques of neuroliberalism than merely a concern with intolerance, and we will discuss these at greater length as we move through this volume. At this point, however, it is important to note that those in the ethicist camp claim that neuroliberalism may be far less benign than the behaviouralists suggest.

Having studied various aspects of neuroliberalism since 2008, our work has led us, at times, into both the behaviouralist and ethicist camps. When we started out our research we were generally critical and suspicious of neuroliberal expressions of power. Drawing on Foucauldian accounts of the disempowering nature of neoliberal government, we outlined some of the dangers associated with the fusion of behavioural knowledge and state power (Jones et al., 2011). As we become more aware of the diverse nature of neuroliberalism, and some of its more progressive incarnations, we found ourselves increasingly advocating some of its analytical insights to policy-makers and sociologists who were interested in developing more complex understandings of the human condition (Jones et al., 2013). In recent times we have found it difficult to find a permanent home in either the behaviouralist or ethicist camps. Aware of the all too narrow accounts of human behaviour often found in expressions of neuroliberalism, and the ethical issues they invariably raise, it has become clear that we are not true behaviouralists. At the same time, however, we feel that many in the ethicist camp have developed a caricatured critique of neuroliberalism, which underestimates both its diversity of insights and its potential significance, while overestimating some of its moral implications. Ultimately, we have attempted to pitch our analytical tent in a space between (or, perhaps, more accurately, a space constructed by both) the behaviourist and ethicist perspectives. From this point of view neuroliberalism represents a more significant shift in the nature of government than many in the ethicist camp claim. It also appears to embody much greater moral and constitutional challenges than behaviouralists tend to acknowledge. To put things another way, we claim that neuroliberalism reflects a more significant shift in the nature of modern government than either behaviouralists or ethicists appear willing to concede.

Ultimately the space that we occupy in relation to neuroliberalism is an interdisciplinary one. This is a space that is open to a critical – but not cynical – dialogue between the neurological and political sciences; between psychology and sociology; and between cognitive science and the humanities. In many ways this could also be thought of as an *intra*disciplinary arena, to the extent that it is defined by the often unacknowledged spaces between disciplines, as well as where they meet. There are two important things to note about the inter and intra disciplinary perspectives developed in this volume. First, neuroliberalism is itself a product of a diverse set of interdisciplinary encounters. While the primary focus of these encounters had been between psychology and economics (see Chapter 2) (Jones et al., 2013), neuroliberalism has also been shaped by interactions between the insights of architecture, design and engineering, marketing, animal studies and neuroscience, inter alia. In developing an interdisciplinary engagement with neuroliberalism, our intention is to open it up to the wider insights of sociology, history, geography, meditative studies and the political sciences. In widening the field of interdisciplinary engagement we hope to contribute to new forms of practical dialogue between behavioural studies and government, and to develop novel critical engagements with existing practices of neuroliberal statehood. The second goal of the perspective that we develop on neuroliberalism is to actively avoid the construction of what Fitzgerald and Callard refer to as the 'arid rhetoric of interdisciplinarity' (2015: 3). In their insightful analysis of emerging interdisciplinary engagements between the social and neurological sciences, Fitzgerald and Callard note how interdisciplinary perspectives (when not marked by totalizing critique) can quickly descend into a form of 'bloodless' engagement that fails to acknowledge the challenges of moving beyond entrenched disciplinary perspectives on the world (ibid.). Our hope in this book is to try to establish an interdisciplinary perspective on neuroliberalism that acknowledges and exploits the often opposing perspectives that different disciplines bring. In this context, while we pitch our tent between behaviouralists and social scientists, pragmatists and ethicists, and applied and metaphysical perspectives on neuroliberalism, we do not claim that this space reflects an epistemological nirvana where these varied viewpoints can be simplistically held together. Instead we see it as a terrain where competing disciplinary insights can be assessed and creatively brought to bear on fragments of neuroliberal life and government.

Geography, space and neuroliberalism

While we set out an interdisciplinary perspective on neuroliberalism in this volume, it is important to be candid about the particularities, and peculiarities, of own disciplinary points of origin. We are, as it happens, already an interdisciplinary team, with our areas of expertise spanning geography (Jones, Pykett and Whitehead), social psychology (Howell), and media and contemplative studies (Lilley). But from within this disciplinary mix we are particularly interested in exploring the contribution that geography can make within the critical analysis of neuroliberalism. Our desire to develop geographical interpretations of neuroliberalism requires some explanation. While geographers have for some time been interested in the connections between the behavioural sciences, political power and government (Amin and Thrift, 2013; Anderson, 2014; Huxley, 2006; Jones et al., 2013), they rarely appear in the interdisciplinary exchanges that surround and inform neuroliberalism. This is surprising given the centrality of geographical themes to questions of neuroliberal government. As we will see as we move through this volume, neuroliberalism is often based upon the construction and reconstruction of so-called *choice architectures* as a basis for new forms of behavioural government. The idea of choice architecture (or choice environment as it is also known) is an inherently geographical notion that draws attention to the ways in which the design and location of physical objects in space shapes and conditions choice and human behaviour. Neuroliberalism involves the construction of choice architectures at a range of different scales and in a number of different contexts. Choice architecture is now a consideration for planners thinking about the best design of streets and cities (see Jones et al., 2013; Minton, 2009); nutritionists who lay out school canteens; and transport consultants who are keen to promote the use of public transport systems and cycle paths. What is striking about the accounts of space, architecture and environment within discussions of neuroliberalism is how they remain relatively unproblematized. They are simplified to the extent that are seen to be fairly malleable to the desires of the choice architect and engineer, while their transformation is interpreted in mainly technical/experimental as opposed to political terms (see Chapter 8 in this volume). Throughout this volume we aim to develop new perspectives on the reconstructions of space that are associated with neuroliberalism. These perspectives will explore the inertia that many pre-existing spatial forms present to the desires of choice engineers, and consider more broadly what the physical spaces of neuroliberalism might tell us about emerging forms of social power and resistance (see Allen, 2006).

In addition to analysing the relationship between neuroliberalism and transformations in physical spaces, the geographical perspective developed within this volume also draws attention to the connection between more ephemeral aspects of spatial context and neuroliberalism. In its desire to move beyond the decontextualized actions of a universalized homo economicus (see above), neuroliberalism draws attention to the difference that context makes to human action. Context is seen as important within neuroliberal systems of government to the extent that it takes into account the role local history, traditions and cultural practices play in shaping human behaviour. Over shorter timespans, spatial context is also seen as being important to understanding human behaviour to the extent that it frames the often unnoticed affects that condition decision-making. Neuroliberalism recognizes that behaviours are shaped to a significant extent by the affective push of the world, expressed in the often-intangible realms of peer pressure, soundscapes, smells, lighting and broader *structures of feeling*. Unlike the durable infrastructure of choice architecture, the affective qualities of a space are much more fleeting. As particular outcomes of the coming together of different emotional forces in space, affects are more akin to events than feats of design and engineering (Anderson, 2014). While many expressions of neuroliberalism suggest that affect can be routinely manipulated so as to condition human conduct, geographical analyses suggest that affective power is not so easily wielded. In this volume we will reflect on emerging work on the geographies of affect in order to offer new insights into the relationship between psychological governance and spatial context.

A final geographical perspective we bring to the analysis of neuroliberalism is a concern with spatial difference. As with all meta-concepts, there is a danger that a study of neuroliberalism could quickly take on an air of universalism. In such a situation the determination of neuroliberalism as a particular style of behavioural government can lead to it becoming a kind of ideal form that is used to delimit and explain all related manifestations of behavioural power. In this volume we use neuroliberalism more as an analytical category than an ontological test case. As an analytical device neuroliberalism provides a framework within which we can connect together, explore and critically assess emerging manifestations of behavioural government. Being attuned to spatial difference is important in this context because it enables us to consider the adaptive qualities of neuroliberal ideas and how they are used in different ways in different places. Looking at iterations of neuroliberalism from a spatial perspective does not necessarily prevent us from noting the similarities that exist between different mobilizations of its core principles. It does, however, afford us the chance to consider the opportunities that exist to develop alternative forms of neuroliberalism that serve various political, economic and moral ends.

Analytical themes and structure of the book

This volume has been organized around a series of thematic topics that provide a distinctive viewpoint on our empirical research into the geographical spread of neuroliberal forms of government (see Methodological Appendix for methodological detail concerning how the research reported in this book was gathered). These have been designed to offer a broad range of entry points through which to introduce, explore and critically analyse neuroliberalism. Chapters 4 through to 8 have been grouped together in order to facilitate an analysis of the *implications of neuroliberalism*. This section of the volume commences with a discussion of the relationship between neuroliberal ideas and changing understandings of human nature. Chapter 4 considers the ways in which neuroliberal practices are challenging established notions of citizenship and the more and less empowering ways in which related forms of behavioural government frame human subjectivity. Analysis then moves on to consider how neuroliberalism is challenging and redefining the liberal orthodoxies of freedom (Chapter 5). Particular attention is given in this context to the ways in which emerging scientific understandings of human agency are reshaping political interpretations of autonomy and the governmental mobilization of choice. The two chapters that follow consider how emerging neuroliberal ideas and practices are increasingly blurring the boundaries between states, corporation and society (Chapters 6 and 7). In these chapters particular attention is given to the connections between neuroliberalism and the emergence of more experimentally oriented forms of government and more governmentally oriented corporations. Chapter 8 considers the connections between neuroliberalism and the design industries and broader conceptions of the material world.

Chapter 9 is different from the other chapters in the book. While Chapters 1–8 reflect our analysis of emerging forms of neuroliberalism, Chapter 9 reports on our own intervention in neuroliberal government. Reflecting on a series of experimental trials we have carried out with policy-makers and behaviour change experts, this chapter considers the extent to which it may be possible to imagine the development of more personally empowering and democratically oriented forms of neuroliberal government that are based on new forms of relations between the self and behaviour.

The next two chapters of this book are devoted to developing an account of the *rise of neuroliberalism*. This chapter has, in a fairly piecemeal way, commenced this task. Chapters 2 and 3 offer a more comprehensive and systematic account of the history and geography of neuroliberal ideas and practices. These chapters also introduce the reader to some of the key conceptual ideas and themes that will run through each of the chapters in this volume. And so it is to these matters that we now turn.

Note

1 We note here, however, that the emerging insights of the behavioural sciences that inform neuroliberalism are also being used to justify more authoritarian systems of government such as coercive paternalism (see Conly, 2012) We discuss this issue at greater length in Chapters 2 and 5.

2

AN HISTORICAL GEOGRAPHY OF NEUROLIBERALISM I

Applying behavioural insights

Influencing people's behaviour is nothing new to government, which has often used tools such as legislation, regulation or taxation to achieve desired policy outcomes. But many of the biggest policy challenges we are now facing – such as the increased numbers of people with chronic health conditions – will only be resolved if we are successful in persuading people to change their behaviour, their lifestyles or their existing habits. Fortunately, over the last decade, our understanding of influences on behaviour has increased significantly and this points the way to new approaches and new solutions ... To realize that potential, we have to build our capacity and ensure that we have a sophisticated understanding of what influences behaviour.

(O'Donnell and Bichard, in Dolan et al., 2010).

Introduction: mindspace and other origin stories

When introducing a phenomenon such as neuroliberalism it is always tempting to try and find a suitable point of origin from which to tell the story of its evolution and development. As we will see within this chapter (and Chapter 3), when it comes to neuroliberalism there is no shortage of possible anchor points upon which to moor our story. We could choose, for example, the pioneering work on bounded rationality of Nobel prize-winning economist, come political scientist-cum-computer pioneer Herbert Simon; the groundbreaking fusion of economics and psychology developed by Daniel Kahneman and Amos Tversky in the 1970s; the publication of the influential book *Nudge* in 2008, or the appointment of one of its co-authors Cass Sunstein as head of the US government's OIRA the following year; the formation of the UK Government's Behavioural Insights Team in 2010; or the World Bank's embrace of the behavioural sciences in 2015 (see Chapter 1). These anchor points are attractive because they offer linearity to the histories we seek to tell, and points of geographical ground zeros from where our stories can proceed to radiate out. When it comes to neuroliberalism, however, there are actually no Galapagos Islands on which to base our genealogy. As we described in the previous chapter, as an evolving system of behavioural government, which fuses psychological power and insight with a consistent commitment to political and economic freedom, neuroliberalism represents the contingent coming together of a range of processes, technologies, personalities and ideas that cut across the public, private and third sectors. In light of this, it is important to acknowledge the inevitably arbitrary nature of the point in time and space where we have chosen to commence our spatial history of neuroliberal ideas, institutions and policies.

Our history begins in London in 2009. While, to some extent, capricious, this starting point is important because it was at this point that the UK Government's Cabinet Office commissioned the Institute for Government to produce a report 'exploring the application of behavioural theory to public policy for senior public sector leaders and policy-makers' (Dolan et al., 2010: 5). The commissioned report was published in 2010 under the title *Mindspace: Influencing Behaviour through Public Policy*. The report commences with the quote that opens this chapter, which was written by the then Head of the Home Civil Service, Gus O'Donnell (along with Sir Michael Bichard, who was the Executive Director of the Institute for Government). The report is significant for at least three reasons. First, it reflects the high levels of bureaucratic support that the behavioural sciences were beginning to receive within the UK. Second, *Mindspace* was not only an attempt to initiate a turn towards the behavioural sciences in government, but to get a much firmer grasp on what had already been going on. Third, the report provides us with some valuable insights into the nature and form of neuroliberal policies.

Gus O'Donnell, an economist by training, had been advocating dialogue between the behavioural sciences and public policy-makers in the UK since he became Cabinet Secretary in 2005 (see Jones et al., 2013). To these ends it is clear that neuroliberal thinking was already starting to have an impact on approaches to government in one state as long as ten years ago. In addition to indicating the level of influence that neuroliberal orthodoxies were having at the centre of the British state, the *Mindspace* report also indicates that neuroliberalism was already an active part of a series of policy initiatives across a range of sectors in the UK and wider world by 2010. The report reviews a series of extant policy initiatives that bear the hallmarks of neuroliberal thinking. *Mindspace* explores attempts to tackle gang violence in Strathclyde through the establishment of new social norms among youth groups and the use of salient moral messengers; the adoption of opt-out private pension schemes; the application of Parenting Contracts to commit guardians to tackling truancy and poor behaviour in schools; and the promotion of female contraception in Africa through the use of hairdressers (Dolan, et al., 2010). These diverse, and ostensibly unrelated, behavioural initiatives are connected by their understanding of the more-than-rational dimensions of human decision making and action (particularly social influences and inertia) that are at the heart of the neuroliberal project.

In Chapter 1 of this volume we introduced the broad dimensions of neuroliberalism (relating specifically to its attempts to govern in and through emotions; the emphasis that it places on preserving personal freedom; and its links to neoliberal political and economic reason). The *Mindspace* report takes us a little deeper into the neuroliberal universe, and provides us with key insights into the practical dimensions of, and motivations for, neuroliberalism. *The Mindspace* report thus observes:

> For policy-makers facing policy challenges such as crime, obesity, or environmental sustainability, behavioural approaches offer a potentially powerful new set of tools. Applying these tools can lead to low cost, low pain ways of 'nudging' citizens – or ourselves – into new ways of acting by going with the grain of how we think and act. This is an important idea at any time, but is especially relevant in a period of fiscal constraint.
>
> *(ibid.: 7)*

There are two dimensions of this passage that are worth reflecting upon. The first thing to note is the emphasis that the report places on the links between new forms of behavioural government, fiscal constraint and low-cost strategies. While the forms of behavioural government associated with neuroliberalism were initially justified on the basis of their greater effectiveness, in an age of increasing austerity within the public sector (at least within Western governments) they have gradually become associated with the building of more cost-effective states. It is argued that neuroliberal policies can support moves towards greater fiscal constraint within the public sector because they are relatively cheap to implement (particularly when compared to more regulatory forms of state intervention), and will save the state money in the long term (in the context of reduced spending on policing, health care and public pension provision). In this context, certain brands of neuroliberalism have much in common with what has been described as minimalist, *EasyJet* styles of government, which take their inspiration from budget airlines.[1] There is actually a broader debate concerning whether the strategies associated with neuroliberalism reflect a more or less interventionist form of government (we will address this issue in greater depth in Chapter 6).

The second thing of note here is the emphasis that the *Mindspace* report places on 'going with the grain of how people think and act' (Dolan et al., 2010: 7). This notion of going with the grain of human cognition and behaviour is a popular mantra within neuroliberal discourse. It essentially reflects the ways in which neuroliberal policies attempt to acknowledge the automatic, habitual and emotional nature of human behaviour and rather than seek to correct it through rational prompts and regulations, work with it to achieve governmental goals. Neuroliberalism deliberately attempts to work with the desire lines of human behaviour (such as inertia, herd instincts, emotional responses and short-term thinking) instead of investing significant amounts of governmental resources in suppressing them. Going with the grain of human nature has, however, seen neuroliberalism do more than introduce sensitivity to the more-than-rational aspects of human behaviour into the policy-making process. Neuroliberalism displays a commitment to work with the world as it is rather than how policy-makers may wish it to be. As such, neuroliberalism has placed particular emphasis on the observation and study of so-called 'positive deviants' within populations (see Hilton, 2015: 37). Positive deviants are those small segments of a population who already display the forms of behaviours that those who govern desire. Learning from this virtuous minority is perceived within neuroliberal policy development as a far more efficient and effective basis for delivering behaviour change than the implementation of preconceived, externally generated policy programmes.

The *Mindspace* report draws a further line of distinction between new forms of behavioural policy and more conventional forms of regulation. While established mechanisms of incentives and education focus on 'changing minds', new behavioural policies prioritize 'changing contexts' and 'the environment within which we make decisions and respond to cues' (ibid.: 8). This focus on changing context rather than people is precisely why neuroliberal techniques have proven popular on both the political right and left: preserving as it does the importance of personal liberty and self-determination, while acknowledging a continued role for the state in supporting the frailties of the human condition (Taylor, 2009). In relation to changed contexts, evidence of neuroliberalism can now been seen within the behaviourally informed design of offices and canteens, computer hardware and software, household devices and personal health monitors, the design of cities and streets, administrative procedures and application forms, and even in the driving seat of your car (see Chapter 8 in this volume).[2]

A final aspect of neuroliberal government that *Mindspace* emphasizes is the importance of policy *exploration* and *evaluation* (ibid.: 9). Governmental exploration and evaluation are, perhaps, best understood as a move towards a more formal experimental style of policy development and application (see Chapter 6 in this volume). While policy evaluation is nothing new, there has been a strong emphasis within neuroliberalism on trialling innovative and often counter-intuitive policies, and the use of formal policy experiments. Perhaps one of the key hallmarks of contemporary neuroliberalism is the emphasis that it places on randomized controlled trials (see Haynes et al., 2012; John, 2013). In many ways the application of randomized controlled trials (RCTs) reflects the transfer of a preferred evaluative methodology from the behavioural and psychological sciences into the field of public policy. The prioritization of RCTs does, however, also appear to reflect a desire to ground neuroliberalism on a sound evidence base and to characterize associated forms of policy as less a *psychological state* and more a pragmatic, *what works* style of government. As we move through this volume we will discuss the ideological nature of attempts to position neuroliberalism outside of the realm of ideology and into the sphere of evidence-based pragmatism. We will also discuss some of the ethical and constitutional implications of establishing a more formally experimental system of government (see Chapter 6 in this volume).

Ultimately the *Mindspace* report provides us with some traits in and through which we might begin to identify and analyse neuroliberalism. These traits include, inter alia, cost saving; 'working with the grain' of human cognition and behaviour; changing the context of decision making; the use of formal experimentation and trials; and the pragmatic orientation of *what works* government. In identifying these traits of neuroliberalism it is important to be clear about how we understand the nature of the relation between these characteristics and the things they denote. First, we must acknowledge that each of these characteristics of government has its own history and is by no means unique to neuroliberalism. On these terms it is clear that identifying any one of these traits is not equivalent to uncovering neuroliberal practice. At the same time, we do not wish to claim that neuroliberalism is itself limited to instances of government where each of these traits is evident. As we discussed in Chapter 1 of this volume, there are actually very different expressions of neuroliberalism evident in the world today. Specific expressions of neuroliberal government always reflect the contingent coming together of certain traits of neuroliberalism in particular circumstances, in order to address specific issues.

Box 2.1 Key practical and discursive traits of neuroliberalism

Working with emotional grain of human cognition
Changing behaviours through redesigning of choice environments
The study of positive behavioural deviants
Emphasis on low cost government/austerity state
Use of formal policy experimentation and policy trials
A pragmatic orientation within policy making ('what works' government)

As a concept, we propose neuroliberalism as a way to better understand the systemic connections between actually existing forms of behavioural government. Understanding neuroliberalism on these terms does not only open up space for the empirical investigation of its effects. It also affords us the opportunity to develop novel metaphysical perspectives on the varied ways in which it arises in the world around us. In this way, the concept of neuroliberalism offers a vantage point for asking analytical questions about the broader social, economic and political significance of the things that are themselves given meaning within evolving systems of behavioural government.[3]

This chapter and Chapter 3 chart the variegated spatial histories of neuroliberalism. In this chapter we focus on the *practical history* of neuroliberal government, and the particular ways in which related policies have evolved and been implemented in a series of different behavioural contexts. Chapter 3 positions the practical account developed within this chapter in the context of the broader *history of ideas* that have informed the development of neuroliberal government. In the remainder of this chapter we provide an all-too-brief overview of the key practical developments that have informed and enabled the establishment of neuroliberal styles of government. This is a history that spans the work of marketing companies and advertising agencies, design specialists, aid workers, behaviour change start-ups, NGOs and government policy-makers. While some of this history has been directly influenced by the academic insights and ideas that underpin neuroliberalism, much of it has evolved separately from developments in the formal sciences of human behaviour (see Chapter 3). This practical history is thus as much about the intuitive actions of policy-makers confronted with public policy crises, and companies desperate to change consumer behaviours, as the formal application of the behavioural sciences to the problems of modern government.

Depth Boys: a pre-history of neuroliberal practices

For some, neuroliberal government represents the application of commercial techniques of persuasion and sales to the challenges of public sector government. As we will see, this vision of a unidirectional transfer of behavioural insights from the private to public sector is a largely inaccurate depiction of neuroliberalism's past. Nevertheless, it is important to acknowledge that the commercial sector was an important test bed for the ways in which emerging psychological insights into the human condition could be used to shape public behaviours on a relatively large scale.

The American journalist Vance Packard offered one of the earliest, and indeed, most compelling accounts of the commercial exploitation of psychological insights in order to change public behaviours. In his much discussed 1957 book *The Hidden Persuaders* Packard described how in the immediate post-war years there was a coming together of the insights of mass psychoanalysis and the desire of corporations to produce large-scale markets for their goods. Packard identified the emergence of a cadre of professional persuaders/manipulators who were able to use scientific insights into the nature of the human unconscious (developed within the motivational analyses of psychologists and social scientists) to develop more effective ways to stimulate consumption and sell goods. Packard described this new professional cadre – who were compromised of academics turned commercial consultants, and psychologically savvy advertisers – as 'Depth Boys' (Packard, 1957: 8). For Packard the notion of depth refers to two key dimensions of this newly emerging community. First, it denotes the new depth of analysis that was being offered into the working of the human unconscious. In keeping with the basic insights of neuroliberalism, the Depth Boys suggested a new vision of the human subject:

> [T]he typical American citizen is commonly depicted as an uncommonly shrewd person. He or she is dramatized as a thoughtful voter, rugged individualist, and, above all, as a careful, hardheaded consumer ... Typically [the Depth Boys] see us as bundles of daydreams, misty hidden yearnings, guilt complexes, irrational emotional blockages ... image lovers given to impulsive and compulsive acts.
>
> *(ibid.: 6–7)*

This new 'deeper' understanding of the human condition clearly has much in common with the emotionally focused account of the subject that has informed the neuroliberal project. Second, Packard also uses the term depth to refer to the ways in which this new band of behaviour change experts use subterranean 'depth channels' to subtly influence people's behaviour without alerting them to acts of manipulation. The targeting of unconscious depth channels is, of course, also a hallmark of many strands of neuroliberalism.

Ultimately the Depth Boys sought to sell products not just on the basis of cost or utility (as would be expected within classical economics), but through the emotional connections they constructed between consumers and merchandise. Quoting an advertising executive, Packard notes, 'The cosmetic manufacturers are not selling lanolin, they are selling hope ... We no longer buy oranges, we buy vitality. We do not buy just an auto, we buy prestige' (1957: 8). Over time the commercial exploitation of these psychological insights has combined with the novel understandings of the human condition that have emerged from the behavioural and neurological sciences (see du Plessis, 2011). Collectively these developments have led to the emergence of countless real world trials and campaigns that have sought to find out more about, and ultimately exploit, the role of the emotional, unconscious, habitual and automatic within consumer behaviour. The contemporary legacy of the Depth Boys can thus be seen in the design and layout of contemporary supermarkets, the creative connections that are now being made between brands and smell (a sense whose direct connection to the limbic system apparently makes it a particularly valuable pathway to emotional response) (see Lindstrom, 2005, 2008; Anderson, 2014: 25–6), and the ways in which lifestyle advertising seeks to exploit pleasure chemicals through the generation of so-called 'dopamine moments' (du Plessis, 2011: 89–93).

The behavioural experiments of the Depth Boys, and the wider marketing and sales industry, are clearly important precursors to neuroliberalism. It is important to note that the work of the Depth Boys and their successors within neuromarketing is not limited to the commercial sector. Since the 1950s and 1960s marketing has become increasingly influential within the political sphere, as candidates and political ideas were sold through the same psychological strategies as clothes and cars (Amin and Thrift, 2013). There are, however, important lines of distinction between neuroliberalism and the acts of psycho/neuro-seduction. The Depth Boys sought to exploit the emotional orientation of the human subject as a kind of behavioural foible that could be targeted in order to facilitate a commercial sale. In this context the irrational comportment of the individual is seen as a kind of temporary aberration – a brief letting down of the guard of the savvy self – that could be utilized by the advertising industry without necessarily undermining the autonomy or welfare of the citizen. Within the neuroliberal worldview things change. Suddenly, the behavioural foibles uncovered within the psychological and social sciences become the consistent errors identified by behavioural economists (see Chapter 3). These consistent errors are not aberrations, but a fundamental feature of the human condition. Furthermore, human emotions and irrationality are interpreted as not only weaknesses that can be exploited by the marketing industry, but as a cause of consistent error within decision making that results in people leading less healthy, less financially secure and less environmentally sustainable lifestyles. It is the shift from seeing human irrationality as a marketing opportunity to recognizing it as a consistent cause of harm-to-self among humans that distinguishes the practices of the Depth Boys from neuroliberalists. It is a shift that also leads to emerging insights into human behaviour being as much a concern of government as of commerce.

While Packard's *Hidden Persuaders* start from some of the same basic assumptions about the human condition as neuroliberalists, they do not share the same governmental instincts. Understanding neuroliberalism as a fundamentally governmental project (which interestingly involves both the state and corporations) helps us to recognize a further line of distinction between it and the marketing industry. While often accused of manipulation, the marketing industry is not constitutionally required to concern itself in any fundamental way with the impacts that its sales actions have on the freedom of its customers (so long as the veneer of free market competition is preserved and monopolies avoided) (see Davies, 2014). By contrast, as a form of government, neuroliberalism has a constitutional commitment to ensuring that its deployment of psychological insights does not undermine the autonomy of the people who are subject to its actions (see Chapters 4 and 5). The constant desire to find ways of combining new behavioural insights alongside the preservation of personal freedom (variously defined) is thus a distinguishing feature of the neuroliberal project.

While there are clear lines of connection between developments in the marketing industry and neuroliberal government, the notion that neuroliberalism reflects the emergence of some kind of *supermarket state* is clearly inaccurate. Neuroliberalism has drawn, and continues to draw, on many of the same forms of scientific insights and commercial practices that have informed the marketing industry over the last seventy years. But with its particular concern with questions of personal freedom and citizenly care, neuroliberalism is functionally distinct from its commercial precursors. Indeed, in many ways neuroliberalism actually reflects a form of governmental reaction to the neuro-commercialization that is now such a common feature of the world around us (du Plessis, 2011). One of the most common justifications for neuroliberal government is consequently the assertion that it represents a partial antidote to the excessive and damaging lifestyles that have emerged in the wake of the marketing industry's great success in exploiting human emotions in order to promote excessive consumption and financial irresponsibility (see Thaler and Sunstein, 2008). On these terms neuroliberalism is perhaps best conceived of as both a close relation of, but ultimate oppositional force to, the commercial marketing sector.

Social segmentation and branded condoms: the rise of social marketing

Although, as the previous section outlined, neuroliberalism stands in distinction from the marketing industry, during the 1960s a series of policy developments saw the formal fusing of government policies with marketing practices. This fusion between public policy and marketing is now commonly referred to as *social marketing*. Social marketing involves the strategic combination of the governmental pursuit of social care with the sales nous of the marketing industry. To the extent that it combines the pursuit of various forms of public good with an appreciation of the emotional nature of the human subject, social marketing represents one of the earliest practical manifestations of neuroliberal government. The birth of social marketing is, by popular consent, usually traced back to India in 1963. In 1963 the Indian government was struggling with the pressures of a population explosion, and the decision was made to explore novel approaches to family planning policy. In collaboration with the Ford Foundation, the Indian Institute of Management developed a 145-page report entitled 'Proposal for family planning promotion: a marketing plan' (see Chandy et al., 1965). This report had an impact on public health promotion policy that is still being felt today.

Rather than pursue traditional educational routes for promoting the use of contraception, or more coercive methods of population control, the Indian Institute of Management's report supported the use of a highly corporatist strategy for promoting the use of condoms. First of all the report suggested the use of targeted retail marketing, with particular attention being given to urban middle- and lower-income married couples with two or three children. Second, the report supported the production of condoms that were clearly branded through a government-owned trademark. Third, the progamme involved a multimedia publicity campaign, which not only promoted the use of condoms, but the specific use of government-branded merchandise. Fourth, and finally, the report supported the distribution of condoms to a wide range of retail outlets (including kiranas (dry grocers), village shops, cigarette vendors, cooperatives and tea stalls), where the brand would be heavily promoted (ibid.). It was hoped that the distribution of condoms to a wide range of outlets would not only make them more accessible to the general population, but also normalize their use within daily life.

Many aspects of this campaign reflect the practices and principles of neuroliberalism. The use of targeted retail marking, for example, embodies the forms of segmentation and personalized government that have become hallmarks of neuroliberalism (technological developments, of course, mean that the potential for personalized systems of social marketing and behavioural government is now far greater than it was in the 1960s). The production of a specific government brand of condom echoes the emphasis that neuroliberalism places on the role of emotions in human behaviour. In order to promote changes in the nature of sexual conduct, 'Proposal for family planning promotion' appears to have understood how important it was that people first of all identified with and then trusted the product that they were being encouraged to use (the use of government branding, as itself a trusted agency, may have been particularly important here given the socio-cultural taboos that surrounded the use of contraception). The wide distribution of condoms to vendors within a range of everyday spaces also mirrors neuroliberalism's assertion that social context and norms are crucial within the determination of behaviours. Through the programme, condoms became an ordinary feature of everyday social life, and supported the development of a new social norm: the assumption was that condoms were being widely used, and that their use was entirely normal.

To characterize 'Proposal for family planning promotion' as echoing and reflecting neuroliberalism is, in many ways, misleading. Rather than an echo, 'Proposal for family planning promotion' is actually one of a series of early practical iterations that would inform the development of neuroliberalism. What is clear is that 'Proposal for family planning promotion' led to an emerging series of practical experiments in the fusing of public policy and marketing that contributed to the gradual development of neuroliberal styles of government. Following this initial trial in the possibilities of social marketing, a series of prominent organizations such as the World Bank, the Advertising Council of America, the World Health Organization, and the international development agencies of various national governments adopted similar policy initiatives during the 1960s and 1970s (Kotler and Zaltman, 1971). It was not, however, until the 1980s that we began to see the widespread application of social marketing techniques to a series of problems of behavioural government. During the 1980s social marketing techniques were used in developing countries to tackle a range of pressing public health issues including the spread of HIV/AIDS, diarrhoea and malaria. In more economically developed countries the 1980s were also witness to the increasing use of marketing techniques by governments keen to address the public health challenges relating to skin cancer, high blood pressure and smoking.

Throughout the 1990s social marketing techniques continued to be used to address a range of issue-specific problems. It was not, however, until the turn of the millennium that social marketing began to shape national public policy in a coordinated way. During the first decade of the twenty-first century states such as Canada, Australia, New Zealand, the US and the UK instigated national initiatives that sought to apply the principles of social marketing more systematically to a series of public health challenges (see Jones et al.'s 2013 discussion of New Labour's 2004 *Choosing Health* initiative: 113–21). One of the most significant moments within the systematic governmental application of social marketing was the establishment in 2006 of the UK Government's National Social Marketing Centre (now known by the abbreviation NSMC). Much of the early work of the NSMC was funded through the UK's Department for Health, but now the Centre applies social marketing techniques across a range of different policy sectors as a Community Interest Company. While the NSMC's formation was in part driven by the emerging body of research evidence that demonstrated the effectiveness of social marketing, it was also informed by increasing government recognition of the cost-effectiveness of focusing public spending on preventive behavioural policy measures (as opposed to having to spend public money on actual treatment) (see National Consumer Council, 2006).

While representing an important moment in the international history of neuroliberalism, it is important to emphasize that the NSMC was an ultimately constrained articulation of neuroliberal government. We spoke at length to one representative from the NSMC who had been involved in its original formation. This representative made the following observation:

> The National Social Marketing Centre, when it was set up, we basically had to try and compete with health promotion. And go for the same pot of money as that. And it was focused on public health. And public health, you know, they liked evidence-based things. And marketing is as much a science as it is [an] art. And that made them [public sector funders] nervous. So, what happened at the Centre [NSMC] is we developed a planning process model, which was five stages, and now six … And we did that for, as I said, for political reasons. And that was the correct thing to do at that time. However, when we did that, we moved it more away from actually what social marketing is about, and made it more kind of a process, and totally process driven. So, it took away … it took away the kind of anthropology, the psychology background of it …
>
> *(NSMC representative, interview, 2014)*

It appears that in order to be taken seriously within the scientifically oriented public health sector in the UK, social marketing had to be separated from its association with creative marketing and intuition and given a much more positivist feel. The representative of the NSMC went on to observe:

> And still people, when I do training courses, they struggle because you know, public health people, they like to think about it as this systematic and stage process. And when you talk about insights, and you say, 'Well, no [behavioural] insights, in the way you go with your gut feeling, you know, what do you think will be the tipping point, the cue that will trigger the behaviour and make it sustainable?' They find that bit really difficult … So, basically, to answer your question, the NSMC took it [social marketing], ironically, away from human behaviour to make it this kind of organized structure. I feel too much. And you know, and I was to blame for that, like I was one of the developers of it.
>
> *(NSMC representative, interview, 2014)*

Here we see how in the UK the mainstreaming of social marketing (at least through the NSMC) involved the occlusion of some of the key behavioural insights that inform neuroliberalism (particularly in relation to the role of emotions, gut feelings and unconscious habits in driving human behaviour). New scientific insights into the role of emotions and habits would ultimately give greater political credence to the behavioural assumptions upon which social marketing was based. As we will see, however, these new scientific insights would ultimately be used to support a new strand of neuroliberal government, which, while connected to social marketing, would ultimately become something of a rival.

Nudge squads and neuroliberal policy experiments

Nudger-in-Chief: US beginnings

The next key stage in the practical history of neuroliberalism came in Washington, D.C. in 2009 during what would ordinarily be a fairly routine Senate confirmation process. The Senate confirmation process was focusing on the appointment of Barack Obama's nomination to head the White House Office of Information and Regulatory Affairs (OIRA). OIRA is a powerful, if often overlooked, branch of the US Federal Government. Established by Ronald Reagan in 1981, OIRA's primary focus is to test the validity of governmental regulation. While initially part of Reagan's push to reduce governmental intervention, over time OIRA has become a crucial conduit in and through which state regulation is tested and evaluated in the US. The Senate confirmation of the head of OIRA is normally a relatively routine affair, and certainly not an event that generates much public interest. But in 2009 things were different. The reason that things were different was that Barack Obama had chosen to nominate Cass Sunstein, the co-author of *Nudge*, to head up OIRA. Obama had known Sunstein from his time at the University of Chicago, and Sunstein had campaigned on his behalf during his run for the Presidency. It was Sunstein's advocacy of nudge-style policies – which combined insights into the irrational nature of human decision making with design-based interventions into human behaviour (among other things) – that made his nomination controversial. The TV host and writer Glenn Beck ran a series of features in which he described Sunstein as 'the most dangerous man in America': claiming that the neuroliberal strategy of nudging was manipulative and insidious (Sunstein, 2013: 24). Certain Republican senators placed holds on Sunstein's confirmation, and Sunstein himself began receiving hate mail and death threats in the post (ibid.). While the nature of Sunstein's appointment as head of OIRA is, in many ways, an unsavoury episode in the history of neuroliberal government, it does perhaps reflect one of the few times when the principles of neuroliberalism have been subject to a significant period of public scrutiny and debate.

Once in post at the OIRA Sunstein became a kind of regulatory tsar (although Richard Thaler preferred the term Nudger-in-Chief), who sought to systematically apply new behavioural insights to various forms of regulatory policy. Sunstein's tenure as head of OIRA (between 10 September 2009 and 10 August 2012) represents one of the most significant periods in the practical history of neuroliberal government. During this period Sunstein was able to implement neuroliberal policy innovations at large spatial scales, and across many branches of the Federal Government. Before we discuss some prominent examples of Sunstein's neuroliberal policies, it is important to note the way in which he positioned his initiatives politically. Foremost, Sunstein wanted to distance himself from proponents of a more psychologically interventionist state:

Some people think that behavioural economics and an appreciation of System 1 justify a greater role for government. If we know that people are likely to err, shouldn't government do a lot more to correct their mistakes?

(ibid.: 71)

Sunstein was keen to avoid the accusation that behaviourally informed policies were overtly regulatory in nature (this was a particularly significant issue given OIRA's regulatory oversight). While acknowledging that neuroliberal styles of policy have emerged in response to consistently observed *behavioural market failures* (from failure to adequately invest in pensions, to the slow take-up of more fuel-efficient cars), Sunstein did not believe that they necessarily had to involve more regulation. Sunstein thus observed:

[i]t remains true that even if we have to supplement the standard accounts of market failures, it does not necessarily follow that more regulation is justified. Maybe reliance on the private sector is best. The regulatory cure may be worse than the disease. It might be poorly designed and ineffective; it might be too expensive …

(ibid.: 73)

While OIRA was responsible for overseeing federal regulatory policy, Sunstein did not see the behavioural policies he trialled as being necessarily regulatory. Instead what Sunstein instigated was a programme to test the extent to which behavioural insights could be used to inform the design of regulatory policies (ibid.: 73). According to Sunstein then:

It would be absurd to say that behaviourally informed regulation is more aggressive than regulation that if not so informed. The argument is instead that such an understanding can help to inform the design of regulatory programs – and make them more likely to succeed. And in some contexts, we will be able to come up with new nudges, taking the form of creative solutions to seemingly intractable problems.

(ibid.: 73)

Understanding the ways in which Sunstein connects neuroliberalism and regulation is not merely contextual, it has had a substantive impact on the evolving nature and remit of related styles of government in the US and around the world. Consequently, while drawing on the insights of behavioural sciences, Sunstein's brand of neuroliberalism was carefully constructed in order to avoid accusations of manipulative state intervention. In Sunstein's eloquent reflections on his time in government in his book *Simpler: The Future of Government*, the future of government is primarily positioned as a form of scientifically grounded, empirically oriented system of policy development that relies heavily on cost–benefit analysis and experimentation (Sunstein 2013; see also Sunstein, 2014). For Sunstein then, the policy nudges that he developed were not about more or less government and/or regulation, but about developing:

> [a]ccurate, rather than fanciful, understandings of how human beings think and act. They are subject to careful empirical testing. What matters is whether they work. The best nudges have high benefits and low costs.
>
> *(Sunstein, 2013: 9)*

The positioning of this nudge-oriented brand of neuroliberalism as a form of pragmatic government appears to have been crucial to its gaining political acceptability and legitimacy. The key for Sunstein was making sure that where regulatory policies did exist they were behvaiourally effective.

As head of the OIRA Sunstein instigated a programme of regulatory reform that emphasized the importance of recognizing new insights into the nature of human behaviour and motivation (particularly the power of inertia and procrastination; the significance of framing and presentation; social influences; and the difficulties that people experience when trying to accurately assess probability) (Sunstein, 2013). These initiatives related to the salient framing of energy efficiency and nutritional information to customers; the strategic resetting of defaults in relation to health care schemes and free school meal provision; and a simplification of the processes through which people applied for federal student aid. It is also important to note that Obama's flagship Patient Protection and Affordable Health Care Act (2010) contained several neuroliberal features (including its use of disclosure requirements and the resetting of the default for enrolments in health care schemes from opt-in to opt-out).[4]

While it is important to acknowledge that neuroliberal forms of policy existed in the US long before Sunstein's appointment to the OIRA (see for example the 2006 Pension Protection Act's use of automatic enrolment; and the use of Save More Tomorrow initiatives within certain company pension schemes),[5] it is clear that Sunstein's tenure helped to institutionalize neuroliberal thinking into the heart of the US Federal Government. While the forms of policies that Sunstein promoted were inspired by similar insights into the emotional nature of human decision making as those that informed earlier social marketing policies, there are key differences between these neuroliberal policy regimes. The types of policies that emerged from Sunstein's OIRA placed less emphasis on general marketing strategies and publicity campaigns, and focused much more on redesigning the choice architectures that surround human decision making. The policies developed by OIRA were informed less by the practical insights of the marketing industry (on how to sell an idea, practice or product), and more by formal scientific insights into specific behavioural tendencies and heuristics. According to reports issued by OIRA, the styles of neuroliberal regulation promoted within Sunstein's tenure resulted in billions of dollars of benefit to the US treasury and economy (Halpern, 2015: Loc 639).

Behavioural insights in the UK: The **Personal Responsibility and Changing Behaviour** *report*

If the US was a key practical test bed for nudge-oriented policy development, the UK was also home to key developments in the practical evolution of neuroliberalism. The UK Government's engagement with neuroliberal ideas does, in many ways, predate those in the US (see Jones et al., 2013). During the early years of the 2000s, under Tony Blair's New Labour government, a group of civil servants working in the Prime Minister's Cabinet Office Strategy Unit started to explore the potential of applying neuroliberal styles of policies in the design and implementation of public policy. Two key figures in the Strategy Unit were David Halpern and Geoff Mulgan. David Halpern is a social psychologist and was Chief Analyst in the Prime Minister's Strategy Unit between 2001 and 2008. Geoff Mulgan is an academic and policy advisor and was Director of the Strategy Unit. Together they were instrumental in the production of the 2004 report *Personal Responsibility and Changing Behaviour: The State of Knowledge and its Implications for Public Policy* (Halpern et al., 2004). At the heart of this report was a desire to explore how governments could best support individuals to instigate forms of behaviour change that are in their best long-term interests. The report asserted that there were limits to the role that traditional forms of government action (including public spending and regulation) could have when it came to achieving key social and economic goals. Given that many of these government goals (whether it be improving the general health of the population, securing the financial security of families or protecting the environment) ultimately depend on the decisions and actions of individuals, the *Personal Responsibility and Changing Behaviour* report considered how best to enable people to take greater responsibility for their behavioural choices (ibid.: 3–4).

Alongside a desire to refocus government action onto personal behaviour and responsibility, the report outlined the ways in which new behavioural insights could make policy delivery much more effective. In language that is clearly neuroliberal, the report identified the limits of regulatory policies that assumed a 'rational man' model of human behaviour, and instead promoted an *ecological* vision of human motivation (ibid.: 16–18). Ecology is used in the report as a kind of framework of analogy through which to understand the complexities of 'non-rational' forms of human behaviour. At one level the ecological analogy draws attention (deliberate or otherwise) to the evolutionary psychology that has informed the development of forms of human decision making that may not be optimal, but have served to ensure our collective survival. The ecological perspective on human behaviour is also used in the report to draw attention to the integrated mix of social, cultural and environmental influences that routinely, and often unconsciously, shape our behaviour. The *Personal Responsibility and Changing Behaviour* report's reference to ecology is also used to highlight the ways in which humans (like other animals in an eco-system) seek consistently to save both time and energy within the process of decision making (and thus use behavioural heuristics or shortcuts) (ibid.: 16).

Ultimately, the report offers an account of human behaviour that is both holistic and grounded in behavioural and evolutionary psychology.

The *Personal Responsibility and Changing Behaviour* report is significant not only because it marks the first systematic articulation of neuroliberal ideas by a branch of the British state, but also because it provides us with some clues as to why neuroliberalism became seen as a governmental option in the early years of the new millennium. The Strategy Unit team argued that a key force driving the emergence of new styles of behavioural government was welfare conditionality (ibid.: 6). Welfare conditionality is about connecting the reception of some form of governmental benefit (perhaps unemployment support or incapacity benefit), with a series of desired behaviours (perhaps seeking a job, or pursuing training support). Welfare conditionality schemes presented public policy-makers with an opportunity and a challenge. The opportunity related to the fact that with new conditions being attached to the receipt of welfare, policy-makers had a captive audience with whom they could trial new policy initiatives. The challenge was presented by the fact that welfare conditionality was seeking to change a series of behaviours (in particular the habitual receipt of welfare) that had historically been recalcitrant to transformation. It was specifically in relation to such behavioural challenges that the authors of *Personal Responsibility and Changing Behaviour* argued that more complex and ecologically oriented understanding of human decision making could be particularly valuable within the policy-making process. In addition to welfare conditionality, the *Personal Responsibility and Changing Behaviour* report suggested that the ongoing desire to rein in the excesses of public spending made the cost-effectiveness of neuroliberal styles of government (particularly when compared to the expenses of monitoring, regulation and education) very attractive (as we will see shortly, the emergence of austerity systems of government following the 2008 credit crunch would only add to the economic appeal of new behavioural policies) (ibid.).

Despite laying the intellectual and practical ground for the development of more neuroliberal styles of government in the UK, the *Personal Responsibility and Changing Behaviour* report actually got somewhat derailed by a reference it made to the use of 'fat taxes' within health promotion campaigns (see Jones et al., 2013). Due to the media controversy that was stirred up by the report's reference to calorific taxes, many in Westminster (and particularly those close to the Prime Minister) distanced themselves from the publication. Certain policy strategists in key government departments such as the Department for Health and the Department for Environment Food and Rural Affairs did, however, see great potential in the report's suggestions. Consequently between 2004 and 2010, and while lacking formal support from the Prime Minster's Office, the principles of neuroliberalism began to be quietly tested and developed within a series of Whitehall departments who were keen to find solutions to recalcitrant behavioural problems.

While the *Personal Responsibility and Changing Behaviour* report is routinely referred to as a key publication within the history of neuroliberal styles of government, it actually contains an often overlooked, and certainly unresolved, tension. According to one of the reports authors with whom we spoke:

[t]here is a tension in the [report] which reflects a political tension itself, which is that it was a paper about *personal responsibility and behaviour change*, so there's those two things in it, and now, those don't sit perfectly together actually if you reflect about it. So politically the drive amongst particularly Labour backbenchers and others, is rooted in, well, anti-social behaviour – let's stop all these horrible people doing nasty things or, let's get everybody to recycle more or whatever it is. But ... actually often it was rooted especially for Tony [Blair], it has to be said, in as I said, this model of stopping these bad people doing bad things, and rooted in a slightly moralistic ... And so one of the things, in a subtler way, a lot of behaviour change, well, famously they use the phrase nudge, you nudge, you manipulate, encourage people to do something differently. And in fact that might be subverting or by-passing personal responsibility in the normal moral sense.

(Co-author, Personal Responsibility and Changing Behaviour *report, interview, 2009)*

The tension between the moral reform of the subject (as implied within the notion of taking greater personal responsibility) and changing behaviour (as something that may involve bypassing the moral autonomy of the individual: see Furedi, 2011) is never really resolved within the report. For us the report's discussion of personal responsibility alongside behaviour change is suggestive of a deeper debate about behavioural capacity and incapacity that runs through the behavioural sciences. This debate concerns the extent to which new insights into the emotional and often unconscious nature of much human decision making mandates a more paternalist style of government (which can counterbalance inevitably flawed human decision making), or a more behaviourally empowering state (which seeks to build greater understandings of, and control over, personal habits and routine behaviours). While this issue is not directly addressed within the *Personal Responsibility and Changing Behaviour* report, it is a theme that we will return to consistently in this volume (see in particular Chapters 3 and 4).

David Cameron and the 'next age of government'

In February 2010 the then leader of the British Conservative Party David Cameron delivered a now famous TED talk entitled 'The Next Age of Government'. The talk was designed to set out his vision for a new age of government and to establish an intellectual framework for his broader political project.[6] In many ways this talk laid the foundations for the UK's neuroliberal policy agenda, which Cameron would usher in when he came to power later that year. Cameron's vision actually echoes closely the sentiments of the *Personal Responsibility and Changing Behaviour* report. He argued that in the wake of the financial crisis of 2008, new systems of lower-cost government had to be developed. He also claimed that the information revolution provided new opportunities for the development of personalized systems of government (see Domehl, 2014). And, drawing on the work of Cass

Sunstein, Richard Thaler and Daniel Kahneman (et al.) (and directly echoing the sentiments of the *Mindspace* report), he asserted that the emerging insights of the behavioural sciences would enable public policy to increasingly 'work with the grain of human nature' as opposed to pushing helplessly against it.

Ultimately, Cameron extolled the virtues of a more human, post-bureaucratic style of government within which the acts of governing are increasingly delivered through smart networks of collaborating citizens working on a variety of different scales (see Hilton, 2015: 9–12). As we will see later in this volume the motif of the post-bureaucratic state has become strongly associated with the practices of neuroliberalism (see Chapter 6 in this volume). The post-bureaucratic ideal can be seen within neuroliberal policies to the extent that they emphasize the role of social influences, norms and peer networks in shaping and regulating human conduct – as opposed to seeing power trickling down from on high or radiating out from a government centre. The notion of the post-bureaucratic is, however, evident in a more literal sense through the neuroliberal association with the formation of institutions of government that adopt flat bureaucratic structures, functional independence and the ethos of innovative business start-ups (see Chapter 6 in this volume). As we will see, the practical history of neuroliberalism has not involved governments simply delivering policies that reflect a more complex understanding of the human subject. It has also involved attempts to reshape government structures themselves (through the formation of citizens' juries, Skunkwork units, embedded government and community-focused governance systems) in order to facilitate a greater sensitivity to the everyday human condition. As we will discuss at greater length in Chapter 8 of this volume, in attempting to develop more humanly oriented systems of government, neuroliberal policies have become associated with the practices of human-centred design and the ethnographic techniques of study that it involves (Hilton, 2015: 30–5). In this context, it is clear that neuroliberalism is as much about the procedures of governing as it is about theoretical assumptions concerning the human subject.

At around the same time that David Cameron gave his TED talk he had a meeting with the authors of the poplar behavioural economics book *Freakonomics,* Steven Levitt and Stephen J. Dubner (Levitt and Dubner, 2007). Reports of this meeting suggested that when Cameron arrived he endearingly asked 'Where are the clever people?' (Runciman, 2014). Despite its cheery start, this was not to be a productive meeting. As the conversation turned to the UK's National Health Service (hereafter NHS) Dubner and Levitt provided a typical behavioural economist analysis of why the health care system was in such dire financial straits. Dubner and Levitt described to Cameron how the financial problems of the NHS stemmed from the fact that when confronted with a free service, people tend to consume it in relatively inefficient ways. It appears that Dubner and Levitt's point was not to suggest that people should pay the market value for medical care in the NHS, but that if a small (even nominal) charge were introduced people's behavioural tendency to over-consume would be removed and greater savings in costs could be made. According to Dubner and Levitt, Cameron's response to their suggested reforms to the NHS was not supportive, '[h]e didn't say anything at all. The smile did not leave David Cameron's face, but it did leave his eyes … In any case he offered a quick handshake and hurried off' (Runciman, 2014). We recount this story here not because it is necessarily a significant point in the practical history of neuroliberalism – ultimately it would reflect nothing more than a small bump in the road – but to indicate that the history of neuroliberalism cannot be understood in isolation from broader political considerations. In the UK, for example, to suggest reforms to the NHS that would involve the implementation of fees (even if only nominal) would be tantamount to political suicide. This is at least one of the reasons why Cameron gave such a lukewarm response to Dubner and Levitt's suggestions. Here we see how the history of neuroliberalism is a both a scientific and political story. And for new scientific ideas and practices to take hold it is clear that the political conditions must be supportive.

Notwithstanding the abortive meeting with Dubner and Levitt, once elected as Prime Minister, David Cameron oversaw one of the most significant fusions of the behavioural sciences and government witnessed anywhere in the world. This fusion of science and policy would centre on the newly formed Behavioural Insights Team. Much of the Conservative Party's interest in the behavioural sciences in general, and behavioural economics in particular, was instigated by two policy advisors: Steve Hilton and Rohan Silva. Hilton and Silva served as policy advisors to David Cameron and George Osborne in the build-up to the 2010 election. Hilton and Silva had visited the US in order to find out about the latest policy developments on the other side of Atlantic. It was on this trip that the two advisors would meet Richard Thaler, who would eventually become a key advisor within the Behavioural Insights Team (Halpern, 2015). In addition to exploring the potential for the transatlantic transfer of new policy ideas, Hilton and Silva became interested in new behavioural policy thinking much closer to home. Rohan Silva was aware of the of the work of David Halpern, who had at this point left the civil service to work at the Institute for Government (a UK-based independent think tank). Silva's interest in what Halpern had to say was spiked again in early 2010 with the publication of the aforementioned *Mindspace* report. Given his appreciation of the emerging insights of the behavioural sciences (as a social psychologist) and his understanding of the internal workings of the British government (as a former civil servant), Halpern become an obvious person to lead the Behavioural Insights Team.

The Behavioural Insights Team (hereafter BIT)[7] was formally launched in the summer of 2010. With an initial budget of just £0.5 million, the unit was set the tasks of 'transforming two major policy areas'; 'spreading an understanding of behavioural approaches across Whitehall'; and 'achiev[ing] at least a tenfold return on the costs of the unit' (Halpern, 2015: Loc 831). The BIT had a sunset clause built into its constitution, which would mean that if it failed to meet its stated objectives it would be closed down after two years. This sunset clause was never activated as the BIT steadily grew in national and international significance. Now a social purpose company (jointly owned by the UK state and the innovation charity NESTA, which is headed by Halpern's former Strategy Unit colleague, Geoff Mulgan), the BIT has a multi-million pound budget, a staff of over fifty people, and offices in London, Sydney and New York. Before considering some of the early work of the BIT, it is important to recognize the particular, and to some degree unusual, political circumstances that came together to facilitate its formation. As we have already mentioned, the BIT was in part the product of the election of a Conservative Party keen to promote new, cost-effective styles of government. It is, however, often overlooked that the Conservative Party's junior coalition partners (the Liberal Democrats) liked the idea of the BIT (in particular they appear to have been drawn to the libertarian ethos of the policies it promoted and the empiricism on which it was to be based) (ibid.: Loc. 769). The BIT also had strong support from within the civil service, with the aforementioned Cabinet Secretary Gus O'Donnell being an advocate of new behavioural insights (O'Donnell went on to chair the BIT's Academic Advisory Panel).

Since 2010 the BIT has been engaged in developing a series of policy initiatives and trials with a range of government departments. It has, for example, developed policies that sought to help reduce household energy use; support the government's consumer empowerment strategy; reduce incidents of fraud, error and debt; promote charitable giving; improve levels of educational attainment; and combat mobile phone theft. The BIT has also conducted RCTs on the use of behavioural insights in attempts to increase rates of organ donation and support the growth of small businesses. The specific work of the BIT in relation to issues of fraud, error and debt is indicative of the new forms of government practices that the unit has been promoting. The BIT has liaised with the National Health Service, the UK tax authorities and Britain's Driver and Vehicle Licensing Agency (DVLA) to try and combat the challenges associated with fraud and error and the billions of pounds it costs law-abiding taxpayers every year.

In collaboration with Her Majesty's Revenue and Customs Risk and Intelligence Service, the BIT sought to tackle the specific problem of undeclared income among doctors and dentists. This specific problem stems from the fact that doctors and dentists have two primary streams of income. The first comes through their salaried work within the NHS or clinics, and the other is through the additional work they take on an ad hoc basis. While their salaried work is taxed at source, it has proven difficult to increase the payment of tax on additional earnings (Halpern, 2015: Loc. 1271). Conventional (neoliberal) approaches to undeclared tax repayments have tended to interpret undeclared tax as a deliberate attempt to game the revenue system, and have deployed legal sanctions and advertising campaigns (which seek to generate a fear of being caught) to address the matter. Drawing on neoliberal insights, the BIT claimed that the failure to declare earnings to the tax authorities has at least as much to do with the complexities associated with the tax payment systems than a deliberate attempt to deceive. They have also argued that reframing tax repayment schemes around social norms may be much more effective than using fear. In order to make declaring extra income easier, the BIT have explored the ways in which it may be possible to pre-populate tax forms (with relevant, personal information) and develop apps that facilitate the real-time capture tax information. In relation to the use of social norms, the BIT have also run a series of trials within which the failure to repay tax has been framed within personalized tax letters as an 'oversight' (rather than a criminal activity), with emphasis placed on the trust and honesty that is typically associated with the medical professions (BIT, 2012). The emphasis that is placed here on the promotion of cognitive and practical ease, and the use of tailored social norms, are both hallmarks of neuroliberal government. The work of BIT to date has demonstrated that such initiatives can increase tax repayment rates significantly.

The BIT have also worked with the DVLA to try and target people who fail consistently to pay their car tax (estimates in 2011 suggested that there were approximately 249,000 unregistered vehicles in the UK collectively costing the state £40 million in lost revenue: BIT, 2012: 25). Deploying an RCT, the BIT explored the impact of sending out personalized car tax letters to the owners of untaxed vehicles. A photograph of the untaxed car (taken automatically by DVLA cameras) was affixed to the tax payment letter (alongside some changes in the language and layout of the letter). This strategy has resulted in 20 per cent increases in car tax payments. The idea of a more personalized form of government within which the individual loses their sense of anonymity in relation to the state (and the forms of cognitive protection this seems to afford) is an emerging practical characteristic of neuroliberalism.

Globalizing neuroliberal practices

While developments in the US and UK have played an important part in the evolution and development of neuroliberalism, neuroliberal government practices are evident in many other countries throughout the world. At the end of 2013 we conducted an extensive survey of neuroliberal styles of government to see just how globalized neuroliberalism had become (see Whitehead et al., 2014 for the full details of our findings and an explanation of the methodology that we deployed). Our study was primarily interested in two things: (1) which countries showed some form of evidence of neuroliberal forms of policy operating somewhere within their borders; and (2) which nations had developed some form of centrally orchestrated application of neuroliberal policies across their public sectors (as in the cases of the US and UK). In order to carry out this survey we identified a series of policy proxies, which were used to determine the presence or absence of neuroliberal policies within states around the world (see Figure 2.1). Utilizing these proxies we discovered that as of late 2013, 135 independent states including Taiwan (that is 69 per cent of all states) were witness to some form of neuroliberal policy within their territory (see Figure 2.2) (Whitehead et al., 2014). We further discovered that fifty-one states had some forms of centrally orchestrated neuroliberal policy in operation (that is over a quarter of all states in the world) (see Figure 2.3). This survey represents a minimum baseline assessment of where we can see neuroliberal styles of government in action (it can usefully be read alongside other international reviews of behavioural insights in public policy) (Joint Research Centre, 2016; Lunn, 2014). In this context, it is highly likely that neuroliberalism is influencing public policy in states that our survey did not identify.

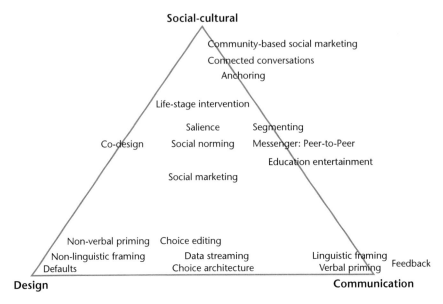

Social-cultural

Community-based social marketing
Connected conversations
Anchoring

Life-stage intervention

Salience   Segmenting
Co-design   Social norming   Messenger: Peer-to-Peer
                              Education entertainment

Social marketing

Non-verbal priming   Choice editing
Non-linguistic framing   Data streaming   Linguistic framing
Defaults   Choice architecture   Verbal priming   Feedback

Design   **Communication**

FIGURE 2.1 Policy proxies used to identify the global spread of neuroliberal government
Source: Whitehead et al., 2014.

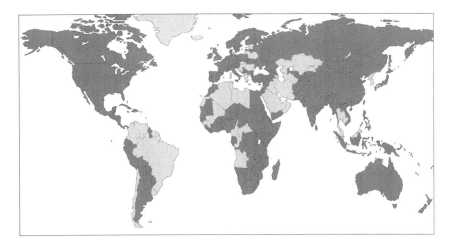

FIGURE 2.2 Independent states (darker shading) where evidence was found of the impact of the new behavioural sciences on the design and/or implementation of public policy

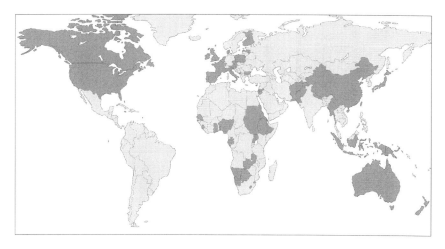

FIGURE 2.3 Independent states (darker shading) with centrally orchestrated neuroliberal-type policy initiatives

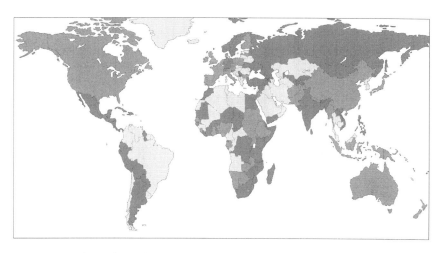

FIGURE 2.4 The independent states with centrally orchestrated behaviour change programmes (midtone shading) and those states where there has been a more ad hoc adoption of neuroliberal-type policies (darker shading)

In exploring the global spread of nudge-type policies two things become immediately apparent. The first is that neuroliberalism is not the preserve of more economically developed countries. Neuroliberal styles of government are evident throughout large swathes of Africa, South America and Asia. The prominence of neuroliberal policies in places such as Africa reflects attempts to use new behavioural insights to tackle a range of pressing public health issues, such as HIV/AIDS, malaria and diarrhoea. These policies have been supported by prominent development agencies such as USAID, the United Nations Development Programme, AusAID, the Japanese Social Development Fund and the World Bank, but there has also been advocacy from national health authorities.[8] Many of these public health initiatives actually predate the rise of neuroliberalism in more economically developed states, particularly in Africa where they have been used to tackle the HIV/AIDS crisis since the late 1980s. In this context, it appears that many of the early iterations of actually existing neuroliberalism were born out of the practical struggle to tackle pressing public health problems and not the formal transfer of behavioural science into government. The second thing of note is the fact that neuroliberal styles of government have become a feature of policy making in more authoritarian states (particularly China and Singapore).

In addition to international development agencies, the globalization of neuroliberalism has been supported by a series of significant organizations. Prominent among these have been the OECD, the World Economic Forum (Agenda Council on Neuroscience and Behaviour) and the European Commission (see Van Bavel et al., 2013; Lunn, 2014). Other smaller organizations including the Danish Nudging Network, Behaviour Works and Change Labs have also played a role in supporting the global spread of neuroliberal practices. More recently the BIT has been playing a leading role in supporting the internationalization of neuroliberalism. The BIT has been advising national governments on how best to deploy new behavioural insights to various public policy programmes (they have, for example, been advising the Guatemalan state on how to apply behavioural insights to tax policy). They have also been counselling a series of states (including the Netherlands and the New South Wales government in Australia) on how to establish behavioural insight units of their own. In an interesting development, the BIT offered support to the Federal Government in the US as they sought to establish their own behavioural insights unit. This new unit is known formally as the Social and Behavioural Sciences Team. While the Social and Behavioural Sciences Team is building on the aforementioned work of Cass Sunstein, its form and function closely resemble the BIT. The work of this new team has been partly enabled by the release of a Presidential Executive Order – Using Behavioral Science Insights to Better Serve the American People – by Barack Obama in September 2015 (White House, 2015).

According to the Executive Order:

> To more fully realize the benefits of behavioral insights and deliver better results at a lower cost for the American people, the Federal Government should design its policies and programs to reflect our best understanding of how people engage with, participate in, use, and respond to those policies and programs. By improving the effectiveness and efficiency of Government, behavioral science insights can support a range of national priorities, including helping workers to find better jobs; enabling Americans to lead longer, healthier lives; improving access to educational opportunities and support for success in school; and accelerating the transition to a low-carbon economy.
>
> *(White House, 2015)*

Ultimately the Executive Order mandates that the Federal Government should identify important policy areas where neuroliberal styles of government intervention can be implemented, actively recruit behavioural science experts into government, and actively pursue the application of new behavioural policies to relevant public policies.

Conclusion

In this chapter we have set out a detailed – albeit necessarily partial – history of the emergence and spread of neuroliberal ideas, institutions and policies. We have intentionally avoided providing a linear account of neuroliberalism, acknowledging instead the many origin stories that might be told in relation to its development. By focusing on neuroliberal *practices*, we wish to convey a sense of the fragility and contingency of this broad political project. In so doing, we also want to open up space within this book to consider three interrelated themes. The first is the importance of examining empirically the particular geographical circumstances in which neuroliberal practices have become established. These circumstances include the particular political traditions and principal economic circumstances of specific nation states, and the cultural conventions and historical notions of citizenship with which neuroliberal practice have to work (see in particular Chapter 5 in this volume). The second theme opened up by this practical history of neuroliberalism is a discussion of the extent to which various forms of governmental intervention are seen to be justified and under what circumstances human autonomy is either threatened or supported by neuroliberalism (see Chapters 4 and 5 in this volume). In opening up a focus on the contingent and thus politically fecund idea of neuroliberalism, we hope to begin to explore and chart alternative pathways that neuroliberal forms of government might take (see Chapter 9 in this volume).

Notes

1 In 2009 the London Borough of Barnet announced plans to adopt a model of local government that reflected the economic logics of a low cost airline (*The Guardian*, 2009). While plans to provide a basic service that residents could choose to upgrade are not neuroliberal policies, the broader goals of developing of a minimalist, low-cost state are supported within many iterations of neuroliberal government.
2 As we will discuss later in the volume, such policies make a series of significant, and often problematic, assumptions about the malleability of environment and space in public policy making (see Leggett, 2014).
3 As we will discuss later in this chapter, one of the virtues of neuroliberalism is that it leads us to ask important metaphysical questions about emerging forms of behavioural government, which themselves appear to preclude metaphysical perspectives.
4 In this instance the automatic enrolment of employees on to health care schemes applied to employers with workforces greater than 200.
5 Developed by the behavioural economist Richard Thaler and Shlomo Benartzi, the Save More Tomorrow pension scheme attempts to overcome inertia and procrastination relating to the money people save towards their pension by getting people to commit in advance to automatically increasing their pension contributions as their salary rises.

6 Cameron's TED talk can be watched here: https://www.ted.com/talks/david_cameron#t-590568 [accessed 31 January 2017].
7 Various names were mooted for the BIT including the Behaviour Change Team (a title that was rejected by Richard Thaler); the Behavioural Economics Team (according to Halpern too narrow in suggested focus); and the Behavioural Science Team (with problematic connotations of abbreviating to the BS Team!) (see Halpern, 2015: Loc. 806).
8 More recently the Gates Foundation has shown an interest in related policies.

3

AN HISTORICAL GEOGRAPHY OF NEUROLIBERALISM II

On new behavioural ideas

Introduction: a history of neuroliberal ideas

In many ways it is unwise to try and separate out the practical history of neuroliberalism (outlined in the previous chapter) from its intellectual antecedents. It is clear, for example, that the emerging practices of neuroliberal government have been consistently informed by academic enquiry into the nature of human behaviour, and that the intellectual evolution of neuroliberalism has been informed by numerous practical experiments in behavioural government. Notwithstanding this, it is also apparent that the scientific and philosophical history of neuroliberalism has maintained a degree of autonomy from the evolving practices of behavioural government. This chapter outlines the key scientific and philosophical ideas that have informed the emergence of neuroliberalism. This endeavour seeks to reveal the crucial role that academia has played in legitimizing neuroliberal forms of government, and to expose the complex of debates and controversies that lie beneath the surface of the sciences of neuroliberalism.

In charting the intellectual and scientific history of neuroliberalism, this chapter will essentially reflect upon a long and ongoing set of interactions between political science, economics and various strands of psychology that ran through large parts of the twentieth century. At the centre of these interactions has been an ongoing concern with how best to understand human behaviour, and how to use this knowledge in ways that may serve the common good without undermining the basic principles of a free and liberal society. Ultimately, this confluence of the sciences of government and behaviour is primarily concerned with how it may be possible to incorporate an appreciation of the suboptimal, automatic and emotional constitution of human conduct within rationally oriented systems of political and economic governance. As this chapter will show, these intellectual and scientific concerns have not been limited to the field of politics, economics and psychology, but have also incorporated insights from evolutionary biology, neuroscience, anthropology and the design sciences. Ultimately, this chapter will show that the intellectual history of neuroliberalism is not a neat and uncontroversial one. Analysis demonstrates that neuroliberalism is often an uneasy compromise between an economic commitment to free market values, a political concern with personal liberty and a behavioural interest in more-than-rational behaviours. It will further demonstrate that the dominant brands of neuroliberalism appearing in the world around us are just some of the many ways in which the economic and behavioural sciences could be forged into a governmental project.

This chapter commences with an account of the key figures that have shaped the intellectual and scientific landscape within which neuroliberalism has emerged. At this point we want to acknowledge that the history of ideas presented here is markedly gendered and thus partial; it appears that the established figures in many of the disciplines of significance outlined here are male, and we have reservations about reproducing this narrative in this book. There remains important work to be done in charting the role of female academics in developing the intellectual tenets of neuroliberalism, as well as in understanding the consequences for the nature of behavioural insights of this historical gendering – most obviously in attitudes towards rationality as an economic and political goal. The second section of the chapter considers the ways in which the behavioural sciences associated with neuroliberalism have coalesced with emerging ideas concerning the nature of freedom and the changing role of the state within society to forge a distinctive politico-intellectual project. This politico-intellectual project is often referred to formally as libertarian paternalism, and more colloquially as nudge. The final section of this chapter moves beyond the intellectual history of neuroliberalism to consider the extent to which the concept could not only provide a nomenclature through which to identify emerging systems of behavioural government, but also a framework in and through which to critically analyse related developments.

The intellectual and scientific origins of neuroliberalism: psycho-economic fusions

Foucault and the problem of homo economicus

French philosopher and historian of ideas Michel Foucault provides us with a helpful starting point from which to chart our history of neuroliberal ideas. In his 1978–9 lecture series at the Collège de France, Foucault charted the rise of neoliberal styles of government and their underlying philosophical assumptions (Foucault 2008 [2004]). In a lecture on 28 March 1979, Foucault focused on the problematic, but necessary, figure that sat at the centre of the neoliberal universe: *homo economicus*. As an intellectual project neoliberalism was a movement devoted to trying to re-instigate nineteenth-century forms of liberalism, and encourage the use of decentralized, market-based systems for governing society (Davies, 2014: 1). We will talk more about the main principles of neoliberalism's protagonists later in this chapter. For now, what is important to note about neoliberalism was the assumption that it made about human subjectivity. If a market-based system is going to secure both the efficient delivery of economic goods and services and wider forms of personal freedom, then certain assumptions must be made about the nature of human motivation and behaviour. For market-based societies to function according to the ideals of liberalism and neoliberalism it must be assumed that humans act *rationally* (Friedman, 2000 [1982]). As this chapter will discuss, there has been something of a neoliberal colonization of the notion of rationality. In this colonization process rationality has become associated with certain forms of conscious, market-compliant decision making, which tend to deny a range of other forms of rationality that may be less conscious and less market oriented. At this point, however, we simply want to observe the parameters of neoliberal notions of rationality. In the neoliberal universe, rationality is associated with deliberate forms of human behaviour, which are formulated in social isolation, based upon relevant knowledge, and motivated by self-interest. Crucially, such idealized forms of behaviour are important for securing (economic) freedom at both the individual level (where the act of being free is associated with the ability to formulate unimpeded behavioural calculations), and the collective level (where

 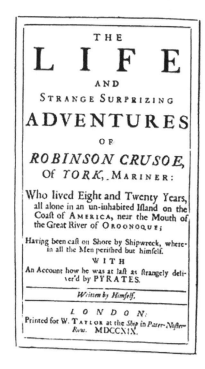

FIGURE 3.1   The figure of homo economicus was, in part, inspired by the literary figure
of the island-bound castaway Robinson Crusoe
Source: Wiki Commons.

the absence of social influence and the prevalence of self-interest prevent collusion and monopoly interests). The figure that became associated with such patterns of economic behaviour was homo economicus (Cohen, 2014).

Homo economicus (or economic man) was, it is fair to say, a necessary myth for the neoliberal thought collective. But while neoliberalists recognized that homo economicus did not exist in the real world, they did believe that related assumptions of rational action provided an accurate enough approximation of human behaviour for their economic philosophy to be validated. But according to Foucault, during the 1960s and 1970s neoliberal scholars started to problematize the figure of homo economicus in significant ways. Foucault traced concern with the notion of homo economicus to 1962 and a series of articles, written by prominent neoliberal thinkers, in the *Journal of Political Economy* (Foucault 2008 [2004]: 268). Reflecting on the related work of the prominent American neoliberalist Gary Becker, Foucault observes within neoliberalism a desire to move beyond the 'outdated' and ultimately unrealistic vision of homo economicus, to incorporate an appreciation of non, or more-than-rational human conduct within economic behaviour (Becker, 1962). The critical thing for Becker was that non-rational behaviours could be incorporated into economic analysis (and government) so long as those behaviours consistently 'react to reality in non-random' ways (Foucault 2008 [2004]). Drawing on Becker's concern to incorporate non-random forms of irrational behaviour into economic analysis, Foucault discerns a possibility for the entry of the behavioural and psychological sciences into economics (ibid.: 270). According to Foucault, the systematic analysis of how people respond (both rationally and irrationally) to modifications in their surrounding environment is precisely what the behavioural sciences are devoted to studying (he draws particular attention in this context to the work of the psychologist B. F. Skinner on behavioural conditioning). Essentially, Foucault is preempting here (in the formative years of neoliberalism) a fusion of economics and psychology, which now defines neuroliberalism.

Foucault's analysis has two important implications for the analysis presented in this volume. First his work reveals a crucial point in time within which the neoliberal project started to search for a more behaviourally realistic and nuanced account of human conduct than that found within the figure of homo economicus. Second, his analysis reveals a renewed interest within the neoliberal thought collective in the governability of the economic subject. Classic versions of homo economicus suggested that her spontaneous pursuit of self-interest meant that she was best left alone by the state. But if the human subject was now understood less as a rational deliberator, than as someone who acts irrationally, but 'responds systematically to modifications in the variables of the environment', then they were, in the words of Foucault, 'someone who is eminently governable' (ibid.: 270). An appreciation of the governability of the subject would shape the more state-oriented visions of laissez-faire society (at least when compared to classic, nineteenth-century liberalism) ultimately promoted by the neoliberalists. A belief in the governability of the subject would, however, also inform the emergence of neuroliberal systems of government.

Foucault's analysis of neoliberalism's struggles with homo economicus provides us with an insight into how and why we would ultimately see a fusion of economics and psychology under neuroliberalism. Foucault's analysis does, however, predate the ultimate emergence of neuroliberalism by some thirty years, and post-dates some of the earliest attempts to construct a more psychologically informed version of homo economicus by at least the same length of time. In the remainder of this section we will consider the key parts of the sixty-year story of the psychologization of economics and the economization of psychology, which bookend Foucault's reflections.

Bounded rationality: Herbert Simon and the Old Behavioural Economists

The intellectual history of neuroliberalism starts with one fairly incredible man: Herbert Alexander Simon. Born in Milwaukee in 1916, Simon was the quintessential polymath (Simon, 1991). At one and the same time a social and political scientist, Simon's research also spanned the computer sciences and psychology and made contributions to organizational theory and the philosophy of science. A sense of both the significance and scope of Simon's work can be discerned in the fact that he was the recipient of both a Nobel Memorial Prize for Economics (in recognition of his pioneering work in the varied fields of decision making), and the Turing Award (for his work in the field of artificial intelligence). What united Simon's research interests was his interest in the nature of human decision making and its varied rational and irrational dynamics. Simon's work is a crucial component within the history of neuroliberalism for two reasons: (1) because it paved the way for the development of the study of the more-than-rational processes of decision making with which neuroliberalism is synonymous; and (2) because of the troubled relations between his work and that of the economic scholars of neoliberalism (which in itself provides a valued historical lens on some of the main controversies that have surrounded the troubled evolution of neuroliberalism).

Simon's main contribution to the intellectual evolution of neuroliberal government was the notion of *bounded rationality* (it appears that Simon actually preferred the term *satisficing* to describe his theory). Simon utilized the rather elegant notion of bounded rationality to convey the necessary limits that surround the acts of human decision making. Whereas classical and neoliberal economic theory assumed deliberation, and the availability of adequate time and information in the formulation of human decisions, Simon's theory of bounded rationality recognized how limits in the cognitive capabilities of people and available resources in the immediate environment inevitably compromised optimal forms of human action (Simon, 1957). According to Simon this situation did not mean that humans were hapless victims of practical circumstance, but that they had to develop adaptive responses to their decision-making situations. Rather than optimizing, Simon argued that humans adopted satisficing techniques. As a fusion of satisfying and sufficing, the idea of satisficing conveys the ways in which humans do not search for the best decision-making option, but one that meets their decision-making needs. While economists would expect homo economicus to sift logically

FIGURE 3.2   Portrait of Herbert Simon, January 1987
Source: Creative Commons: Richard Rappaport, Collection of Carnegie Mellon University.

and systematically through all available options before choosing the optimal behavioural path, the satisficer (Simon sometimes used the term 'administrative man') would normally choose the first option that was discovered that met her threshold of acceptability.

The crucial thing to note within Simon's theory of bounded rationality and satisficing is that it recognizes the ways in which the human mind engages in a form of necessary self-restriction (*Economist*, 2009a). Bounded rationality is thus as much recognition of the adaptive capacity of human decision making to cope with imperfect behavioural situations, as it is a statement on the cognitive limitations of the human subject. In addition to questioning the unrealistic psychological assumptions of classical economics, bounded rationality, at least on Simon's terms, offers an invitation to explore the hidden forms of intuitive wisdom and the creative ways of being in the world that are often unthinkingly characterized as irrational. Bounded rationality draws attention to the market incompatibility of many behaviours that appear to be inherent to the human condition. In Simon's world of satisficing, suboptimal forms of economic behaviour are not necessarily second-rate behaviours; they can embody *rational* adaptive responses to the complex worlds that we inhabit, and to the non-market-based values that constitute the human character.

The essence of Simon's analysis of bounded rationality has been taken up most directly in the work of Gerd Gigerenzer. We discussed the work of Gerd Gigerenzer, and in particular his analysis of the so-called recognition heuristic, in Chapter 1. Gigerenzer suggests that bounded rationality is actually composed of two broad forms of human behaviour (2000). The first category, which Simon termed satisficing, relates to those decisions that are made on the basis of *stopping* the decision-making process at the point when a suitable (but not necessarily optimal) choice becomes available. The second category relates to the heuristic cues – including emotional responses, the actions of others, the things we have done in the past – that we all use as necessary shortcuts to the multitude of decisions we must make on a daily basis. A central component of Gigerenzer's work is a desire to connect bounded forms of rationality with forms of evolutionary intelligence in human behaviour. According to Gigerenzer, bounded rationality bears the hallmarks of a form of evolutionary selection of efficient behaviours to the extent that it is characterized by decision making that is *fast, frugal* and *cognitively cheap* (ibid.). It is also, according to Gigerenzer, a reflection of a form of almost Darwinian ecological rationality to the extent that it involves the development of decision-making systems that are best suited to the limitations and opportunities of behavioural environments.

Simon and Gigerenzer's work are both part of what Sent (2004) has described as the Old School of Behavioural Economists (we acknowledge that this title may be something of a misnomer given the contemporaneous nature of much of Gigerenzer's work). As *Old* behavioural economists, Simon and Gigerenzer are both concerned with developing a creative fusion between the psychological and economic sciences that can ultimately contribute to a more sophisticated account of human decision-making within economic theories. The Old School of Behavioural Economics tends to be characterized by two features: (1) an optimistic outlook on the nature of bounded rationality; and (2) a radical commitment to exploring non-market-compliant forms of human decision making as valued parts of life, and not troubling aberrations. As we have discussed, the optimistic ethos of Old Behavioural Economics sees bounded rationality as a form of evolutionary intelligence, or rationality by another means. In the case of the work of Gigerenzer, however, this optimism appears to take on another form. It is clear that much of the behavioural intelligence that is encoded in bounded forms of rationality has evolved at an unconscious level, and remains a predominantly unthinking set of responses to situational decision making. For Gigerenzer, however, an increasing awareness of bounded rationality offers humanity a new evolutionary opportunity to shape and train our bounded rationality more consciously (see also Rowson, 2011). This more reflexive boundedness of rationality suggests that it may be possible to understand better both the positive and negative consequences of certain forms of automatic decision making and selectively apply new forms of *fast, frugal* and *cognitively cheap* forms of decision making that are more beneficial than their predecessors. We will talk at length about these notions of behavioural empowerment later in this volume (see Chapter 4's discussion of neurological reflexivity, and Chapter 9's account of mindfulness).

New School of Behavioural Economics

Following the pioneering work of Herbert Simon in the 1940s and 1950s, the ideas of the Old Behavioural Economics School lay relatively dormant. There are many potential reasons for the quiescence. It is, however, clear that the relative suspicion with which these ideas were treated by economists (particularly of the neoclassical variety) was central to this period of dormancy. We will speak at greater length about the ongoing tensions that exist between psychology and economics (and that continue to shape the behavioural economists' agenda) later in this chapter. At this juncture we want to consider the emergence of what Sent (2004) has described as the New School of Behavioural Economics. This branch of behavioural economics would prove to be vital in building new lines of engagement between psychology and economics from the 1970s onwards.

While the Old School of Behavioural Economics is closely associated with the pioneering work of one person, new wave behavioural economics is synonymous with a much broader cast of characters. Two figures do, at least in the early stages of the movement, stand out. Daniel Kahneman is an Israeli-American psychologist who began his academic career at the Hebrew University of Jerusalem in the early 1960s. Amos Tversky was a cognitive psychologist who studied and taught at the Hebrew University of Jerusalem. In the late 1960s Kahneman invited Tversky to give a guest lecture at the Hebrew University. This meeting would mark the beginning of one of the most productive and influential intellectual relations in the history of behavioural economics and neuroliberalism (see Lewis, 2016). *The*

Economist recently likened the impact of Kahneman's (and by definition Tversky's) work to the truly great thinkers of the past:

> As Copernicus removed the Earth from the centre of the universe and Darwin knocked humans off their biological perch, Mr Kahneman has shown that we are not the paragons of reason we assume ourselves to be.
>
> (Economist, 2011)

While these sentiments are clearly hyperbolic, it is salutary to consider precisely what it is about the Kahneman and Tversky's collaborative work that has made it so influential.

During the 1970s and 1980s Kahneman and Tversky published a series of influential articles that explored the nature of human decision making. Influenced by the work of Simon, Kahneman and Tversky were primarily interested in the ways in which people make judgements under conditions of inevitable uncertainty (see Kahneman et al., 1982). At the centre of Kahneman and Tversky's intellectual project was a concern with the strategies that people deploy to cope with the constrained forms of cognitive capacity that define the human condition. What their work and related experiments show is that humans do not cope with bounded forms of rationality in random ways, but instead deploy a consistent set of heuristics (sometime, in more pejorative terms, also called cognitive biases).

As was discussed in Chapter 1 of this volume, behavioural heuristics reflect the shortcuts we consistently make when confronted with little time and information. Common behavioural heuristics include our tendency to favour the present over the future; to prefer status quo to change; and be strongly influenced by the actions of others. The work of Kahneman and Tversky can be seen as a form of refinement and extension of the work of Simon: unpacking and classifying the forms of behavioural shortcuts that are characteristics of bounded rationality. There are, however, some key ways in which the old and new waves of behavioural economics diverge. In keeping with Simon (and Gigerenzer), Kahneman and Tversky's work clearly recognizes that heuristics play a necessary and valuable part in everyday life and decision making. Their work is, however, primarily concerned with the errors that tend to emerge from the bounded nature of rationality (see Kahneman, 2011).

Kahneman and Tversky's research is particularly concerned with the statistical conditions of judgements, and the ways in which people are rarely able to access or understand the statistical parameters of what would make a good decision (see Jones et al., 2013: 9). According to Sent (2004), and in contradistinction to the Old Behavioural Economist School, Kahneman and Tversky start with the rationality assumption and study systematic departures from it. While acknowledging the inevitability of cognitive biases and errors, Kahneman and Tversky's work tends to see heuristics as error-prone free radicals that escape the grasps of aspiring rational actors. Deliberative forms of rationality, however, remain the gravitational centre around which human actions revolve and behavioural government operates. On this basis the new wave of behavioural economics was based upon a partial resuscitation of homo economicus, at least as a goal of governmental policy. It is, we think, important to note that the pioneering work of Kahnemen and Tversky was concerned primarily with cognitive illusions and error as opposed to adaptive forms of heuristics. By paying less attention to the utility of adaptive heuristics, their work has become much more associated with corrective strategies to mitigate against the bounded nature of rationality, as opposed to a broader study of irrational wisdom. Interestingly, and perhaps as a product of starting with the rationality assumption, Kahneman and Tversky's parameters for defining optimal decisions tend to revolve around market-based goals of profit, self-interest and utility maximization. In uncovering the systematic nature of heuristic mistakes Kahneman and Tversky's work would ultimately lay the foundation for a new vision of governmental intervention that could more effectively see and predict human irrationality and conceive of shifting it into more desirable economic directions.

It is interesting to think about what an equivalent study of the systematic use of beneficial heuristics, which did not assume optimal market behaviours as a normative goal, but perhaps considered the importance of belonging, sharing and caring, would look like. At this point, however, we note that while the foundational work of Kahneman and Tversky was not necessarily celebrated in classical economic thought, it was much more aligned with the core assumptions of neoliberalism and homo economicus. By assuming that deliberative forms of self-interested utility maximization were behavioural norms, New Behavioural Economics not only reasserted the rationality assumption (at least as a yardstick against which to measure irrationality), but also supported the assumption that rationality was synonymous with market-oriented conduct. These core values would become central to the fusion of neoliberalism and psychological governance that would lay the foundations for emerging systems of neuroliberalism.

The neoliberal thought collective

Although neuroliberalism is in part a reaction to the shortcomings of certain facets of neoliberalism, as an intellectual project it is deeply wedded to its neoliberal counterpart. Chapter 1 provided a brief introduction to the concept of neoliberalism. In this section we consider in greater detail the intellectual currents that bind together neoliberalism and neuroliberalism. One of the problems of trying to explore the connections between neoliberalism and neuroliberalism is that significant forms of internal diversity and disagreement characterize both intellectual movements (see Davies, 2014; Peck, 2010). In this section we consequently focus on what we perceive to be the core intellectual assumptions of the more influential branches of both projects.

The neoliberal intellectual project originated in the 1930s and 1940s in response to the rise of various forms of collectivism (in the forms of Keynesian social and economic policy and communism), and authoritarianism (expressed in various fascist and socialist state systems).[1] In its early guises neoliberalism was most closely associated with the work of two Austrian exiles: Friedrich von Hayek and Ludwig von Mises. Through the collective work of Hayek and Von Mises neoliberalism became associated with '[t]he elevation of market-based principles and techniques of evaluation to the level of state-endorsed norms' (Davies, 2014: 37). For neoliberalists markets offered a system within which it was possible to achieve a balance between socio-economic stability and freedom. According to neoliberalism, while collectivism and authoritarianism delivered certain forms of constancy in social and economic life they did so at the cost of personal liberty. Markets are central to the neoliberal credo because of their purported ability to deliver freedom and efficiency. In relation to freedom, Hayek and Von Mises claimed that the 'impersonal and anonymous' nature of markets ensured that they delivered a kind of blind justice in and through which hard work and innovation are rewarded and nepotism and monopolies are avoided (see Davies, 2014). The market-based forms of liberty prioritized within neoliberalism are, of course, much more concerned with economic than political life. But for the neoliberalist it is in the sphere of the economy that the most important expressions of freedom in everyday life are realized (Friedman, 2002 [1982]). As a place of open and relatively unhindered competition the market delivers freedom in the forms of consumer choice and preference, and the opportunities to participate and compete within market exchanges. Neoliberalism recognizes that the market generates economic winners and losers, but it argues these forms of success and failure are a product of fair competition and not elite control and influence.[2]

If Hayek and Von Mises provided much of the early intellectual infrastructure for neoliberalism, 1947 marked the point at which the project would start to build political impetus. In 1947 Hayek established the Mont Pèlerin Society in order to bring together academics, politicians and business leaders who were committed to a neoliberal worldview (see Mirowski and Plehwe, 2009).[3] With funding support secured from wealthy backers, the society was successful in mobilizing academics, journalists, political activists and the business community (Monbiot, 2016). Neoliberal ideas gained further support through the formation of a series of interconnected think tanks including the Institute of Economic Affairs, the Cato Institute, and the Manhattan Institute for Policy Research. Ultimately, the neoliberal project would gain one of its strongest footholds at the University of Chicago. With the support of Hayek, Robert Hutchins (the Chancellor of the University) and Henry Simons of the Chicago Law School, the University of Chicago supported the appointment of a faculty with a strong interest in neoclassical economics and the principles of neoliberalism. Over time, this group of academics would become known as the Chicago School of Economics, or more colloquially as the *Chicago Boys* (Klein, 2007). Supported by this broad range of institutions, neoliberalism rapidly became an international movement of ideas, which following the crises of planned Keynesian economics in the 1970s would be seized upon by leaders such as Margaret Thatcher, Ronald Reagan and Augusto Pinochet as a basis for developing more market-oriented societies (Burgin, 2012; Peck, 2010).

It is our contention within this volume that while neuroliberalism stands in partial distinction from neoliberalism, these two intellectual projects are deeply interconnected. Table 3.1 indicates some of the key features that distinguish neo- and neuroliberalism. We talk more about these distinctions in the chapters that follow. At this point, however, we consider some of the commonalities between the two intellectual projects. First, it is clear that key branches of neuroliberalism are shaped by the kinds of market-oriented policy making that defined the neoliberal project. The market orientation of dominant brands of neuroliberalism is evident in the fact that although it recognizes the rational shortcomings of people it sees these shortcomings largely as a failure to engage effectively in the marketplace (particularly in relation to financial investments, pension planning and long-term cost assessments). As Wilby (2010) so aptly puts it when talking about the nudge philosophies that are synonymous with neuroliberalism, '[Nudge] argues that there's nothing wrong with markets, only with people, and the state's role is to make people fit for markets, not the other way around'. Building on the insights of the New Behavioural Economists, neuroliberalism recognizes that people do not operate in ways that are compatible with the effective functioning of markets, but in classical neoliberal terms still sees markets as the best way of achieving social order and freedom. The market orientation of important branches of neuroliberalism is perhaps cemented by the fact that they show no discernable support for the redistribution of wealth as a way of securing behavioural goals, but do advocate the wider application of commercial techniques (particularly relating to marketing, persuasion and entrepreneurial experimentation) within behavioural government.

TABLE 3.1 Key distinctions between neo and neuroliberalism

	Neoliberalism	*Neuroliberalism*
Targeted behavioural system	Deliberative/utility maximizing	Automatic/emotional
Assumed human context for decision-making	Individual	Social
Fictitious figure	Rational – homo economicus	More-than-rational Homer Simpson
Experimental style	Informally experimental	Formally experimental
Economic orientation	Market-oriented	Market/austerity-oriented
Vectors for behaviour change	Incentive/information based decision-making	Context-based decision-making, behavioural environments
Cognitive target	Conscious	More-than-conscious
Target population	Aggregate population	Personalized

A second crucial way in which neo- and neuroliberalism are connected intellectually is in relation to their respective views on the state. There is some debate concerning precisely what neuroliberalism means for the state, with some arguing that, contra neoliberalism, it represents an attempt to extend the power and influence of the state into the details of daily life (Leggett, 2014: 8). More commonly, neuroliberal styles of government (particularly in the context of austerity programmes) have become synonymous with a much smaller, less substantively interventionist style of state (ibid.). The fact that neuroliberalism tends to eschew mandates and bans and instead prefers subtle forms of behavioural intervention would also support the idea that it is closely wedded to minimalist forms of government. While neoliberalism is often associated with the vision of a stateless society within which the market is allowed to operate as freely as possible, this actually denies the crucial role that that neoliberalists (and in particular Hayek) saw for government in society. For many neoliberalists the state has a crucial role in securing the necessary conditions (or rules of the game) within which free markets can operate (particularly in relation to the preclusion of monopolies and the litigious processes that secure contracts). In many ways neuroliberalism shares with neoliberalism a very similar vision for the state. While neoliberalism supports the presence of the state to the extent that it ensures markets can operate with limited distortion, neuroliberalism invokes the behavioural state to ensure that individuals act in ways that are market-compliant (for more on the relationship between neuroliberalism and the state see Chapter 6 in this volume).

A further area where there is common ground between neo- and neuroliberalism is in relation to questions of freedom. While we argue in Chapter 5 that neuroliberalism has been involved in the subtle process of redefining liberal notions of freedom, at this point we want to point out how its particular interpretation of freedom resonates with neoliberalism. For neoliberalists *total freedom* (that is the combination of political and economic freedom) is determined primarily by the nature of economic exchange (Friedman, 2002 [1982]: 9). For neoliberalists, markets offer the best route to economic (and then political) freedom because they are based upon 'bilateral voluntary and informed' modes of transactions (ibid.: 13). According to neoliberalism, markets deliver freedom to the extent that they provide systems of coordination that do not require coercion (ibid.). On these terms neoliberalism tethers freedom to the notion of choice: the ability to become involved voluntarily in a given economic activity and/or to select a particular product for consumption. While neuroliberalism begins to question the neoliberal understanding of freedom (particularly in relation to recognized cognitive barriers and inertias that limit apparent choice), in many of its forms it ultimately confirms the neoliberal vision of what freedom is. Accordingly, neuroliberalism equates freedom with an ability to be able to choose (often between a series of preset options), and also with an ability to participate in market-oriented activities. What neo- and neuroliberalism thus have in common is a belief that freedom can be secured so long as people are not subject to either economic or political coercion. What neither addresses, however, are the ways in which freedom (and degrees of choice) are facilitated and denied by different levels of capacity to act in markets or political spheres (see Chapters 4 and 5 in this volume). Like a game of survival of the fittest, both assume that all are equally fit (or unfit in the case of neuroliberalism) at the outset. As we discuss later in this volume, there is potential for alternative forms of neuroliberalism to address questions of behavioural capacity, but at present this issue is addressed only to a limited extent within neuroliberal systems of government (see Chapter 4).

Recognizing both the intellectual connections and schisms that exist between neoliberalism and neuroliberalism, this volume argues that in practice these two movements are inextricably linked. Peck argues that rather than thinking about neoliberalism from a purist Chicago School perspective, it is more accurate to understand it as a system of adaptive and ever changing market-oriented government (Peck, 2010). Peck goes on to claim that as an adaptive process 'the reinvention of neoliberal practices often occurs, in fact, at the limits of the processes of neoliberalization' (ibid.: xviii). We contend that many of the dominant brands of neuroliberalism that we see in the world today are actually adapted forms of neoliberalism, which have embraced a revised understanding of the human subject. Leggett goes as far as to claim that the nudge-type policies that are often regarded as synonymous with neuroliberalism are 'at the leading edge of roll-out neoliberalism: human irrationality and emotional complexity are not seen as a refutation of neoliberal economic theory, but as a means of re-legitimizing it' (Leggett, 2014: 9). If neuroliberalism offers the relegitimization of neoliberalism it is perhaps no surprise that, just as neoliberal ideas had proven so popular following the crises of Keynesian economic policies, neuroliberal government should have risen to prominence in the wake of a neoliberal global economic crisis.

The sciences of the brain and human

Over the last thirty years the intellectual foundations of neuroliberalism (developed primarily within economics and psychology) have been supported by findings within the applied sciences of the brain. The neurosciences have provided empirical evidence to support the observations of behavioural economists and social psychologists. As we will see, however, the neurosciences have also provided grounds to challenge some of the assumptions of certain strains of neuroliberal thinking.

In Chapter 1 we claimed that neuroliberalism is a system of government that is grounded in evolving understandings of the central nervous system. In this context the neurosciences have gradually provided the biological foundations for neuroliberal thought and action. As the science of the central nervous system, neuroscience has a long history of operation within the interdisciplinary spaces of biology, chemistry and the cognitive sciences (see Rose and Abi-Rached, 2013). The last two decades have, however, been witness to the rising power and influence of the neurosciences in society (ibid.). Technological developments in brain scanning that commenced with Positron Emission Tomography (and associated PET scans) entered a new phase with the advent of Functional Magnetic Resonance Imaging (fMRI) in the early 1990s. These technologies have essentially enabled the brain to be visible to scientific scrutiny in entirely new ways. Developments in the use and application of fMRI technology have been particularly significant in relation to neuroliberalism. fMRI scans measure the flow of oxygenated blood within the brain – which acts as a reliable indicator of cerebral activity (Camerer, 2007: 30). The particular nature of this technology has enabled neuroscience to monitor brain activity at much finer neurological scales than had been possible previously, and to notice changes in brain functioning over much shorter periods of time.[4]

The ability of fMRI to make the operation of brain regions and related neural inputs visible has opened up significant potential to study the neurological corollaries of the observed behaviours described in behavioural economics and related psychological sciences. Over the last twenty years a series of neurological studies has been conducted to explicitly analyze the neurological foundations of the more-than-rational behaviours described within neuroliberalism. As Camerer notes, the coming together of certain branches of behavioural economics and the

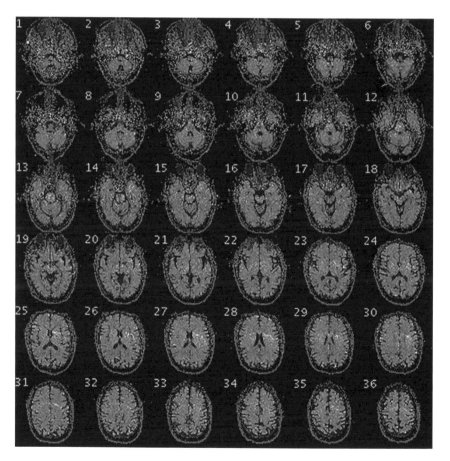

FIGURE 3.3   Governing through the brain: fMRI scans of the brain of a participant on the Personal Genome Project

Source: Wiki Commons, 2016.

neurosciences has had significant benefits for both parties: with behavioural economists being able to ground their observational studies in the empirical sciences of the brain, while the neurosciences have been able to connect fine-grain neurobiological studies with theories of 'higher order cognition' (ibid.: 26).

While the insights of the neurological sciences are often depicted as supporting the assumptions of neuroliberalism, the relationship between the neurosciences and neuroliberalism is actually more complex. Various neuroscientific studies have been able to demonstrate that when it comes to the use of behavioural heuristics activity in more emotionally oriented regions of the brain is clearly evident (particularly in the limbic system) (ibid.: 32–5; see also McClure et al., 2004). In this context, fMRI has been able to demonstrate that in situations where classical economics would expect calculation and deliberation, humans are actually engaging much more affectively attuned neurological circuitry. But the insights emerging out of the neurosciences go much further than this. Studies of brain function under various economic decision-making scenarios often demonstrate that while emotionality is clearly a part of how decisions are made, under such circumstances brain regions associated with more rational cognition are also active (McClure et at 2004). It appears that in many decision-making situations where behavioural heuristics are being used brain activity actually reflects a form of 'splicing' of cognitive function, which combines emotionality with more strategic action (Camerer, 2007: 32).

The neurosciences indicate that human behaviour is never the simple outcome of the operation of either emotionally or deliberately oriented brain activity. According to Damasio (1994),

> [t]he reasoning system evolved as an extension of the automatic emotional system, with emotion playing diverse roles in the reasoning process. For example, emotion may increase the saliency of a premise and, in so doing, bias the conclusion in favor of the premise. Emotion also assists with the process of holding in mind the multiple facts that must be considered in order to reach a decision.
>
> *(Loc. 134)*

Understanding reasoning and emotion as part of an interconnected and evolving system of human behaviour does of course complicate the dual system of decision making depicted within many branches of neuroliberalism. While neuroscience may find evidence of hot *System 1* emotionality and cooler *System 2* calculation, it would suggest that their concurrent existence in brain imaging undermines the very idea of their being two states, or systems of human behaviour.[5] Neuroscientific analysis instead appears to suggest the importance of searching for the role of the emotional in the reasoning process, and the role of deliberation in emotionality. Furthermore brain imaging problematizes the pejorative depiction of System 1 thinking as an error-prone basis for decision making. Damasio consequently observes:

The obligate participation of emotion in the reasoning process can be advantageous or nefarious depending both on the circumstances of the decision and on the past history of the decider.

(Ibid.: Loc. 134)

It is clearly dangerous to try and characterize the insights of the neurosciences in any totalizing way. It does, however, appear to be fairly clear that the neurosciences neither support the notion of a dual decision-making system, nor see emotionality and automaticity as behaviourally problematic. It must be acknowledged that the behavioural economists and psychologists who study biases and heuristics also recognize the valuable role of System 1 thinking in human life (see Kahneman, 2011). The challenge for neuroliberal policy would appear to be to how to develop systems of behaviour change that recognize the ongoing cognitive mixes of emotions, deliberations, conscious thought and unconscious instincts that constitute decisions. In this light, behaviour change becomes less about the short-term fix of moving from one mode of decision making to another (generally from System 1 to System 2), and more about enabling more reflective systems of personal and collective understanding of human behavioural patterns (see Chapter 4).

It should, perhaps, not come as a great surprise that the neurosciences provide something of a scientific foundation for many of the behavioural assumptions associated with neuroliberalism. When classical economics chose the path of presumed rationality and homo economicus it did not do so because that was assumed to actually be the nature of human behaviour. This path was travelled precisely because it was believed that in the absence of being able to actually see the brain this was an adequate approximation of human conduct (Camerer, 2007: 26–7). What is perhaps more unexpected is that the neurosciences have not themselves had more direct impact on behavioural government. While the neurosciences are starting to inform systems of behavioural government, their insights have had most influence through their association with behavioural economics and psychology. To these ends, it is clear that the intellectual foundations of neuroliberalism reflect a hybrid fusion of neurological, psychological, behavioural and social sciences.

Neuroliberalism as politico-intellectual project

It is one thing to establish the more-than-rational nature of human decision making and behaviour; it is quite another to convert this knowledge into a political project. While we outlined the emerging political applications of neuroliberalism in Chapter 2, in this section we consider the intellectual origins of this political project. To speak of the intellectual origins of a political project is to recognize that all scientific insights have to find political support and acceptability before they can wield power and influence. This section demonstrates that the political influence of neuroliberalism is based upon important intellectual elaborations of the behavioural economist and neuroscientific project outlined in the previous section.

As we shall argue, however, it was through the design sciences that these intellectual elaborations become grounded in policy and practice.

Cognitive design and the environment as behavioural target

Many of the most important scientific developments that would ultimately enable the practical application of neuroliberalism occurred outside its intellectual heartlands. While psychology, behavioural science, behavioural economics and the neurosciences all informed the academic evolution of neuroliberal thinking, it was actually the design sciences that would prove crucial to its practical application. In Chapter 8 we critically analyze the role of neuroliberalism and the redesign of the everyday environments in which we live. At this point, however, we are interested primarily in the ways in which the academic field of design has formed politically acceptable techniques for the application of neuroliberal insights.

To be able to act effectively on the more-than-rational aspects of human behaviour requires considerable effort. Behavioural heuristics are not easily addressed within liberal societies for the reasons we set out in Chapter 1. The ability to cause harm to oneself (through overeating, not saving, or gambling, inter alia) is an intrinsic part of how liberal society, for better or worse, defines freedom. The problem here for the neuroliberalist is that while they may have identified the mechanisms that produce human behaviours that are consistently detrimental to those who practice them, to act on these insights would be in contravention of the core principles of liberalism: it would essentially deny our right to be wrong. To become a practical project neuroliberalism essentially had to resolve the paradox of liberalism: how to protect people from themselves. We talk at greater length about neuroliberal attempts to circumvent the liberalist paradox, and the moral implications of these strategies, in Chapters 4 and 5. At this point we are primarily interested in how developments within cognitive design and engineering contributed not just to the partial resolution of the paradox of liberalism, but also to the formation of neuroliberalism as a project in and of itself.

During the 1970s and 1980s the emerging fields of cognitive design and engineering had been exploring the same forms of consistent human error and behavioural shortcomings as behavioural economists. Crucially, while behavioural economists were concerned primarily with the internal computational limits of human reason that generated error-prone decision making, the field of cognitive design approached things from the opposite direction. While behavioural economists looked within humans for the causes of our predictable forms of irrationality, cognitive designers were much more concerned with the ergonomic environments in which we lived our lives. According to the emerging field of cognitive design, human error was at least as much a product of the poorly constructed environments in which we live as it was the cognitive limitations of human beings.

A central figure in the cognitive design movement was Donald Norman. Donald Norman is a cognitive engineer who pioneered the development of User-Centered Design. Norman is currently the Director of the Design Lab at the

University of California, San Diego, but is also a formal advisor to the Toyota Information Technology Center. In addition to his academic career, Norman was employed during the 1990s as an *Apple Fellow* (working as a 'user experience architect'), before becoming Vice President of the company's Advanced Technology Group. The notion of user experience architecture effectively captures the essence of his academic and corporate work. According to Norman, our collective design environments (including the estimated 20,000 objects we encounter on a daily basis) actively contribute to the behavioural errors that humans make (Norman, 2002). Whether it be counter-intuitive software interfaces, the opaque operation of household thermostats or the obscure location of stairs in buildings, Norman argues that design worlds have consistently been shaped on the basis of assumed rationality, aesthetics and cost, and not on the basis of how people actually behave (ibid.). As a user experience architect, Norman has advocated the need to design our world on the basis of how people actually behave, not on how designers and engineers may wish they did. Through the use of contextual and participatory design methods (which involve the trialling and analysis of products and environments *in situ*, and alongside end-users), Norman's work has been central in demonstrating the power of environmental redesign in reshaping behaviours. These methods have been most notable in the institutionalization of design approaches to public policy in Denmark's MindLab, Singapore's Human Experience Lab (see Chapter 5), and PolicyLab in the UK.

It is not difficult to draw a direct line of connection between the forms of contextual and participatory design methodologies developed by Norman and others working in the field of cognitive design and engineering. As with behavioural economics, cognitive design supports neuroliberalism's commitment to the practical observation of actually existing behaviours and experimental empiricism (see Chapter 6). But more importantly the forms of user-centred design and engineering pioneered by Norman enabled inchoate strands of neuroliberalism to circumvent the paradox of liberalism. If human behavioural flaws are, in part, a product of our interface with the design systems that surround us, then cognitive design suggests that behavioural government can be delivered through reforms to that environment. So long as the redesign of personal behavioural environments does not involve the denial of choice (an issue we will return to in Chapters 4 and 5), then cognitive design revealed the possibility of forms of behavioural government that did not deny our right to be wrong, but just made it easier to be right. Cognitive design, and by extension neuroliberalism, works around the paradox of liberalism to the extent that it seeks to reform environments and not the individual.

Nudge and the libertarian paternalist project

While the emergence of cognitive and user-centred design was central to the fusion of behavioural science and liberalism, it would be wrong to think that the work of Norman and others in the field produced a coherent philosophy of liberally oriented behavioural government. Others would realize this project with two prominent advocates of behavioural economics playing a particularly important role. In 2008 Richard Thaler and Cass Sunstein published what would prove to be the single most important book in the history of neuroliberalism. While the volume was initially going to be titled under the more politically explicit moniker *Libertarian Paternalism*, under the advice of publishers it was eventually called *Nudge: Improving Decisions about Health, Wealth and Happiness* (Thaler and Sunstein, 2008). Although nudge (and the associated philosophy of libertarian paternalism) is only one branch of neuroliberalism, it is undoubtedly one of the most influential. It is also clear that, in distilling the complex scientific and philosophical insights that are associated with neuroliberalism in a simple term 'nudge', Thaler and Sunstein did as much as anyone else to popularize neuroliberal approaches to behavioural government.

In Chapter 2 we talked about how following the publication of *Nudge* Cass Sunstein went on to head up Barack Obama's Office of Information and Regulation Affairs (OIRA) and to introduce neuroliberal practices in Federal Government policies. At this point we want to focus briefly on Sunstein's co-author, Richard Thaler. If Herbert Simon is the founding father of neuroliberalism, and Daniel Kahneman is its great scientific pioneer, then Richard Thaler is undoubtedly the mobilizer-in-chief. Certainly, no one has done more both to consolidate the neuroliberal project and to ensure that it has been adopted by policy-makers around the world. From the early stages of his career Thaler was concerned with the origin and role of unexpected forms of economic behaviour. He describes compiling a list on his wall of observed human behaviours that do not conform to classical economic expectations (from the obscure economics of gift giving, to the distances we are, or are not, prepared to travel in search of a bargain (Thaler, 2015)). In trying to better understand these behavioural patterns, Thaler describes how he quickly found himself moving from the economics section of his university library in Rochester (USA) to the psychology stacks and the work of Kahneman and Tversky (ibid.). At the heart of Thaler's intellectual project was a desire to incorporate what he described as 'supposedly irrelevant factors' (or SIFs), into accounts of human behaviour (ibid.).

Before we outline the key intellectual contributions of Thaler and Sunstein to neuroliberalism, it is important to note that both spent important parts of their academic careers, including the period leading up the publication of *Nudge*, at the University of Chicago. Given that they were developing behavioural economic research in the shadow of the classical economic bastion of the Chicago School, both Thaler and Sunstein provide some interesting first-hand accounts of the relationship between neuroliberalism and neoliberalism. In his recent book on the development of nudge-style policies in the Federal State, *Simpler*, Sunstein describes the antagonistic response that his and Thaler's work received from the Chicago Boys of the neoliberal school (Sunstein, 2013). The opposition encountered here was in part political, as neoliberalists railed against the forms of government intervention apparently suggested by neuroliberal ideas. Reflecting on the classical economists' responses to Herbert Simon, however, Thaler suggests that these tensions also had an intellectual root:

I believe that many economists ignored Simon because it was too easy to brush aside bounded rationality as a 'true but unimportant' concept. Economists were fine with the idea that their models were imprecise and that the predictions of those models would contain error. In the statistical models used by economists, this is handled simply by adding what is called an 'error' term to the equation.

(Thaler, 2015: Loc. 442)

For Thaler and Sunstein, however, the irrational behaviours outlined by behavioural economists were not error terms – they were a representation of a significant chunk of social reality. It was in this context that they worked on developing a political philosophy that would enable the application of behavioural economic insights to a system of liberal government. The simple idea of a nudge would be crucial to the realization of this politico-intellectual project.

According to Thaler and Sunstein a nudge is:

[a]ny aspect of the choice architecture that alters people's behaviour in predictable ways without forbidding options or significantly changing their economic incentives. To count as a mere nudge, the intervention must be easy or cheap to avoid. Nudges are not mandates. Putting the fruit at eye level counts a nudge. Banning junk food does not.

(Thaler and Sunstein, 2008: 6)

Nudges essentially embody tactics that use behavioural insights simultaneously to identify consistently problematic behaviours and to find ways of changing them. But nudges are actually only the practical end of a broader governmental philosophy espoused by Thaler and Sunstein: the aforementioned notion of *libertarian paternalism*.

For some, libertarian paternalism is a contradiction in terms. For others it is neither truly libertarian (to the extent the it seeks to enhance political and economic freedom), nor paternalistic (to the extent that it attempts to enforce beneficial behaviours that the subject does not want to pursue, much like a parent forcing their children to eat their greens). For Thaler and Sunstein, however the idea of libertarian paternalism reflects a political 'third way' between the laissez-faire of the right and the interventionism of the left (ibid.: 13–14). For Thaler and Sunstein, libertarian paternalism is paternalistic to the extent:

that it is legitimate for choice architects to try to influence people's behaviour in order to make their lives longer, healthier, and better. In other words we argue for self-conscious efforts, by institutions in the private sector and also by government, to steer people's choices in directions that will improve their lives.

(ibid.: 5)

They further claim that their governmental vision is paternalistic in the sense that nudges are 'relatively weak, soft, and nonintrusive' and are based on the preservation of personal choice. Libertarian paternalism (and associated nudges) personifies the broader project of neuroliberalism in its mobilization of styles of government that draw on psychological tactics at the same time as seeking to preserve the freedom of the subject (we discuss in Chapters 4 and 5 the problematic association that is made here between freedom and choice). By seeking to redesign the choice environments in which we live, and by perceiving behavioural biases and heuristics not just as behavioural flaws, but also as active tools of government, libertarian paternalism has proved a very popular strand of neuroliberal government.

As we move through this volume we analyze the emergence of libertarian paternalist policies, but we also consider the different ways in which psychological government can be fused with notions of liberalism and freedom. At this point however it is salutary to mention one style of behavioural government, which has been associated with the forms of psychological insight we have outlined in the last three chapters, but could not be considered neuroliberal. In her recent book *Against Autonomy*, Sarah Conly argues that the tyranny of human automaticity should make us question more deeply our social commitment to liberty. Conly claims that while behavioural psychologists have demonstrated that we are not the autonomous agents that our Enlightenment tradition has led us to believe, they have 'hesitated to draw conclusions from this that would radically alter the way we design government' (Conly, 2012: 2). In light of the insights of the behavioural sciences, Conly suggests a much more radical vision of state:

> [W]e need … a democratically elected government, but one in which the government is allowed to pass legislation that protects citizens from themselves, just as we allow legislation to protect us from others. I argue for the justifiability of *coercive paternalism*, for laws that force people to do what is good for them.
>
> *(ibid.: 5) (emphasis added)*

While controversial, what Conly's work does demonstrate is that the behavioural insights that are closely associated with neuroliberalism do not lead axiomatically to the fusion of psychological government and political and economic liberty with which it is associated. These behavioural insights could also be used to justify a much more coercive and behaviourally interventionist state.

Neuroliberalism as critical intellectual project

So far in this volume we have presented neuroliberalism in two ways. In Chapter 2 neuroliberalism was depicted as a series of extant and emerging processes of government that can be seen in the world around us. In this chapter we have outlined the notion of neuroliberalism as a series of interconnected scientific and philosophical developments that are beginning to shape systems of liberally oriented psychological government. Understanding neuroliberalism in these ways is important because it enables us to connect together a series of processes of behavioural government with psychological, political and economic thinking, which may seem disconnected, but actually share common genealogies and goals. But our use of neuroliberalism extends beyond the realm of ontological yardstick. We thus understand neuroliberalism to be as much a critical concept through which to interpret reality as a feature of the world around us. By way of concluding this chapter, we briefly outline the analytical purchase that the concept of neuroliberalism brings to analysing emerging systems of behavioural government.

The idea of neuroliberalism as a critical theory of neuroliberal government may seem peculiar. In order to understand the notion of neuroliberalism as a form of critical framework it is necessary to reflect on the nature of critical theory more broadly. In general terms critical theory[6] emerged as a neo-Marxist tradition in Europe in the middle decades of the twentieth century. Critical theory has three key characteristics: (1) it is interdisciplinary in its orientation; (2) it is deliberately abstract and abstracting in the ways in which it seeks to interpret the world (with a particular interest in uncovering contradictions and contestations); and (3) it emphasizes a concern with how the world could be different to how we find it, or perceive it to be (Brenner, 2009).

It may seem strange to talk about developing an interdisciplinary perspective on neuroliberalism. Throughout this chapter we have outlined the inherently interdisciplinary nature of neuroliberalism as an intellectual and scientific project: spanning as it does psychology, economics, the design sciences, neuroscience and the broader behavioural sciences. As a critical theory, however, neuroliberalism could draw on a very different set of disciplinary perspectives that sometimes have much more totalizing and normative ambitions. These disciplines, which would include but not be limited to the political sciences, philosophy, human geography and social science, do not focus on positivist excavations of the laws that govern how the world works (as happens when behavioural economists undercover another behavioural heuristics, for example). Instead they are concerned with understanding the world in order that it can be transformed. The judgemental and transformative agenda associated with critical theory is connected to its penchant for abstraction. While the positivist sciences involve forms of abstraction (to observe a behavioural bias and then to suggest that it reflects a facet of human nature, for example, is an abstraction), critical theory abstracts in a very different way. Critical theory seeks to utilize particular observations of the world around us in order to understand, and critique, the systems through which social, economic and political life are organized and governed. While the positivist sciences of neuroliberalism abstract to generate knowledge of how people behave, a critical theory of neuroliberalism is more interested in what particular instances of behaviour or behavioural policy tell us about how social order and stability are produced, and the winners and losers of these processes.

Finally, critical theory is concerned with revealing the arbitrary nature of the world around us, and how things could be different. This aforementioned commitment to social transformation derives from critical theory's concern with social, economic and political domination and how best to achieve human liberation. While early forms of critical theory were concerned primarily with the ways in which people are enslaved by the market and state, more recent approaches have addressed a variety of often overlooked and decentralized processes through which social control is achieved and liberty is eroded. Understood on these terms, neuroliberalism as critical theory is perhaps best conceived of as a project that is dedicated to exposing the limitations of the knowledge systems that have informed the emergence of neuroliberalism as a practical project. Furthermore, it is a project that questions the forms of liberty that are associated with neuroliberal styles of governing. Ultimately, as a critical theory, neuroliberalism enables us to think reflectively about what evolving systems of behavioural government tell us about changing understandings of the human subject, the emerging nature of the state and its relationship to economic markets, and the role of corporations in society, inter alia.

We are not, of course, the first to attempt to develop a critical theory of the application of behavioural and psychological power (Mettler, 2011; Nolan 1998; Rose, 1998). Furthermore, this book is not the first attempt to develop a critical theoretical analysis of emerging forms of behavioural government (Jones et al., 2011; Whitehead et al., 2011; Jones et al., 2013; Leggett, 2014). This volume is, however, the first to attempt to understand and interpret these emerging fragments of psychological power through the critical lens of neuroliberalism. It is also the first analysis to position these systems of behavioural government in international comparative context. In so doing, we openly acknowledge the dangers of developing and deploying a critical theory of neuroliberalism. As with critical theories of neoliberalism, there is a risk that neuroliberalism can rapidly become an explanatory category that crudely homogenizes a series of processes into a single analytical frame. This process can have two consequences. First, neuroliberalism can quickly be seen as both omnipotent and omnipresent (see Clarke, 2008), and the project's hopes for emancipation quickly blunted. Second, as a critical category neuroliberalism can lead to a totalizing process in and through which the diversity of practices, ideas and beliefs with which it is associated are lost in the process of analytical abstraction. In this volume it is our desire to ground our critical project within a diverse range of empirical perspectives (including over one hundred in-depth interviews; seven behavioural trials; and numerous case examples – for more on our research approach see the Methodological Appendix at the end of this volume). We hope this empirical commitment will enable us to discern the emancipatory alternatives that neuroliberalism can offer for its own worst effects.

Notes

1 The term neoliberalism was first coined at a meeting in Paris 1938 and represented an attempt to try and reboot the classical liberal orthodoxies of the nineteenth century.
2 Neoliberalists argue that markets support freedom at two main levels: (1) through the profit motivation, they promote the provision of necessary economic goods and services without the need for coercive action; and (2) through the efficient provision of low-cost goods and services they enhance the freedom of choice and opportunity of consumers. In

a market-based society the freedom of producers is secured in the liberty of choice associated with consumers, while the freedom of consumers is undergirded by the unencumbered nature of corporate activity.

3 The *Mont Pèlerin Society* gained its name from the Swiss resort within which is founding meeting was convened.

4 PET scans, which use an injected radioactive solution in order to scan the brain, have much lower temporal and spatial resolution than fMRI) (ibid.).

5 System 1 and System 2 are characterizations of human decision-making used within behavioural economics and psychology. System 1 refers to immediate and intuitive forms of decisions, while System 2 involves more knowledge-intensive forms of deliberation.

6 Or more specifically *social critical theory* (to distinguish it from literary forms of critical theory).

4

THE NEUROLIBERAL SUBJECT

Rethinking human nature and reinventing the self

Introduction: self and behaviour

The first three chapters of this volume have demonstrated how neuroliberalism is predicated on new understandings of human nature. This chapter considers what these changing understandings of human nature mean in relation to how subjects are governed and how they self-govern. This chapter demonstrates that, while offering new insights into human nature, neuroliberalism does not uncover an undisputed vision of the human self on which we can all agree and act. Rather, neuroliberalism involves the use of new behavioural insights to actively construct novel forms of human subjectivity. As we will see, in the construction of new ways of being in the world, neuroliberalism is actually associated with the production of a variety of forms of self. What we are interested in primarily is the differential impacts (or potential impacts) of these different constructions of selfhood on human *character, agency and dignity*.

While the themes addressed in this chapter have relevance for how neuroliberalism relates and ultimately seeks to redefine freedom, the issue of freedom is explored in greater depth in the following chapter (see Chapter 5). Our primary concern in this chapter is people's relationship with their behaviour. It may seem strange to speak of a person's relationship to their behaviour, as behaviour is often considered to be synonymous with the self: we are our behaviour and our behaviour is us. In this chapter we consider how different strands of neuroliberalism conceptualise and approach our relations to behaviour. Some approaches suggest that it is wrong to even speak possessively of 'our' behaviour, and claim that behaviour is either something that escapes our conscious grasp, or is shaped by systematic forces that are beyond our control. Other branches of neuroliberalism are predicated on the assumption that humans have the capacity to control and moderate behaviours reflexively in a range of individually and collectively beneficial ways. The ways in which people are seen to relate to their behaviours have significant implications for how behaviours may be governed, and the extent to which behavioural government contributes to the corrosion or augmentation of human character.

Governing the late modern subject: corroding character or building human capacity?

Character, values and the disoriented self

In his 1998 book *The Corrosion of Character* Richard Sennett considers the impacts that new systems of flexible and knowledge-based capitalism are having on human character. According to Sennett, '[c]haracter concerns the personal traits which we value in ourselves and for which we want to be valued by others' (1998: Loc. 75). Sennett's analysis suggests that systems of economic organization that are founded on flexible working and short-term contracts, and encourage multiple career changes over the course of a working life, have generated systemic uncertainty over the personal traits that people feel that they should exhibit themselves and, in turn, value in others. Traditional patterns of Fordist work, which were based upon long-term commitment and assumed security, valued loyalty, sacrifice, and commitment. By contrast, the shorter-term horizons of the new economy are characterized by self-interest, disloyalty and distrust (ibid.). Sennett argues that this shift in working patterns makes it increasingly difficult for people to exhibit the forms of personal character they would like to be known for.

Unpacking the notion of character further Sennett argues that '[c]haracter particularly focuses on the long-term aspect of our emotional experience. Character is expressed by loyalty and mutual commitment, or through the pursuit of long-term goals, or for the practice of delayed gratification for the sake of a future end' (ibid.: Loc. 74). It appears that for Sennett the notion of character has two distinct modalities. First it represents an unspecified set of personal traits that we value. Second it refers to a normative set of personal traits that specifically value loyalty and an ability to shape long-term goals proactively. This distinction is perhaps best captured in the difference between asking for a description of a person's character (a reference to a more open-ended sense of a person's nature), and suggesting that a person possesses character (a kind of virtuous trait of perseverance). In this chapter we are interested in both notions of character. We are specifically concerned with the implications of neuroliberalism for how we see ourselves and how we assess our ability to develop certain forms of behavioural traits.

In essence Sennett is concerned with the ways in which changes in the macro and micro economy are generating a series of uncertainties that threaten our collective and personal sense of self. In more general terms the impacts of the uncertainty of (late) modern selfhood has also animated the work of Anthony Giddens (1998). According to Giddens, globalization, the *detraditionalization* of society and the transformation of the natural world (and the associated loss of a sense of naturalness) have already contributed to an increased sense of risk and uncertainty about how best to behave. As the moral compass of nature or custom are no longer reliable guides to effective self-conduct, Giddens describes how the modern era is defined by an increasing amount of uncertainty about our ability to shape our lifeworlds autonomously and reliably (ibid.). If Giddens and Sennett describe how socio-economic and ecological forces have led to a crisis of the self, then neuroliberalism suggests a psychological and neurological dimension to this crisis. Neuroliberalism suggests that not only is the world around us more uncertain, but we may be less able to shape our own lives effectively than we previously thought. If character is, for example, understood as a form of long-term self-determination, then many of the sciences that neuroliberalism are based upon suggest that the our collective 'present bias' means that humans are psychologically ill-equipped to plan for the long-term future, and by definition be characterful.

In this chapter we consider the corrosion of character as both the partial loss of a future-oriented self (cf. Osman, 2014) and a more general sense of decline in our ability to self-author our lives and destinies. On these terms neuroliberalism is understood both as a governmental response to the corrosion of character outlined above, and as an arena that itself presents new threats to self-autonomy and determination. In the remainder of this section we position the relationships between neuroliberalism and character in the context of broader historical and theoretical discussions of psychological government and the self.

Governing the self: history, psychology and regimes of subjectification

A valuable starting point for thinking critically about emerging neuroliberal regimes for governing the self is offered in Rose's volume *Inventing Ourselves: Psychology, Power and Personhood* (1998). In this Foucauldian-inspired volume Rose presents a genealogy of subjectivity in which he uncovers the historical emergence of different regimes of the self and explains how they have been connected to associated regimes of government and the formation of social, political and economic order. Rose's reflections are important for how we approach neuroliberal regimes of subjectification to the extent that they raise critical questions concerning how we might understand both the idea of self and related systems of government.

The primary focus of Rose's analysis is the role played by the psychological sciences in the construction of the rational, calculating subject of liberal societies – homo economicus (see Chapters 1 and 3). Rose's analysis is novel to the extent that it argues that the historical emergence of homo economicus does not reflect the gradual scientific uncovering of a truer, more accurate sense of human nature, but the contingent intersection between economic science, moral norms and government. In this context, more ancient notions of the self as the subject of divine should not necessarily be seen as less truthful (or more fabricated) than liberal constructions of the self. Both divinely and liberally oriented notions of the self reflect historically specific constructions of the subject, which are not a reflection of the true nature of humanity, but are rather products of varied practices of power. To these ends it is important to acknowledge that despite being grounded in the sciences of the brain, and meticulous empirical observations of the behavioural sciences, the neuroliberal subject is still a construction of the self and not an ahistorical, universal category. The neuroliberal subject is not a self that has merely been waiting for developments in brain-scanning technology to emerge so that it could be discovered. It is a self that has to be actively produced by myriad social, economic and cultural practices that believe in its existence.

At the heart of Rose's analysis is the challenge that faces all systems of liberal government – namely how free individuals can be encouraged to use their freedom appropriately (1998: 12). The problem of liberal government is that as soon as one pursues freedom as the primary organizing goal of political and economic life it becomes necessary to produce selves who are 'enjoined to govern themselves as subjects simultaneously of liberty and responsibility' (ibid.: 12). The liberal self is then one who is able to realize its freedom in a way that is immediately expressed in the self-curtailing of that freedom. So while the liberal subject is constitutionally free everywhere he finds himself ensnared in the self-imposed regulations of inhibition, sobriety and self-mastery (ibid.). The psychological sciences played an important role in the historical production of the liberal self to the extent that they asserted the existence of a subject that was a 'coherent, bounded, individualised, intentional [entity], the locus of thought, action and belief, the origins of its own actions, the beneficiary of a unique biography' (ibid.: 3), and as such was able to shoulder the burden of liberty and responsibility. With their unique insight into the interiority of the subject, the *psy* sciences also offered a fertile ground for those keen to inculcate the values of self-fulfilment and restraint into the liberal self.

Rose's work is important for our discussion of neuroliberal subjectivity because it demonstrates how we might start to analyze the emergence of the neuroliberal self, and how this self is different from its liberal predecessor. To paraphrase Rose's reflections inversely, the neuroliberal self differs from its liberal ancestor to the extent that it is perceived to be incoherent, unbounded, socialized, unintentional, one point in the broader flow of thought, action and belief, and the beneficiary of a unique, but largely illusionary, biography (ibid.: 3). The notion of the neuroliberal subject critically brings into question the idea of an *interiorized* self that is able to balance liberty and responsibility rationally, and suggests instead the notion of an *exteriorized* self, shaped by social and environmental forces that are out of its control, whose lack of responsibility erodes its freedom. The value of Rose's work does, however, extend beyond merely offering an historical counterpoint to the neuroliberal project of the self. Rose argues that attempts to produce a 'unification of life conduct around a single model of appropriate subjectivity' (be in Puritan, neoliberal or neuroliberal) belie extensive forms of heterogeneity in desired forms of personhood. To speak of neuroliberal subjectivity is not then to suggest the total demise of the neoliberal subject, but instead to acknowledge the emergence of a new project of personhood (with its own internal diversity) whose practices are being used to address a specific set of behavioural problems that lie partially outside of the gestalt of the neoliberal project (ibid.: 28). It is to be expected that an age of neuroliberalism is likely to be characterized by regimes of neoliberalism and neuroliberal subjectivity that promote different forms of subjectivity to achieve solutions to different problems. The relationship between neo- and neuroliberalism may be as much about coexistence and mutual fusion as it is about distinction and tension (see Chapter 3).

In addition to casting critical light on the notion of the self, Rose's historical analysis also raises important questions concerning how the practices of governing the self should be interpreted. Drawing on Michael Foucault's theory of governmentality, Rose argues that governing should not be conflated with practices of statehood, but should instead be interpreted as a broader set of processes:

> Government here does not indicate a theory, but a certain perspective from which one might make intelligible the diversity of attempts by authorities of different sorts to act upon the actions of others in relation to objectives of national prosperity, harmony, virtue, productivity, social order, discipline, emancipation, self-realization and so forth.
>
> *(ibid.: 29)*

There are aspects of Foucauldian approaches to government that have significance for our current discussion. The first is that government does not reflect a form of power that radiates out from the central apparatus of a state, but is instead the product of a heterogeneous set of actors. When exploring practices of government Foucauldian analysis incorporates a broad set of agencies of power including doctors, lawyers, teachers, planners and counsellors. In relation to neuroliberal regimes of subjective government this list may be extended to include designers, app technicians, behavioural scientists, policy consultants, software engineers and life coaches, among many others. Second, Foucauldians suggest that modern regimes of government tend towards systems of self-government, in and through which the desires of government are realized within the self-regulating conduct of individuals. If liberal systems of government are concerned with the emergence of a self that is trained to self-govern more carefully, neuroliberalism raises important questions concerning our ability to achieve effective self-government. Thus while neuroliberalism is concerned with rethinking the ways in which we relate to our behaviour, it raises important questions about what self-mastery may involve (particularly in relation to forms of meta-cognition), and whether it is really possible in the long term.

The remainder of this chapter draws on the insights of Rose's analysis in order to consider the contested construction and practices of neuroliberal selfhood, and what they can tell us about nascent neuroliberal systems of government.

The limited self: nudging and the unchanging subject

One of the more significant attempts to construct the neuroliberal subject has emerged out of libertarian paternalist thinking and associated nudge strategies (see Chapter 3). These diverse forms of behavioural intervention are now being deployed throughout the world, but have been pioneered by the UK's Behavioural Insights Team, the US Government's Office of Information and Regulatory Affairs and Social and Behavioural Sciences Team (see Chapter 2), and numerous third sector organizations and consultancies including iNudgeyou (Denmark), GreeNudge (Norway), Ogilvy Change (UK) and the Behavioural Architects (UK and Australia). It would be a gross misrepresentation to suggest that these organizations only use nudging tactics. Most of these agencies use nudge techniques alongside other behavioural tools, with many, such as the BIT, being at times keen to distance themselves from the phrase nudging. What this section seeks to do, however, is to identify the assumptions that these organizations appear to make about the human subject when they are employing libertarian paternalist styles of behavioural government, and to explain how these assumptions shape the systems of self-government that they support.

Econs, real people and the opt-out self

A helpful starting point from which to understand the libertarian paternalists' approach to the self can be found in Thaler and Sunstein's aforementioned book *Nudge*. Thaler and Sunstein observe:

> If you look at economics text books, you will learn that homo economicus can think like Albert Einstein, store as much memory as IBM's Big Blue, and exercise the willpower of Mahatma Gandhi. Really. But the folks that we know are not like that. Real people have trouble with long division if they don't have a calculator, sometimes forget their spouse's birthday, have a hangover on New Year's Day. They are not homo economicus; they are homo sapiens.
>
> *(2008: 6–7)*

The libertarian paternalist subject is an inherently limited self. Underpinning this limited vision of the self is not so much a realization that we cannot consistently attain the rational expectations of homo economicus, as an understanding that humans are systematically limited in their behavioural capacity. Our limitations are not errant shortcomings; they are part of our humanity. There are two particular things to note in Thaler and Sunstein's reflections, which are characteristic of nudge-oriented practices of behavioural government. The first is the tendency to construct a self-effacing subject with which we can all relate (the forgetful spouse, and the over-enthusiastic New Year's reveller, or perhaps the over-spender and the under-saver). This involves a candid exposure of the human subject, which suggests that although we may try to hide behind our masks of competence, our true self is ultimately flawed. The second is the attempt to ground the subject in the hard realities of biology: here is the figure of homo sapiens. These seemingly innocuous and unsurprisingly overlooked tendencies conceal the fact that the 'real human self' depicted by the libertarian paternalist is also an approximation of the subject. While this construction of the self may be more nuanced than those proffered within classical economics, and seem truer to our contemporary sense of who we are, it is still a highly generalized and politically conditioned construction.

If we are to understand the nudging self as a scientific and political construction, it is important to be clear about what the key features of this construction are. At the heart of nudge-style policies is a vision of a self that has a problematic relationship with its own behaviour. Related policies are based upon the assumption that a significant portion of our daily behaviours (particularly those associated with habit and routine, but also including complex decision making) largely eludes our self-regulatory grasp and available cognitive capacities. A representative of the Norwegian foundation GreeNudge explained this line of thinking in the following terms:

> [W]e very much believe we need to start with behaviour change and not attitude change. That attitudes primarily follow behaviour rather than the other way around, so it's behaviour action-based rather than intentions or belief-based.
>
> *(GreeNudge, interview, 2014)*

Here we see the subject of nudge as a person whose sense of self is actually derived from behaviours, as opposed to understanding selfhood as emerging from the internal drives of intentions or attitude.

Crucially, it is claimed that not only do many forms of behaviour elude our control, but that they do so in fairly irredeemable forms. When talking about behavioural biases, for example, Daniel Kahneman asks:

> What can be done about biases? How can we improve judgements and decisions, both our own and those of the institutions that we serve and that serve us? *The short answer is that little can be achieved without a considerable investment of effort. As I know from experience, System 1 is not readily educable* … The voice of reason may be much fainter than the loud and clear voice of an erroneous intuition, and questioning your intuitions is unpleasant when you face the stress of a big decision.
>
> *(2011: 417, emphasis added)*

For Kahneman the neuroliberal subject is doubly limited to the extent that a significant portion of its behaviour is shaped by unconscious biases, and there is limited capacity for these biases to be overcome through pedagogic regulation. The idea of the doubly limited self is related to the emerging practices of libertarian paternalist governmental practices. Nudging does not seek to change the self on moral terms (by defining what is right and wrong and shaping human character accordingly), but instead works to reshape the social and physical environments in which behaviours are conducted. As a now senior figure in the UK's BIT observed:

> [T]he current debate is much less about personal responsibility in that sense and has moved into, you know, let's put aside those sort of moral hang up

things, let's just concentrate on how we change behaviour. Well if you look at nudge in particular, a good example since it is obviously very high profile, it doesn't really have a strong line on moral responsibility.

(Institute for Government representative, interview, 2009)

The nudged self is thus someone who is partially absolved from the moral expectation that they can reliably control their actions. Behavioural government in this instance is not about redirecting a subject's relationship with itself, but instead seeks to outsource behavioural control to the social and material environments within which people carry out their daily decisions. Grist observed this notion of displaced moral agency when he stated that:

If understanding remains only with a certain reified camp, then better-designed services and systems may result, and this seems to be the remit of 'nudge' – to educate the influential and let them guide the rest of us, in as far as they can, to the social outcomes we want.

(Grist, 2009: 35–6)

While the idea of a behaviourally educated influential class 'guiding the rest of us' may raise significant ethical concerns, this statement does reveal why nudge may have become such a popular policy option. On these terms nudge is suggestive of a style of behavioural government that is relatively low cost (with a particular emphasis on more efficiently designed systems) and thus appealing to austerity-oriented governments. In addition, a nudging government does not seek to change the moral orientation of the subject, which has obvious resonance with liberal norms.

The resetting of defaults is perhaps the nudge technique that most closely reflects a belief in a limited, unchanging self. Building on the behavioural insight that recognizes the status quo bias (the human tendency to prefer stasis as opposed to change), defaults are being reset in a range of public policies in order to generate desired shifts in behaviour. Recently, for example, in Wales the Human Transplantation (Wales) Act (2013) resets the default position on organ donation from opt-out to opt-in. This subtle, but significant, shift in policy has resulted in tens of thousands of extra people joining the Organ Donor Register. The policy is based upon the realization that while most people have a stated preference to donate their organs after death, very few actually put their names on donation registers. This policy has been successfully implemented in a range of states throughout the world. Opt-out has also been used as a mechanism for promoting company pension scheme membership in the UK and US. The resetting of defaults from opt-in to opt-out has, however, proved controversial in some instances. In the US, for example, the No Child Left Behind Act instigated an opt-out system in relation to the release of children's contact information to the military for purposes of recruitment (this, unsurprisingly, led to stiff opposition from parents, who no longer had to give their consent for the release of information pertaining to their children (see Thaler and Sunstein, 2008: 85–6)). Our concern here, however, is not with the specific ways in which defaults can be deployed. Instead we are interested in the broader impacts of opt-out environments on human subjectivity and agency.

As our world gradually, and often for good reasons, becomes characterized by systems of opt-out as opposed to opt-in, it is important to recognize that this shift reflects a subtle diminution in accepted systems of human self-determination. Many systems of so-called soft opt-out are justified on the basis that it remains very easy to choose not to go along with the resetting of defaults and thus to leave company pension schemes or organ donor registers. But this rather misses the point that there is a big difference between opting out and opting in. First, the notion of opting out is based on the use of a behavioural flaw in order to stimulate a form of behavioural response (or non-response in this instance). Thus, while defaults may be used to achieve the behavioural ends that people profess they desire, they still reflect the exploitation of people's behavioural frailties. Second, it is clear in terms of agency that there is something very different about the positive decision to opt in and the more passive failure to opt out. The resetting of defaults is thus predicated on a form of negative human agency, whereby human action is defined less by what we choose to do and more by our tendency towards inertia. As one interviewee observed:

> I mean clearly they're not the same. Opting out of something is not the same as not opting in to it. And those … you know, the effect might be the same, but the way, the process by which you do something is important. Because humans have a memory, don't they?
>
> *(Behaviour Change designer and academic, interview, 2014)*

The point being made here is not only that opting out rests on a fairly thin vision of human agency (one, in fact, that appears to hope for a lack of agency), but that a consistent failure to have to express positive forms of agency can be detrimental to learned human behaviour and character in the long run. The human memory of decisions and their effects is clearly an important part of the establishment of any subject's sense of appropriate conduct in the world. By making socially desired decisions more easy, opt-out systems reflect the emergence of a process of governing that could encourage behavioural inertia and discourage personal responsibility for one's behaviour. At the very least, such tactics raise interesting questions concerning the mobilization of passivity as a governmental tool.

Inside the Self-Regulation Lab: meta-nudging and the divided self

Another important feature of the nudging subject is internal division. The nudging subject is a divided self to the extent that it is associated with an ongoing struggle between two behavioural systems: the automatic and impulsive System 1; and the deliberate and slower System 2. Systems of opt-out government involve recognizing the dominant role played in human decision making by System 1 thinking, and associated attempts to regulate these behavioural drivers by external mechanisms and prompts. There are other techniques of nudging that seek to facilitate forms of self-government by supporting the use of System 2 behaviours. These styles of government (in keeping with a fairly limited view of the human subject) do not envisage a form of wilful triumph of System 2 over System 1, but instead instigate strategic victories that are based upon the fluctuating strengths of deliberative and automatic forms of action. An interesting example of these forms of nudge is the use of self-exclusion in gambling communities (Jones et al., 2013: 68). Self-exclusion is used by many problem gamblers as a way of trying to control the impulsive System 1 through the planning capacities of System 2 thinking. Self-exclusion works on the basis that gamblers are able to pre-emptively exclude themselves from gambling establishments in those moments when their sense of self-restraint and will is strong, so that when the highly emotional temptation to gamble occurs their behaviour can be externally regulated. Self-exclusion schemes have been deployed in a series of countries around the world, and were enshrined in UK legislation in the Gambling Act of 2005 (ibid.). Self-exclusion would not be seen by many as being a true nudge as it involves the use of a hard ban on gambling. We would argue, however, that as something that is easy to avoid (either by not self-excluding, or by taking oneself off a self-exclusion register), self-exclusion is a particular form of neuroliberal policy manifestation that blends psychological insights with the freedom to choose. Self-exclusion is similar to a broader family of nudging policies known as self-nudges. These forms of nudge involve subjects voluntarily setting up their own nudging systems (perhaps an automated email letting them know their levels of household energy use). The interesting things about self-nudges are that they allow for much more meaningful forms of agency than government opt-out systems. Self-nudges and systems of self-exclusion essentially support the idea that the will of System 2 can be effectively used against the impulses of System 1, so long as the deliberations of System 2 are sufficiently separated in time from the corrupting influences of temptation.

A nuanced set of perspectives on the divided self and systems of self-nudging have been developed within the Self-Regulation Lab (hereafter SRL). The SRL is a research and teaching establishment based at Utrecht University in the Netherlands. Working primarily in the field of health psychology, the SRL was established in 2003 and is currently made up of eighteen members of staff. The Lab is primarily responsible for carrying out a series of trials to explore various forms of health behaviour (ranging from unhealthy eating to bedtime procrastination). At the heart of the Lab's work is a desire to explore the ways in which psychological insights can be better used in order to empower individuals to gain greater forms of control over their unhealthy habits. What is perhaps most interesting about the work of the SRL is that it combines nudging techniques – and an associated appreciation of the limited cognitive capacities of subjects – with a more empowered vision of the self. Crucially, the Lab is also interested in challenging the established roles that are ascribed to System 1 and System 2 behaviours in accounts of human conduct.

While working within a broadly dual-system vision of the subject, the SRL's research seeks to question the behavioural assumptions that are made about the divided neuroliberal subject. One representative of the SRL stated:

> I was always vaguely annoyed by the strict distinction between wise and cool, and emotional and impulsive. And you know there is some research like Damasio's [about how] emotions and intuitions can help us ... So most of the time we are intuitive and emotional and think fast, but I have always hated the idea that that was equated with bad behavior.
>
> *(SRL representative, interview, 2014)*

The SRL is, in part, interested in understanding the beneficial role of System 1 thinking in guiding human actions (see Chapter 3 for a broader discussion of this perspective). What is, however, most striking about the work of the Lab is a concomitant desire to reveal the behavioural problems that are associated with cool and deliberative systems of human decision making:

> You know, the idea is most of the time when you're going to have a cool head, when you have got the resources, you do the right thing. And if you are emotional and impulsive, you do the wrong thing. And our research has challenged this quite simple idea. We have some research on justification. Sometimes when you have a cool head and you have a reason to abandon your goal, then you do it ... And we also think that the hot impulsive system ... you can use it and exploit it in low self-control situations to help people behave in the right way.
>
> *(SRL representative, interview, 2014)*

It is interesting to think of the role of deliberation and cool-headed thought as a way of mollifying the beneficial behavioural prompts that we may receive from our emotional systems. In a recent study carried out by members of the SRL the team considered the impacts that an unconsciously triggered behaviour had on subjects when this behaviour directly contradicted a long-term goal or value of that person (for example a dieter eating excessively, or a polite person being prompted to be rude) (see Adriaanse et al., 2014). In this study the team recognized the role of the automatic system in alerting the subject to the problematic nature of their behaviour through the onset of a negative affect or 'mystery mood' (ibid.: 255–6). Interestingly, the SRL also discovered that in the presence of an 'explanatory vacuum' for this uncharacteristic behaviour, that the deliberative self would 'confabulate' (that is make a false claim without knowing that it is false) as a justification for the action (ibid.: 255). In this situation we can observe an emotive response that is contributing to a form of self-regulation, and a deliberative response that is trying to placate a negative affect, with the potential consequence of making such behaviours seem more acceptable in the future.

In recognizing the positive and negative contributions of System 1 and System 2 thinking to self-control, those working in the SRL are interested not only in the ways in which we relate to automatic forms of behaviour, but also in the relationship between the self and thinking processes. Nudges are thus still seen as a valuable tool of behavioural government, but in new ways. As one representative of the SRL observed:

> And that is where the nudge comes in. If for most of the time, we are not so clever, we are tired, or have other things on our mind, then we can use those things to help them a little bit [to] do the right thing. So we've evolved a bit, so we still use the dual system, but we play around a little bit with it.
>
> *(SRL representative, interview, 2014)*

Playing around with the dual system theory of behaviour has involved members of the SRL considering new ways in which nudges can be used. At the centre of these experiments is a realization that humans can be effective authors of their own behaviours (countering many assumptions of the New Behavioural Economist School, see Chapter 3). They further argue that in order to be effective authors of our behavioural destinies, and in order to build character, we cannot rely on the practices of inhibition to regulate our long-term conduct. As a representative of the SRL stated:

> I'm very much in favour of the idea that people can regulate their own lives. But what I am struggling with is the idea that there is so much emphasis on inhibition … but … inhibition is such a frail system. We are not built to resist things so, we … if you rely both as a person and theoretically that inhibition is what drives civilization and attaining your goals, then we probably do not do so well.
>
> *(SRL representative, interview, 2014)*

Those working in the SRL liken forms of behavioural inhibition and control to a muscle, which may be effective in the short-term, but quickly gets tired and loses its strength. This is not so much the *lazy controller* described by Kahneman (2011: 39–49), as the *fatigued regulator*, whose resistive capacities are eroded by time and temptation. Returning to our interviewee:

> So, I think that self-regulation is all about being smart and not circumventing your inhibition, in a way, and relying on environmental support or installing habits, and making sure that you don't need to resist all the time, because one way or another you are going to give up.
>
> *(SRL representative, interview, 2014)*

Ultimately the SRL supports the notion of self-nudging, but not in a conventional fashion. While established forms of self-nudging involve a kind of conscious prompt to action (like a notification of your success in achieving a set of exercise goals within a phone app, for example), the SRL has looked at the ways in which more automatic/emotional triggers can be used to support behaviour modification. The Lab is particularly interested in the ways in which self-nudges can be designed to establish certain forms of behaviour without the need for effortful resistance.

An interesting example of the forms of self-nudging envisaged by the SRL relates to healthy eating (see De Ridder et al., 2013). There are presently two favoured ways to try and address the problems of unhealthy eating and the obesity epidemic. The first suggests the importance of controlling the food environment, and in particular the availability of large portion sizes of unhealthy foods, more effectively. The second is to support systems of self-regulation that rely on controlled diet and personal resistance to food temptations. The SRL observes that controlling the food environment is challenging and has only limited success in transforming diets (ibid.). They further note that in light of the widespread availability of unhealthy food, it is very difficult for individuals to use behavioural inhibition consistently as a strategy for controlling overconsumption. It is in these contexts that the SRL recommends the development and use of so-called 'eating appropriateness standards' and related forms of social nudging. Unlike nutritional standards, which convey to consumers information about the content of food (often in scientific and unhelpful ways), eating appropriateness standards seek to establish social norms concerning the type, amount, and timing of food consumption (ibid.). Although the SRL do not tell us how these eating standards could be established, their basic features tell us much about the styles of neuroliberalism the Lab would favour. First, these standards are voluntary and thus preserve the right of consumers to choose not to follow them. Second they seek to use the power of social norms and conventions as a basis for shifting eating behaviours. Once eating standards have been agreed and established, they do not have to be constantly learned and remembered by the individual. Instead, individual eating behaviours are shaped by the conduct of those around us and our common desire to conform with the observed conduct of others (in more general terms, the SRL claims that an important strategy for self-nudging is to mix and socialise with those whose behaviours we wish to replicate in our own lives). Third, eating appropriateness standards reflect an interesting fusion of System 1 and System 2 thinking. While they involve a degree of deliberate calculation and planning, the behavioural effects of such eating standards are felt at a System 1 level, where guilt, habits and herd instincts are all deployed to support behaviour change.

At the heart of the particular brand of neuroliberalism promoted within the SRL is a desire to enable people to recognize their limited ability to control their behaviours, and to use this recognition to construct systems that can support desired behaviours. This form of nudging seeks to unify the divided self in ways that preserve individual autonomy and enhance character in full recognition of the limitations of the subject. On these terms, the work of the SRL embodies examples of what are increasingly being referred to as *meta-nudges*. Meta-nudging involves informing people about their behavioural tendencies and encouraging them to use those insights to self-nudge. This is a form of smart self-government that, rather than pursuing behavioural mastery and autonomy, encourages people to acknowledge and relate to their limited behavioural capacities in creative ways. It is a style of behavioural government that seeks, ironically, to preserve the autonomy of the subject by acknowledging the limited nature of behavioural autonomy.

Against nudging: questions of moral autonomy and intentionality

The practices of nudging have been questioned and criticized from a number of different perspectives. It is pertinent at this point to reflect upon critiques of nudging that have focused specifically on questions of the self, character and autonomy. One of the most prominent protagonists in critiques of nudge policies is the British sociologist Frank Furedi (see Furedi, 2011: 134–47). Certain aspects of Furedi's critique focus explicitly on the impacts of nudging on government constructions of the self. At the centre of Furedi's concerns is the assumption that, however they are constructed, nudges erode the moral autonomy of the self,

> Arguments about the necessity of protecting people from themselves were traditionally conveyed on religious and philosophical grounds. Today the traditional categories of sinners and the morally inferior have been displaced by jargon drawn from behavioural economics, evolutionary psychology, and neuroscience. The resources of these disciplines have been mobilised to effectively discredit the idea of moral autonomy.
>
> *(ibid.: 136)*

According to Furedi, nudges reflect the fact that governments do 'not quite believe that the majority of people possess the capacity for rational responsible behaviour' (ibid.: 135) and afford 'little tolerance towards behaviour deemed irrational or incorrect' (ibid.: 137). Furedi suggests that nudging policies reflect a form of intolerance towards private behavioural preference that has significant implications for democratic assumptions and processes (ibid.: 137). Additionally, Furedi suggests that governments that nudge are likely to inculcate a culture of infantilization in which not only is the moral autonomy of subjects assumed to be weak, but its active development (particularly through the making of behavioural mistakes and the building of associated forms of character) will be stunted (ibid.: 135). While we see some merit in Furedi's perspective, we believe that it is characterized by two shortcomings. First, just because subjects may be prevented from making mistakes and developing effective forms of moral autonomy in some areas of their lives (where they are being nudged) does not mean that autonomy cannot be developed either prior to nudging interventions, or in other areas of non-nudged living. Second, it is clear that while Furedi's critique may be relevant to certain styles of nudging (such as opt-out government), it has less purchase in relation to more self-regulatory systems (and in particular meta-nudging) that assume forms of smart engagement with, and use of, the different registers of human behaviour. In this context, we claim that Furedi's critique is based on too narrow a reading of neoliberal systems of government.

The philosopher and neuroscientist Raymond Tallis offers a further critique of the constructions of the self that are common in nudge (Tallis, 2011). According to Tallis, the behavioural studies and neurosciences upon which neuroliberalism is founded establish a vision of the human subject that is characterized by *universal helplessness* (ibid.: 245). This universal helplessness is predicated upon research into human behaviour in 'unusual situations in which we are less in control than we think we are' (ibid.: 245). Tallis asserts that the selection of situations where our System 1 selves essentially trick our System 2 selves fails to account for the broader, longitudinal context within which human action emerges. Tallis depicts nudge as a form of *political scientism* that misrepresents the nature of human character and underestimates the power of the autonomous self (ibid.: 326). What is missing from nudge then is an appreciation of human intentionality, that is to say 'the sustained and complex resolve that is being maintained over very long periods of time' (ibid.: 248). It is one thing then for someone to succumb to the temptations of eating unhealthily in one situation, but it is quite another to position this momentary lapse in the context of a long and sustained dietary programme. Tallis' critique has implications for both simple nudges and the more complex meta-nudges devised by the SRL. The smart nudges of the SRL are predicated upon the likely exhaustion of the human will to resist long-term temptations. But Tallis argues that humans relate to behaviour through longer-term forms of intentionality, which cannot be effectively discerned within the short-term trials of the behavioural sciences. On these terms, while smart and meta-nudges may suggest the presence of a more autonomous self than opt-out government, they still tend to underestimate the nature of human character.

The neurologically reflexive self: changing the subject and the Social Brain Centre

In this section we outline a set of understandings of the neuroliberal self that build upon, but ultimately transform, the notion of meta-nudging that was discussed in the previous section. The ideas in question concern the notion of *neurological reflexivity*, and the organization that we will discuss is the UK's Royal Society for the Encouragement of Arts, Manufactures and Commerce (RSA) Social Brain Centre.

Introducing the Social Brain Centre

The RSA's *Social Brain Centre* (hereafter SBC) was established in 2009 in order to support research on, and action inspired by, the emerging insights of the behavioural sciences into human nature. The SBC is inspired by the same scientific insights and practical impetuses that animate neuroliberalism generally, but is especially interested in the implications of these insights for the kind of societies we build.[1] The background and thinking behind the SBC was described to us by one representative of the RSA in the following terms:

back in 2008–09, sort of post-crash period there was a sort of moment where everyone was rethinking virtually everything. One of them was will the economy survive? [another was] What are the foundations on which the economy rests? That wasn't the only impetus because at the same time books were coming out, I think *Nudge* was released about then, I think Sunstein was advising Obama in the US. There was a buzz in air about behavioural insights. A lot of it had come from behavioural economics … I wasn't here at the time, but Matthew Taylor,[2] who had just come out of government saw a chance to use this material to help redefine the RSA's mission as being about coming to know ourselves better, but also critiquing much of the social and economic world through those new foundations.

(*SBC, interview, 2014*)

Two things are of particular note about the SBC's mission: (1) it places emphasis on the importance of society becoming much more aware of the behavioural insights that are associated with neuroliberalist thinking (this would be part of the RSA's broader '21st Century Enlightenment' project); and (2) it seeks to use new behavioural insights to develop a political project of critique, which questions the behavioural and neurological functions of social and economic institutions.

The key behavioural foci of the SBC's work were described to us in the following terms:

There's a shift from an emphasis on the individual to an emphasis on the heavily socialized creature, and there's a shift in emphasis from the conscious reasoning to automaticity and habitual behaviour.

(*SBC, interview, 2014*)

The shift in emphasis from conscious to automatic forms of action is of course a hallmark of the forms of neuroliberal approaches to the subject that we have outlined. The approach that the SBC develops to how people might relate to automaticity is, however, original, as it calls for systems of *neurological reflexivity*. The concern with humans as 'heavily socialized creatures' does, however, diverge from mainstream neuroliberalism. While nudging tactics recognize the impact of other people on the behaviours of individuals (through social norms, peer pressure and herd mentalities), nudge techniques tend to understand behaviour as a feature of the individual. The SBC, however, sees society as the primary force in shaping long-term behavioural patterns, and indeed in forming and changing the individual subject itself.

New perspectives on the brain and behaviour: plasticity and socialization

In order to appreciate the originality and significance of the SBC's approach to the behavioural self it is necessary to unpack some of the scientific assumptions upon which the Centre bases its work. The theoretical underpinnings of the SBC were established in its first report, *Changing the Subject: How New Ways of Thinking about Human Behaviour Might Change Politics, Policy and Practice* (Grist, 2010). While reciting the neuroliberal emphasis on automatic brain functions and habitual practices, the *Changing the Subject* report emphasizes two scientific insights into human behaviour: brain plasticity and the social brain. Neuroscience has demonstrated that the brain exhibits plasticity to the extent that the neurological apparatus of the brain evolves and changes through a life course on the basis of experience. The notion of brain plasticity (and in particular the realization that brains can change and evolve in adulthood) has political significance because it suggests that people can change and are not necessarily slaves to their habits and automatic tendencies. The idea of brain plasticity has informed the SBC's assumption that behavioural government can hope to achieve more than merely a changed behavioural environment: it can also realize a changed behavioural subject (Grist, 2009: 41–4).

The idea of the social brain as a focus for the Centre is drawn primarily from evolutionary anthropology, but has been supported by related work within the behavioural sciences. The social brain hypothesis suggests that: (1) sociality is a fundamental component of brain functions; and (2) the human brain has evolved to its unusually large size so as to enable us to deal with our complex relations with other people. While reciprocal forms of altruism and empathy appear to be important in the development of effective forms of behaviour and social interaction, the idea of the social brain recognizes that not all people will have the same opportunity to develop these social skills. This is essentially where the political dynamics of the SBC become apparent. According to the SBC, our ability to achieve effective forms of behavioural control is in part driven through the forms of social interactions we have and the broader *institutions* that support our neurological and social development (including schools, community associations, sports teams and more general social networks). Crucially, according to the SBC, this means that behavioural agency and character are severely diminished by forms of social disadvantage, which may inhibit these opportunities.

Neurological reflexivity, social justice and steering the behavioural self

It is useful at this point to position the SBC's approach to behaviour change in the context of the other neuroliberal techniques that we have so far outlined in this chapter. In keeping with both conventional nudges, and the work of the Self-Regulation Lab, the SBC works from a System 1 and System 2 vision of human thought and behaviour. The SBC Centre also recognizes (in keeping with nudge techniques) that the powerful influence of System 1 on human behaviour can erode human agency and forms of self-authored behaviour (as 'aggression, fear, anxiety and compulsion' render the self unable to direct its life autonomously (Grist, 2009: 59)). As found in the work of the Self-Regulation Lab, however, the SBC also suggests that System 2 cannot realistically be expected to reign in the powerful behavioural drivers associated with the automatic system. The key to effective forms of self-government (at least in the long term) is 'training the way the automatic and controlled brain interact with one another' (Grist, 2009 page 59).

The main point of divergence between the SBC centre and SRL is in how they envision techniques to establish new relations with System 1 behaviours in order to support effective forms of self-government. The SRL (and related meta-nudging approaches) suggests the use of specific collective interventions that use habits, social cues and biases in order to aid self-control. The SBC is much more interested in developing personal meta-awareness of both automatic and deliberative behaviours. Crucially, the SBC suggests that relearning and adjusting automatic forms of behaviour cannot be achieved through formal education (which tends to rely on educating the calculating self). Instead it is argued that it is only in real world spaces and contexts of routine societal interaction that System 1 can change and develop.

As the *Changing the Subject* report observes:

> Not to say that individual effort doesn't matter, but given what we know about the brain this seems misplaced. Developing autonomy and responsibility seems to depend in large part on learning through the absorption of social cues in a responsive and enabling environment … and through repeated activities that allow learning from mistakes[.]
>
> *(ibid.: 63)*

There are two implications from this statement. The first is that it is futile to try to facilitate lasting forms of change in self-government through either formal systems of behavioural government (such as nudges) or behavioural education. Behaviour is shaped in affective fields, which emerge from pre-cognitive and contingent social interactions that largely elude governmental control. The second is that effective forms of behavioural government rely on 'responsive and enabling environments' that are not available to all in society. Here we can begin to discern the political dynamics of the SBC's project.

The SBC essentially makes the political assertion that empowering forms of behaviour change can only be achieved if people have the opportunity to experience effective forms of social learning. Neurological government thus becomes less about a technical exercise in behaviour modification and more one of opportunity creation and social transformation. This transformative mission was captured by one representative of the SBC in an interview we conducted with them:

> Basically, people's idea of what they want is a function of their experience, and those that have had experiences that they value and that they think are of a higher order … it's incumbent upon them to allow others to at least taste that experience so that they may know of another way of being. And if you buy into that broad perspective, then you have a theory of progress really, behavioural progress whereby it's not so much people do things differently,

but their conception of the world is different, their experience of themselves and their relation is different.

(SBC, interview, 2014)

The fundamental assumption here is not that some people are inherently able to attain autonomous agency over their actions and life goals, while others are not. Rather the assumption is that agency and character are defined by social experience, which is itself shaped by differentiated forms of social opportunity. Recognizing the role of social conditions in determining behavioural autonomy also has implications for established political positionalities. As the *Changing the Subject* report notes:

> So neoliberal conservatives find themselves in a conundrum: it is benevolent social conditions that foster self-reliance and individual effort, rather than the other way around. Autonomy and responsibility are achieved with the support of others … On the other hand, left-wing liberals find themselves pushed to accept the traditional conservative value placed on family and other supportive institutions.

(Grist, 2009: 64)

While it is here that the SBC clearly begins to disconnect from neoliberal orthodoxies, from this point we can also begin to see the radical political potential of neuroliberalism.

If behavioural government is essentially concerned with how the self relates to its own behaviour, then the SBC's work suggests that our relationship with our behaviour is filtered through the social relations that we are able to establish and cultivate. The SBC argues that effective behavioural government is best thought of as a form of *neurological reflexivity*. To paraphrase the SBC, neurological reflexivity is a continual activity of making choices based on an awareness that one's choices are shaped by automatic processes that often escape our conscious grasp, that our ability to make neurologically informed choices is critically shaped by the kind of society we live in and the social groups with which we mix, and that our behavioural choices determine the trajectory of our future behaviours (Grist, 2009: 13).

The principle of neurological reflexivity has been the foundation of a series of ongoing SBC projects and reports. In their 2010 report *Steer: Mastering Our Behaviour Through Instinct, Environment and Reason* (Grist 2011), the SBC details the delivery of behavioural workshops based on the principles of neurological reflexivity in which members of the public were encouraged to relate to their behaviour through systems of critical self-awareness. The SBC has also worked with taxi drivers in an attempt to use SBC methodologies of behavioural government to support the more effective driving of taxi cabs in order to reduce carbon emissions (Rowson and Young, 2011). The SBC's application of neurological reflexivity has generated some positive qualitative and quantitative results within the communities where it has been applied. Those encouraged to develop their neurological reflexivity report developing more nuanced understandings of how they make decisions, and being able to invoke strategies to support desired behaviours more effectively (for example by engaging other people in the decision-making process, using mulling techniques to engage the automatic brain creatively, and deploying incremental forms of behaviour change (Grist, 2010)). Despite clearly offering a more empowering form of behaviour change, the real world application of neurological reflexivity does raise some questions. Unlike nudge, the effective scaling-up of the forms of behavioural learning advocated by the SBC are difficult to imagine (at least outside of the formal education system). Furthermore, despite emphasizing the connections between the spread of neurological reflexivity and social justice and opportunity, the SBC remains relatively silent on precisely how new forms of social experience and learning may emerge (with SBC interventions to date being delivered in the absence of a related programme of radical social change).

Conclusion

This chapter has reviewed the implications of neuroliberalism for how, collectively, we understand human nature and construct subjectivity. At the heart of this analysis has been a desire to consider the assumptions that neuroliberal strategies make about human agency and the implications that these assumptions have for human character. Driving this chapter has been the common fear that, in uncovering a less deliberately oriented and rational self, neuroliberalism is based upon a very limited view of the human subject, which is likely to be reinforced by related forms of disempowering behavioural government. In relation to conventional nudge policies this chapter has shown that many neuroliberal styles of government (particularly focusing upon the ideas of the opt-out self) are based upon fairly limited and limiting views of human autonomy and character, and an assumption that the self is not able to develop significant forms of long-term transformation. In this context, behavioural government becomes a system focusing essentially on out-sourcing the self to choice architects and trying to find short-term fixes to socially problematic behaviours that are unlikely to be resolved at an individual level.

Beyond these nudge-based approaches we have, however, seen neuroliberal strategies that are based on more optimistic views of the human subject and ultimately more progressive political programmes. In relation to the work of the Self-Regulation Lab, we have observed policy strategies that call for forms of smart meta-nudging, which enable individuals to work creatively with their behavioural flaws in order to find effective solutions to various lifestyle challenges. The Social Brain Centre suggests that through practices of neurological reflexivity and the opening up of new opportunities for everyday behavioural learning, the neuroliberal self can achieve personal change and development, but can also be an agent of broader forms of social transformation. Running through our analysis has been a desire to reveal both the contested nature of the neuroliberal subject, and its connections with ever-evolving and mutating systems of liberal government (see Rose, 1998). In the chapter that follows we build on this analysis of human agency and character to consider the ways in which neuroliberalism is challenging and redefining liberal understandings of freedom.

Notes

1 The social-orientation of the SBC's work reflects the broader remit of the RSA, which over its 250-year history has sought to facilitate social progress by encouraging multidisciplinary research into social problems.
2 Matthew Taylor was Chief Executive of the RSA at the time of the launch of the SBC, before which he was a key advisor in Tony Blair's government.

5

REDEFINING FREEDOM

Neuroliberal autonomy and citizenship

Introduction: neuroliberalism and the free society

Having set out the implications of neuroliberalism for human character and subjectivity in the previous chapter, we now consider its implications for how we might understand freedom and related notions of autonomy and citizenship. As we have already described, neuroliberalism denotes the use of behavioural science and neuroscientific knowledge to shape and govern conduct in free societies (see Chapter 1). Its novel governmental techniques have a strong political association with the promotion and assurance of freedom and an economic commitment to market liberalism. As we have already seen, however, certain brands of neuroliberalism emphasize the fallible, unconscious and automatic aspects of human decision-making and thus challenge many of the 'classical' assumptions concerning human autonomy (see Chapter 3). Neuroliberalism maintains that governments are warranted in interfering in individual choices in light of the consistent behavioural market failures that require correction.

Neuroliberalism has three broad implications for ideas of freedom and associated notions of autonomy. First, neuroliberalism questions the human capacity to be free (at least at the level of intentionality) in the face of the powerful forces of unconscious bias, emotion and automaticity. Second, many forms of neuroliberalism, with their reliance on unconscious strategies of behavioural adjustment, are associated with manipulation and the partial erosion of freedom. Third, through the particular emphasis that neuroliberals place on the importance of choice in preserving freedom, the neuroliberal project is involved in the (often stealthy) redefinition of freedom. While discussion tends to focus on these three questions of freedom, in this chapter we will consider the broader issues of freedom that are brought to the surface by neuroliberal government. Through case study material, we consider the assumptions of thick and thin autonomy that surround contemporary debates about neuroliberalism, and use these concepts as a way of opening up a critical dialogue around questions of behavioural government and freedom.

This chapter draws on qualitative research interviews with Singaporean and Dutch policy officials, social entrepreneurs and academics in order to explore the impact that neuroliberalism has on emerging understandings and practices of freedom, and how existing cultures of freedom shape neuroliberal policies. We have chosen these as case study states to discuss here because while both have been influenced by neuroliberal ideas and practices, they are characterized by very different cultures of freedom. While both of these states are liberal democracies, they embody very different approaches to freedom and have different expectations of autonomy among their citizenry. Singapore is a form of authoritarian democracy that places much stronger emphasis on economic than political freedom. The Netherlands, on the other hand, is a parliamentary democracy that has a strong political culture of consensus building and welfarism. As two states that have been in the vanguard of neuroliberalism, they provide interesting comparative case studies into how neuroliberalism shapes understandings of freedom, and is in turn moulded by existing political norms of liberty. In exploring the connections between neuroliberalism and freedom, this chapter draws particular attention to the impacts that geographical circumstances have on the construction of norms of freedom within different national contexts. The chapter commences by introducing the two case study examples of the Netherlands and Singapore. The following section considers the different forms of impacts that neuroliberal styles of policies have had on debates about and practices of freedom in these two states.

Behavioural government in practice: from the Netherlands to Singapore

Neuroliberalism has not evolved in a political vacuum. Indeed there is a risk of over-generalising and over-inflating its importance if it is considered universally applicable and geographically uniform − as if it were a coherent and finished political project. There is no doubt that state-orchestrated behavioural forms of governance have enjoyed widespread political popularity across many countries. Yet specific national and local political, social, cultural and economic circumstances are important factors in shaping the ways in which neuroliberalism is manifested, and the issues that it brings to the surface, in particular nation states. The ways in which subjectivity and character might be impacted by neuroliberalism can be shaped by the degree of autonomy, economic freedoms and political culture already *in place*. In the UK, for instance, since the late 2000s neuroliberalism has been shaped by political debates concerning increasing personal responsibility and freedom, personalized public services and cutbacks in public spending. In the USA, meanwhile, it has been more concerned with improvements in state regulation and promoting the idea of behaviourally informed paternalism in a nation that historically views state intervention with suspicion. Already we can see that neuroliberalism is bound up with culturally specific ideas of state and citizen identity, in which broad philosophical debates around ethics might be usefully supplemented with empirical analyses. Furthermore, the development of neuroliberal forms of government is reliant on the specific institutional arrangements of a particular state. The geographical perspective emphasized in this chapter supports the broader goal of this volume to uncover the different species of neuroliberalism that are emerging in the world around us. In this chapter however we seek to demonstrate that the different emergent forms of neuroliberalism are not merely a product of different ways of interpreting psychological and behavioural sciences, but are also the outcome of specific geographical, political, economic and cultural traditions and practices.

The government as choice architect in the Netherlands

The Dutch state has developed a clear interest in neuroliberal styles of government science since around 2009 when the Scientific Council for Government Policy (WRR) held a symposium, 'The Government as Choice Architect' ('De Overhead Als Keuzarchitect'). This event involved a keynote address by behavioural economist Richard Thaler. Yet as one participant at the symposium told us, there was a general suspicion of the potentially manipulative dimensions of 'nudge'-type policies, and the Scientific Council did not advise the Dutch government to adopt behavioural policies as a result of this event:

> There was some kind of aversion to what they [the Scientific Council] would think would be manipulation … the ethical card which is often played.
> *(Former Scientific Council/WRR member, Netherlands, interview, 2014)*

As we will see, this initial apprehension about the manipulative undertones of neuroliberalism and its potential impact upon notions of freedom in Dutch state–citizen relations have contributed to ongoing ethical debates in the Netherlands.

Despite initial concerns, however, just one year after the WRR's symposium the Dutch Ministry of Infrastructure and Environment (as it is now known) established a behaviour change unit within its department. Representatives of the Dutch government also visited the UK's BIT and the USA to discuss the use of behavioural science in public policy. It has been argued that the Dutch government at the time was attracted by the apparent efficiency of such forms of government:

> this administration, they're probably in favour of fewer rules, smaller government, more effective policies. I think this [behavioural government] is something they will go for whether [or not] they grasp the entire consequences first.
> *(Government advisor, Netherlands, interview, 2014)*

An interdepartmental strategy network consisting of civil servants recommended the setting up of a specific behavioural insights initiative, the first meeting of which was held in May 2013. Subsequently, the ministries of internal affairs, infrastructure and environment, and economic affairs were asked to propose policy areas where new behavioural insights could be applied and tested. A series of governmental ministries have now established their own behavioural insights team, with the team of the Department of Economic Affairs acting as the coordinating secretariat for each unit (Joint Research Centre, 2016). In 2014 the Behavioural Insights Network Netherlands was established to coordinate public sector activity around neuroliberal policies across various regulatory bodies. Additionally, a number of government advisory councils have produced reports exploring the pros and cons of deploying neuroliberal techniques of government (see Council for the Environment and Infrastructure 2014; ISS (Council for Social Development) 2014).

By 2015, the Dutch government had used insights from the behavioural sciences across a number of disparate policy areas, including food safety campaigns, domestic energy conservation, the regulation of complex financial products, the promotion of sustainable food products, policies for the unemployed and in the introduction of electronic health records, which used an opt-out model of implementation. The Ministry of Infrastructure and the Environment went as far as to instigate a requirement for all organizations commissioned to deliver services to complete a detailed behavioural analysis of their work programme and goals prior to receiving any state funding. And the Ministry of Transport deployed the Behavioural Insights Model and Individual/Social/Material (ISM) model developed by Andrew Darnton and David Evans for the Scottish government (Darnton and Evans, 2013) in relation to improving the road safety of cyclists. Finally, there has been speculation that behavioural insights will be used within the social housing sector, where a civil servant in the Ministry of Internal Affairs told us that policies could be developed to encourage middle-income groups to leave low rent state housing voluntarily and move into the private housing sector.[1] The neuroliberal aspect of housing policy is premised on the fact that the decision to stay in social housing is not just a financial one, but is also related to issues of inertia (and the hassles of moving) and the emotional connections that people feel towards their home and neighbourhood. It is suggested that neuroliberal policies could be used to: challenge the predominant perception of social housing as a citizen right within the Netherlands; simplify the processes of moving house; and establish new norms among middle-income groups concerning the importance of independence and social betterment. In addition to offering new approaches to tackling a recalcitrant problem, the non-regulatory nature of neuroliberal housing policies are likely to be less controversial than legislative solutions.

What is clear is that in the Netherlands neuroliberalism is not a centrally led state project, but rather a more piecemeal set of efforts, which, as this chapter explores later, is hotly debated even within the Dutch government. As we will see in subsequent sections, the emerging ethical debates around neuroliberalism in the Netherlands raise some interesting questions concerning notions of freedom and autonomy more generally.

Using behavioural science in a 'benevolent dictatorship': from shoving to nudging in Singapore

Although Singapore is a democracy, as a society it has very different cultures and expectations of freedom from those we find in the Netherlands. Singapore actually has something of a bipolar relationship with freedom. This bipolarity is perhaps expressed most clearly in two recent league tables. The first is the Index of Economic Freedom, which in 2015 ranked Singapore as second in the world in terms of the freedom of its economy. The second table is the Economists' 2015 Democracy Index, where we find Singapore ranked seventy-fourth in the world and designated as a 'flawed democracy'. Singapore's lowly ranking on the Democracy Index comes despite the fact that its government is based upon a parliamentary democracy. The People's Action Party has actually won every election since the nation's independence was established in 1959. This political situation has resulted in the emergence of forms of benevolent dictatorial styles of society in Singapore, where economic freedoms and meritocracy sit alongside more limited forms of civil liberty and a general acceptance of governmental orthodoxy. This political situation raises interesting questions concerning precisely why neuroliberalism has proved to be so popular in Singapore and the extent to which it has been seen to be preserving or denying freedom.

In Singapore, behaviourally informed approaches to government were initially explored in the Civil Service College (CSC) around 2010–11. The publication of CSC member, Donald Low's (2011) *Behavioural Economics and Policy Design: Examples from Singapore* urged a break with Singapore's traditional economic rationalism, arguing that 'while the textbook economic models based on rationality may be internally consistent, policymakers have to grapple with the messiness and complications of the societies they serve' (Low, 2011: 5). The CSC is one of a number of parastate institutions that has promoted the use of behavioural insights in government. Along with Singapore Management University and the Lee Kuan Yew School of Public Policy (LKY), the CSC has provided training, professional development courses and an annual symposium on behavioural economics for civil servants. As one leading academic formerly at the CSC and Public Service Division told us, policy-makers would now feel inadequate if they didn't have knowledge of behavioural economics (Academic (public policy), and senior government policy strategist, Public Service Division, Singapore, interview, 2015). There has also been cross-fertilization of policy ideas globally, with Rory Gallagher from the UK's Behavioural Insights Team advising Singapore's Ministry of Manpower (MoM) and Ministry of Transport in 2014, followed by the opening of a Singapore office of the BIT in 2016. Just as in the Netherlands, there is no central behavioural insights team in Singapore. Rather, there are units in specific ministries, such as the Behavioural Insights and Design Unit in the Ministry of Manpower, and the Environmental Behavioural Sciences and Economic Research Unit in the Ministry of the Environment and Water Resources, set up in 2012.[2]

Singapore is also well known for innovating in 'design thinking' within government. This design expertise has facilitated the development of a series of endogenous interventions that embody the principles and methodological practices of neuroliberalism (Bason, 2014: 3) (for a broader discussion of the connections between neuroliberalism and design see Chapter 8 in this volume). Related initiatives focus on 'user' experiences, rapid prototyping, visualization and experimentation to better understand the behaviour of public service users, particularly through co-design practices with users themselves. This also involves rearticulating the nature of policy problems as complex systems, including a wider understanding of the contexts, multiple agents and materials through which policies are enacted (Bason, 2014: 5). The Design Thinking Unit and the Human Experience Lab in the Prime Minister's Public Service Division, as well as the Design Incubation Centre at the National University Singapore, have been significant players in integrating behavioural and design insights into public policy. Finally, social enterprises (sometimes referred to as social innovation labs), think tanks and public service design start-ups such as the Australian-led *Think Place*, the *Sustainable Living Lab*, and *Syinc* have undertaken government contracts using behavioural insights and design thinking to rethink government service provision and regulation.

There are now a plethora of start-ups, social enterprises and parastate bodies involved in public policy-making in Singapore. While the rise of policy think tanks is a long-running global phenomenon crucial to understanding the evolution of political and economic ideas (Stone, 1996), Singapore specifically has been noted as a hotspot for such organizations in relation to its small population size. Singapore's recent strategic government investments in this sector have also been observed (Biswas and Hartley, 2015; McGann, 2016). Behaviourally informed policy making in Singapore has thus been influenced heavily by the changing relationships between non-governmental social enterprises, policy-focused start-ups and the state. While staff at such start-ups regard their role as developing more empathetic relationships with citizens, others question the degree to which they are free to offer independent advice and project delivery in light of their reliance on government funding and contracts. Despite the lack of a central government office for behavioural insights and the apparently silo nature of behavioural science thinking going on in the ministries, some of our interviewees clearly regarded the relationships between the LKY School, the CSC and the Prime Minister's Office as so intrinsically close that as one social entrepreneur put it, the university bodies and civil servants act as a 'soft power mechanism' with strong influence and little independence (co-founder and director of for-profit social enterprise, Singapore, interview, 2015). As such the kind of neuroliberalism emerging in Singapore should be understood in the context of this changing machinery of government. Where soft power has come to mould policy thinking and state–citizen relations, our analyses must necessarily examine both the neuroliberal policies in place within particular nation states, and the institutional apparatus by which such policies are being devised, designed and delivered (for a broader discussion of the relationships between neuroliberalism and governmental structures see Chapter 6 in this volume).

Behaviourally informed regulations and initiatives have been emerging from these policy units and social enterprises since 2012. Those operating within the Ministry of Manpower and Ministry of Transport are perhaps the most well known, but there is little information as yet publicly available about the evaluation of such initiatives. The Behavioural Insights and Design Unit in the Ministry of Manpower has worked on redesigning the experience of foreign workers applying for work permits. Using principles of user experience and design thinking, they have tried out a new approach of people-centred design and seek to improve the quality of service users' experience. As a director at the Ministry of Trade and Industry, Singapore (interviewed in 2015) told us, the MoM project is where nudges and design thinking (MoM were advised initially in 2010 by international design company IDEO) have come together to focus on end-users and to achieve client satisfaction, even if the outcomes for that client are not what they desired. This is one example in which the Singapore government has recognized the need to relate to citizens on a more emotional level, as one social entrepreneur undertaking government contracts told us, by 'differentiating people with different motivational postures' (Partner at Strategic Public Policy Design Consultancy, interview, 2015). So too, communications and design experts have been consulted in order to ensure that personal tax forms are easy and attractive, so that 'the tax office really sets out to delight its customers' (Partner at Strategic Public Policy Design Consultancy, interview, 2015). Another director at a for-profit social enterprise we interviewed was delivering a programme for the National Environment Agency aimed at decreasing the generation of waste by the public. They set out to change social norms away from a notion of environmental awareness achieved through feelings of shame, and towards collaborative, fun action aimed at developing a 'repair culture'. This was intended to build on the popularity of hackathons (workshops that are intended to repurpose either technology or processes, often for a social good: see Chapter 8 in this volume) as ways to both reuse and recycle material goods and as a metaphor for designing innovative solutions to problems. In this context we can again see the synergies between Singapore's cultural affinity with innovative design solutions and the experimental character of neuroliberalism.

Within the health sector too there are examples of neuroliberal insights being used in the development of health promotion campaigns such as the '1 million kilogram challenge', through which the Singapore Sports Council committed funding for personal gym memberships and running exercise competitions in shopping malls. One of the ideas here was to reward healthy living, and the other to make exercise easy and communal. As one social entrepreneur interviewee told us, the cultural concept of 'saving face' is important for Singaporeans, therefore there was an added social pressure to take part in these activities. This same sense of saving face (and in contrast to the move away from 'shaming' within the National Environment Agency's public communications programme) has also been drawn out through anti-littering and anti-spitting initiatives. Rather than rely on the traditionally punitive fines on public litterers and people who spit on the street, citizens were asked to take a photo of offending people, and this was showcased in prominent places and a 'STOP' website. Offenders are also now required to perform community service in highly visible vests, as the public pressure and embarrassment they experience is said to bring about more sustained changes in behaviour. Indeed citizens have been so committed to providing images for what one interviewee described as this 'rogues gallery' that measures have had to be taken to dissuade people from reporting such transgressions because of the burden of administrating all the reports!

The apparent speed and enthusiasm with which behaviourally informed policies and regulations have been adopted in Singapore is seen as inevitable by some commentators, and somewhat surprising by others. As one policy official described, on the one hand it is logical to use a range of (academic) disciplinary perspectives and forms of knowledge to tackle complex governance problems, and it was high time that the Singaporean government developed a more benevolent approach that addressed citizens more consistently as 'whole persons' by using psychology and service-user research to improve wellbeing (director at the Ministry of Trade and Industry, Singapore, interview, 2015). And yet others questioned why Singapore would even need to experiment with nudges, since there was apparently little appetite to avoid the coercion of traditional regulatory levers among a highly conformist citizenry and ultimately authoritarian one-party state:

> And you would have thought that the Government will really not worry about nudging; they'd really just go straight on to shoving ... the Singapore Government – maybe did come from a more authoritarian space, so perhaps differently [from other countries where they've come from a more, you know, liberal environment and then tried to sort of guide choices ...] Singapore's Government has come from an environment where many of the choices were very constrained, but they've tried to come up with ways to move in a more liberal direction, towards the nudge.
>
> *(Academic (behavioural science, economics, health systems),*
> *Singapore, interview, 2015)*

While recent years have seen a more open forum for public and political debate, the authority of this 'benevolent dictatorship' (as described by the co-founder and director of for-profit social enterprise, interviewed 2015) was not yet in question. What appears to be occurring in Singapore is that neuroliberalism has provided an opportunity to fuse Singapore's penchant with design solutions with an attempt to use less authoritarian styles of governing. While this may not reflect a culture shift in Singaporean understandings of freedom, it does perhaps reflect a pragmatic engagement with policy solutions that may be both more effective and more liberally oriented than their predecessors. We will pick up on this issue again in the next section, which examines why behaviourally informed policies have been adopted in both Singapore and the Netherlands at this political moment, while contrasting the political debates concerning freedom that have surrounded their adoption.

Varieties of freedom under conditions of neuroliberalism

Neuroliberalism, choice and freedom in critical context

In order to understand the emerging entanglements between neuroliberalism and freedom in the Netherlands and Singapore, it is important to reflect more generally on the relationships between neuroliberal government and questions of choice and autonomy. A number of recent commentators have reminded us of significant differences between choice and freedom. In *Choosing not to Choose*, Cass Sunstein (2015) reflects on the sometimes overwhelming array of choices that we face in our everyday lives, and considers how too much choice can have disabling affects; we simply don't have the time, attention or inclination to choose every minute detail of our activities. *Not* choosing can free up time and effort to do things that matter more to us. Furthermore, he argues, '*[d]eciding by default* is an omnipresent (and often wonderful) feature of human life' (Sunstein, 2015: XI, original emphasis). His observations on the default settings in many of our choices (choice architectures) and the liberating features of displaced forms of agency chime with debates within political philosophy and classical economics on the nature of first- and second-order preferences (see Chapter 4 in this volume). In these debates 'second-order preferences' relate more to our long-term interests that are often found to conflict with 'first-order' decisions made in the more immediate term (see Dworkin, 1988: 15). As such, neuroliberal interventions often involve designing choice architectures that are said to reorder our preferences in ways that will improve our health, wealth and happiness in the long run.

This conflict between what, in behavioural economics, has been dubbed 'fast and slow thinking' is fundamental to the project of libertarian paternalism that has shaped much of the thought behind neuroliberalism (Kahneman, 2011). As Sunstein has also argued, where nudges are concerned, context remains crucial in determining the ethics of default positions and displaced agency where these have been designed to intervene in 'fast thinking'. Indeed while it might seem obvious to rational choice theorists that these different layers of preferences can coexist, for most of us the *feeling* of choosing and autonomy can be an important principle, any threat to which seems anti-democratic. This leads Sunstein to outline a distinction between thick and thin autonomy. Thick autonomy aligns with the special status afforded to freedom (at any cost) by neoliberal thinkers, and refers to treating autonomy as an end in itself – as a key component of human freedom and dignity (Sunstein, 2015: 127). Those who resist government paternalism in all forms take this view, arguing that denial of choice, even through default or opt-out settings, can leave people feeling infantilized and frustrated (ibid.: 128). Those who favour a thin version of autonomy may well have welfare as the end goal, and must weigh up whether the preference for, and potentially educative effects of, active choosing are balanced by the consequences of those freedoms for individuals. Here we see how the political philosophies surrounding behavioural governance and neuroliberalism begin to diverge substantially from a neoliberal economic rationality.

The *modus operandi* of behavioural forms of governance is to be paternalistic rather than neoliberal – albeit a soft or libertarian form of paternalism that seeks to preserve or even enhance autonomy. This point of clarification helps us to refine further how we understand the relationship between neuro- and neo-liberalisms (see Chapter 3). While both neo- and neuro-liberalism emphasize the importance of personal liberty, neoliberalism tends to see this freedom as being defined by the unencumbered (thick autonomy) ability to participate in the marketplace (indeed, neoliberalists tend to value economic freedom very highly in their overall assessment of *total freedom* (see Friedman, 2002 [1982]: 9)). Neuroliberalism, on the other hand, is paternalistic not because it is anti-libertarian, but because of how it believes liberty can most effectively be achieved. In the absence of the rationality assumption, neuroliberalists suggest that freedom cannot be achieved without the activities of paternalistic agents who can help to secure liberty by behavioural means. Neuroliberalism is premised on the assumption that individuals often find it hard to know what is best for them to do, and that even when they are in possession of this valuable knowledge, still find it challenging to behave in ways that would help them to achieve outcomes that would be best for them. If freedom is to be understood, at a rudimentary level at least, as the ability to align our behaviour with our intention, then neuroliberal policies seek to support subjects in their ability to sync intentions with behaviour. Neuroliberalism often rests on the notion of *thin autonomy*, because it recognizes that people's intentions are not always used to activate behaviour effectively. Neuroliberalism thus seeks to frame choice in order to support the more effective alignment of intention and behaviour, but in ways that tend to promote choice rather than 'thicker' understandings of freedom.

Where prominent forms of neo- and neuroliberalism do begin to realign, however, is in their assumption that enhanced participation in the market (suitably adjusted for our behavioural flaws) should still be the desired end point of behavioural government. As we will see, other more radically oriented strands of neuroliberalism suggest that the goals of behavioural government are found in freedom-enhancing destinations beyond those of the marketplace. These strands of neuroliberalism also tend to challenge the assumption that *thick autonomy* should be associated with the unencumbered forms of freedom that are associated with the 'total freedoms' of neoliberalism. These more radically oriented strands of neuroliberalism suggest a flaw in any definition of freedom that is based simply upon the absence of coercion. As we will see, freedom for these strands of neuroliberalism rests on a concern first and foremost with the material, social and psychological conditions that enable us to be autonomous in the first place.

Before we consider these deeper questions on autonomy and freedom, it is important to reflect in more depth on the emerging relationships between neuroliberalism and questions of choice and manipulation. Some critical perspectives on libertarian paternalist strands of neuroliberalism have tended to rest on a general suspicion of paternalism as a form of manipulation, and as a disempowering denial of choice (White, 2013). By contrast, others have welcomed more coercive forms of paternalism (Conly, 2012) as welfare enhancing, arguing that liberal governments do not currently operate in a sufficiently paternalistic manner. Conly's position is that governments *should* act coercively where it is in individuals' interests, even if they don't think so at the time. Yet the view that paternalism is inherently coercive has been challenged by Quigley (2014), who cautions against the misrepresentation and overuse of the term 'coercion' by critics of behavioural governance. She argues that nudges 'steer' and 'influence' choices rather than mandate them. As such, dismissing nudges as coercive can divert attention away from genuine examples of coercion that are controlling, liberty-infringing, choice limiting and use force – or the credible threat of force – to compel people to act in particular ways (Quigley, 2014: 146–7). Similarly, we claim that a sweeping critique of behavioural governance as inherently coercive would fail to appreciate how coercion depends on power differentials – the capacity of coercers to determine the actions or decisions of the coercee (Anderson in Quigley, 2014: 153). As debate and analysis of behavioural governance evolves, it is increasingly clear that context really matters in considering ethical and political concerns, as Sunstein (2015: 126) points out: 'Whether people feel frustrated by a denial of choice, or instead relieved and grateful, depends on context.' For Quigley too, it is precisely because choice architectures imply a *displacement* of human agency that we must pay closer attention to the contexts in which choices are arranged in particular ways.

Rethinking behavioural freedom in Singapore and the Netherlands

If the value ascribed to choosing depends on context, then there is much to learn from examining how neuroliberalism is manifest in different nation states. Singapore considers itself to be an early adopter of innovations in governance, as shown by its enthusiasm for 'design thinking', 'futures thinking', 'strategic anticipation' and 'adaptive governance' (director at the Ministry of Trade and Industry, Singapore, interview, 2015). This early adopter status appears to reflect the prevailing political culture in Singapore. As one interviewee observed, 'generally, in Singapore, we are about three or four years behind whatever happens in Silicon Valley … we are basically what is called a very copycat society' (co-founder and director of for-profit social enterprise, Singapore, interview, 2015). Interestingly, one civil servant described Singapore as a 'very impatient government' (director at the Ministry of Trade and Industry, Singapore, interview, 2015), and highlighted how its efficiency and hubris stemmed from an historical sense of vulnerability as a nation-state:

> You need, not just strong but enlightened and forward-looking and innovative leadership. So it's been… so they have that sense of, pervasive sense of vulnerability mixed with a sense of paranoia that if we don't have an excellent public sector, we don't have an excellent government. Why would anybody want to… why would anybody take Singapore seriously? … So Singapore's… all this is very well communicated in the public service. Yeah,

we are excellent, alert, we are on top of our game. That Singapore's success is entirely ephemeral, entirely manmade. So we've got to constantly stay ahead of the competition.

(Academic (public policy), and senior government policy strategist, Public Service Division, Singapore, interview, 2015)

There was little public debate surrounding the aforementioned behavioural innovations in governance in Singapore. Trials including RCTs were thus not deemed necessary because the rolling out of novel policy initiatives in a relatively small city-state with a lean and efficient civil service was relatively straightforward. Furthermore, there is little media diversity in Singapore, so traditional public channels of communication and debate have been largely supportive of government policies. The media has seen its role historically as one of building a stronger nation rather than holding the government to account. That is not to say that the media have been disinterested, but that behaviourally informed policies have been largely welcomed as a way to improve the design, utility and responsiveness of government to public needs. In sum, behavioural governance is often not seen as ideological:

I mean, there is no right-wing or left-wing, behavioural insights that you have. It's a tool, right? So there's nothing inherently left-wing or liberal or conservative about Behavioural Economics.

(Academic (public policy), and senior government policy strategist, Public Service Division, Singapore, interview, 2015)

The absence of media scrutiny or social concern over neuroliberalism in Singapore raises broader questions about the associated practices of freedom. The fact that Singaporean society appears to be generally less suspicious of the intentions of government than citizens in other liberal democracies reduces concern over the freedom-restricting potentials of neuroliberalism. It is interesting to consider, however, whether the broader political system in Singapore (particularly the subservient media and *de facto* single-party government) provides less freedom to question the implications of neuroliberal government in the first place. In essence the case of Singapore suggests the importance of thinking about neuroliberalism in relation to different orders of freedom. These orders of freedom stretch from the individual to broader political systems, and encompass questions of everyday autonomy as well as more general liberal checks on government activities.

By contrast, in the Netherlands, formal government circles have been considering ethical debates around behavioural governance for some time before any significant policy changes were made. The Dutch government has sought to learn lessons from the experience of states such as the UK and USA where behavioural policies have been incubated. In Singapore, behavioural governance has been widely accepted. In the Netherlands, however, there has been more division apparent between those who believe it would be unethical *not* to improve governance through new insights from behavioural economics and science, and those who have concerns about the potential impact of behavioural governance on freedom and autonomy.

On the one hand, there are policy advisors who argue that by failing to apply behavioural insights to policy, the government simply reproduces the status quo and fails to tackle inequalities:

> [T]hinking of ethicality what I am worried about is that when you see the evidence of traditional methods based on communication, information, literacy, et cetera, where there is proof of positive evidence it is among people who are already well-off. So, it increases the divide. So, you take taxpayers' money, from all taxpayers, to do something for a group. Either nobody benefits or a group benefits: the high educated, high income.
>
> *(Academic policy advisor, Netherlands, interview, 2014)*

On the other hand, the Dutch Council for Social Development (RMO), which advises the Dutch government on a range of social issues, has argued for a more concerted effort to tackle the potential threats to autonomy posed by nudging in particular:

> It shouldn't be pushing people in the right direction while harming their autonomy but it should be giving people more space, giving people more freedom without leaving them behind … [W]e're not against that [nudging] at all but we say, you should make some checks and balances right and you should be transparent and you should use it in a specific way. Because otherwise, you won't keep your promise to strengthen people's autonomy. That's the promise of nudging.
>
> *(RMO representative, Netherlands, interview, 2014)*

For one author of the RMO's 'Resisting temptation' report (RMO, 2014), behavioural governance raises a number of normative philosophical questions around autonomy and transparency (i.e. openness and fidelity to the genuine *promise* of nudging), which are in fact pertinent to traditional left–right political ideologies. As they recount:

> we formulated an autonomy paradox. And that relates to this distinction of positive and negative freedom where government is increasingly *retreating from the public domain and expects people to take their own responsibility.* That could easily be framed as an expansion of people's negative freedom because there's less and less distortion by government. But the more and more government expect people to take up their own responsibility, they expect people to be autonomous to make conscious choices. And then comes in the positive freedom because … if people don't have the full agency, the awareness, the self-esteem, they can't make those choices.
>
> *(RMO representative, Netherlands, interview, 2014, emphasis added)*

This discussion of the 'autonomy paradox', drawing on the work of Dutch philosopher Ruud Hendricks, highlights the high political stakes associated with the introduction of behavioural governance as it is being discussed in the Netherlands context. There appears to be much more scepticism surrounding the promise of nudging, its political rationale and the potential benefits to the public than is suggested by Singapore's rapid adoption of behavioural forms of governance. The RMO representative's observations imply that the differences between thin and thick autonomy that we described earlier are a significant and unresolved part of political debate in the Netherlands:

> we say as soon as the government tries to make people autonomous, then she does that anyway in a way that decreases the autonomy of people because then, she's going to say, 'Well, this is autonomy and you should be heading this way if you want to be autonomous.' And that's also a paradox because how can you stimulate or increase autonomy? Isn't that a paradox in itself?
>
> *(RMO representative, Netherlands, interview, 2014)*

A civil servant from the Ministry of Internal Affairs in the Netherlands similarly identified this contradiction as a point of contention within behavioural science,

> One of the principles of behavioural sciences is [that] the average citizen is not homo economicus. But then, I think the second is always but we would like to force them to be homo economicus. *And behavioural sciences can be an instrument to force them to be homo economicus.* And that is something I have … I'm not very comfortable with this because, well, rationally, I can condone that. [But] [c]an we use behavioural science to stimulate that? Because it's also against some principles of behavioural science because you have to be transparent, people can retract if they wouldn't like that. No, that's not possible if you put behavioural science as an instrument to stimulate people to act rationally.
>
> *(Ministry of Internal Affairs, Netherlands, interview, 2014, emphasis added)*

Some of our interviewees in the Netherlands adopted the language of liberal philosopher, Isaiah Berlin (1958) who made a clear distinction between negative forms of liberty denoting freedom from interference and constraint, and positive liberty, describing the extent to which some individuals may have the capacity or agency to take a particular course of action:

> And there is another dimension [of the political debate on behavioural governance] and that's more philosophical. I think our advice is more embedded in philosophical literature particularly that on positive versus negative freedom. A little bit of capability approach …
>
> *(RMO representative, Netherlands, interview, 2014)*

In so doing they argue that the principle of autonomy that behavioural governance promotes must be evaluated in substantive positive terms. Rather than focus on coercion and manipulation (threats to negative liberty), they argue for a capability approach, which refers to a person's 'actual ability to achieve various valuable functionings as a part of living' (Sen, 1993: 30). This approach favours forms of governance that will enhance those capabilities and empower citizens to achieve their own goals (see Chapter 4 in this volume). Again, this distinction highlights the persistence of left/right politics in debates concerning the political antecedents and grounded effects of neuroliberalism. It prompts us to ask to what degree states provide people and communities with the tools, opportunities and resources to exercise autonomy and the freedoms that they perceive to be of value?

While negative liberty often refers to supposed threats to individual sovereignty, positive liberty is used more in relation to collective political action, recognizing the social nature of agency and the government's legitimate role in balancing the often competing goals and preferences of individuals. By contrast, the behavioural insights associated with neuroliberalism are meant to address the conflicting preferences held *within* individuals, for instance the wish to live a healthy life alongside the immediate desire for a cigarette. But in so doing, it can be argued that the thinking behind behaviourally informed governance has downplayed the complex political work involved in deciding on public goods and assembling and resolving collective goals and capabilities. In the Netherlands, the notions of collective action and consensus are very prevalent. One policy advisor we spoke to raised the important question of why and when political consensus may be needed to support behavioural policy intervention in the Netherlands:

> [C]ould nudging or behavioural types of intervention [be applied to] goals that are, that everybody subscribes [to], or where there is a consensus about it … Or where consensus is lacking … So, what they say is if you use nudge instruments, you should first have a discussion about the paternalism behind the libertarian side, if you understand what I mean. So, there should be first a discussion about what are the motives, the intentions … Because if it's implicit, then you depoliticise something that is really political.
>
> *(Government policy advisor, Netherlands, interview, 2014)*

Consensus on these terms could of course apply both to the goal of policy (perhaps increasing organ donations/healthy eating) and the policy mechanism (resetting defaults/redesigning choice environments). It is therefore likely that if behavioural policies are to be framed by consensus in the Netherlands then policy initiatives may develop more slowly and focus on less politically divisive issues than has been evident in other states. This issue speaks directly to the question of different orders of freedom that we mentioned previously. Here we can see the potential of psychologically submerged neuroliberal techniques limiting the ability of individuals and social groups to debate and contest, or indeed consent to, the normative purpose of a policy – primarily because they may not even be able to see the policy. Perhaps one of the most significant critiques of neuroliberalism for questions of freedom is that it can remove the visible points of resistance around which conventional forms of democratic debate (consensus or otherwise) can emerge organically.

The political context of Singapore is something of a contrast, and this is reflected in both the speed of adoption of behavioural governance and the level of public debate. As one academic and former senior policy strategist within the Singapore Government explains:

> the Singapore government has ... we've only ever had one party in office and it's quite well known for being a paternalistic one. So the use of defaults, right? The use of defaults about ... where you're automatically enrolled is quite pervasive. So, I guess it's more or less second nature. And because of its long planning horizon, the fact that [the government] expects to be in office not just in the next term ... or you know it expects to be in office, that that should be given a certain flexibility room for manœuvre and you can try a number of these things without fear that you'll be accused of being manipulative or coercive. So you know, certainly, there are quite a few areas where defaults have been applied. So in health insurance and retirement savings and organ donation, these are all quite pervasive.
>
> *(Academic (public policy), and senior government policy strategist,*
> *Public Service Division, Singapore, interview, 2015)*

These observations highlight how default settings, or automaticity in government administration, have a long history in Singapore. They also suggest that these neuroliberal actions (which carry micro-political implications for the freedoms of individuals) have been facilitated because of the pervading political structures of freedom within Singaporean society (which in turn reveal different orders of freedom). Furthermore, debates around negative and positive freedom, or thin and thick autonomy, have not been prevalent in Singapore, and the government is not necessarily judged on the basis of manipulation or coercion. There are some signs that this may be changing. As one of our interviewees observed, Singaporeans have started to question the predominance of the ruling party, particularly since 2011–12, when opposition parties achieved a stronger voice, and when the government instigated nationwide public engagement on the future of policies in Singapore ('Our Singapore Conversation') (founder of not-for-profit social innovation lab, interview, 2015). Yet freedom itself is still not regarded as a traditional political goal in Singapore:

> the majority of the people do still accept that there is a social contract where you trade off certain freedoms and all of that ... for the Government doing a good job and a fine job at it and keeping things going.
>
> *(Co-founder and director of for-profit Social Enterprise,*
> *Singapore, interview, 2015)*

Rather the interviewee points out that social engineering – shaping the behaviour of citizens in accordance with a particular conception of the ideal society – has shaped social policy in Singapore strongly since the 1960s:

> in the early years of governance in Singapore, historically – in the 60s and 70s – they were doing many, many things … You know, it's actually trying to re-write and re-wire society. I mean, people can make their arguments about, you know, freedom and democracy and so on, but they definitely had a clear idea, at least in leadership, back then in Singapore, of what in their eyes would constitute an ideal society, and they did everything in their power, whether rightly or wrongly, to achieve that.
>
> *(Co-founder and director of for-profit social enterprise,*
> *Singapore, interview, 2015)*

Although perhaps a national stereotype, the apparently compliant nature of citizens in Singapore was seen as another significant factor in the popularity of behavioural governance:

> in America and Britain, the idea that citizens trust the state, trust the government is so, such an alien concept … But in Singapore for the last, I would say, until recent leaderships, there's high levels of trust in government. Not just because citizens are compliant, but genuinely because the government has been a very competent, effective one. It may not be very well-liked because it's paternalistic and it sometimes becomes authoritarian and harsh. But generally nobody doubts its ability to get things done. And because of this high level of trust and the fact that this government has got a high degree of what we call performance legitimacy, people have generally accepted the default that there isn't a great suspicion or distrust or cynicism of government using behavioural concepts to get things done and to get compliant. But of course all that is changing. Now the political landscape is more contested … So that liberal suspicion, scepticism of the state is coming to Singapore finally. I think from a very low base or rather from a very high base, we've put a great deal of trust in the state.
>
> *(Academic (public policy), and senior government policy strategist,*
> *Public Service Division, Singapore, interview, 2015)*

The reference here to the performance legitimacy of government raises an interesting question for how we might interpret the differential geographical application of neuroliberalism in Singapore compared to the Netherlands. It is clear that for various political and cultural reasons the Singaporean and Dutch states have different levels of performance legitimacy (which are not necessarily linked to their actual performance). The issue here is that relative states of trust in government can lead to very different social contracts emerging between states and citizens, which see different compromises reached between individual freedom and collective welfare. In the context of these varied social contracts we claim that neuroliberalism should be understood not only in relation to competing visions of the human psyche and behaviour, but also in the context of different notions of liberalism and citizenship. Discussion of neuroliberalism in general terms should thus give way to an account of particular fusions of neurological/behavioural insights with particular cultures and expectations of freedom.

An example of this can be seen where trust in the state, and the reputedly conformist nature of Singapore's citizenry, have been linked by many to a sense of collective idealism characterized by strong peer pressure and an avoidance of shame, or of losing face. These socio-political cultures have generated opportunity spaces within which neuroliberalism can develop. As one interviewee pointed out:

> using peer pressure … is a very important tool in the Singapore behavioural economics or behavioural sciences methods … Because the concept of 'face' is very important in Singapore … So people who have – who are deemed to be – you know, pursuing undesirable behaviour and so on, they are publicly embarrassed … for example, if they find people littering on a … you know, or basically not using a restroom properly or so on, they'll take a photograph of them and they'll just put it up … So all the neighbours can see.
>
> *(Co-founder and director of for-profit social enterprise,*
> *Singapore, interview, 2015)*

It is a moot point as to whether the behavioural exploitation of such conformism should be considered as a form of coercion. If we are to follow Quigley's interpretation of coercion then we might conclude that a behavioural approach to preventing littering would not involve coercion. There are clearly social pressures that shape people's behaviour in particular ways, arguably curtailing individual choice. Indeed even where there is a strong example of mandatory regulation, this may not by necessity be coercive. For example where the government requests your tax return, having designed the forms using behavioural insights (the work of the UK's BIT and the British tax authorities), this can be considered contractual and persuasive rather than coercive. As the partner at a strategic public policy design consultancy put it, the focus should be on ways to make even 'mandatory interaction as pleasant as possible'. While some may ask whether *pleasant mandatory interaction* is simply a covert attempt to make coercion more palatable, a more pertinent question might be to consider whether there are any significant asymmetries of power or inequalities in agency evident in behavioural governance.

For the Netherlands and Singapore alike, this kind of question has begun to surface among academics, social entrepreneurs, civil servants and leading commentators, encouraging them to argue for empowering forms of 'behavioural literacy' and 'collaborative nudging' (see Chapter 4 in this volume). A director at the Ministry of Trade and Industry, Singapore (interviewed 2015) regarded the rise of behavioural governance as just one among many useful new approaches to governance. He argued that the population must also be exposed to behavioural thinking, for instance in schools, so that they may understand their own behavioural tendencies better and become a more mature polity. In the Netherlands, the idea of collaborative nudging has been suggested whereby citizens and civic organizations are involved in the experimental design of nudges. Furthermore, it is suggested that the way forward for behavioural governance in this context is to understand better how behaviours are constituted at a social rather than an individual level:

> So, we say that if you have these controversial topics, you should involve citizens more and civic organizations more and collaborate with them and use little experiments before you roll out the whole programme for the whole country and because, first, you have to know what the effects are and if the effects are the effects you want … Experiments with people, not just about people or around them or for them but with them.
>
> *(RMO representative, Netherlands, interview, 2014)*

More of a convergence of political voices is evident here between Singapore and the Netherlands. In both cases a concern for the substantive and perceived freedom and autonomy of citizens has evolved, which is sensitive to both individual capability and collective decision-making processes; i.e. the means by which personal and public goals will be achieved.

Conclusion

In this chapter we have explored how neuroliberalism is manifest in different nation-state contexts and considered how different degrees of political freedom, autonomy and citizen identity can shape its various forms. Our focus has not only been the extent to which behavioural governance can *impact* autonomy (as in Chapter 4), but how predominant political cultures, understandings of autonomy and citizenship can themselves shape how neuroliberalism becomes manifest in certain states. The chapter has argued that the forms of paternalism promoted by neuroliberalism diverge substantially from the neoliberal economic ideals from which neuroliberalism has stemmed (see Chapters 1–3). It has been important to unpack definitions of coercion, freedom, choice, autonomy and paternalism in order to ascertain the political stakes of neuroliberalism. We have for instance been sceptical of the charges of coercive manipulation aimed at libertarian paternalism, since there is no clear force or curtailment of choice involved in most of the global policy initiatives that have been influenced by this broad political project. So too we have followed Sunstein (2015) and others in distinguishing between thin and thick forms of autonomy in order to understand better the potential role of government in shaping the welfare and capabilities of citizens. We have, however, questioned the ways in which thick and thin autonomy are defined, and suggested that in the absence of an understanding of potentially unequal distribution of capacities and capabilities, so-called 'thick autonomy' can actually look very thin.

In their detailed discussion of the politics of paternalism, Le Grand and New similarly differentiate clearly between means-and-ends paternalism, arguing that the latter can never be justified in liberal democracies. Rather, the basis for political discussion should focus on exactly how autonomy and wellbeing are balanced in each empirical example of government paternalism, '[t]he government's aim should be to develop paternalistic policies that maximize wellbeing while having a minimal impact on autonomy' (Le Grand and New, 2015: 177). As such they regard that both hard and soft forms of paternalism as indeed 'offend[ing]' autonomy (ibid.: 178) insofar as even nudges can threaten people's own perceptions and feelings of being interfered with. Their discussion highlights the need to examine the nature and consequences of government paternalism empirically *in situ* in order to ascertain where, when and why such paternalism can be justified (ibid.: 179). In exploring the adoption of neuroliberalism in the Singaporean and Dutch policy context, it is possible to identify some key principles by which neuroliberalism might be critically analysed and compared internationally.

First, it is necessary to examine the stated political rationale behind the introduction of behavioural forms of governance. Are the arguments made couched in the language of political scientism (as explored in Chapter 3), as a logical consequence of the apparent progress of human knowledge? If so, there should be a deep consideration of the history and dangers of such an approach. Or are the reasons more fiscal – to do with saving public funds or pursuing austere forms of government (and at what social and personal cost?). Have arguments been made for liberalizing government, improving the empathy of government with complex human needs (as in the case of Singapore), or is behavioural governance seen as a necessary correction to too many decades of rampant individualism and small government (as is argued in the USA). Second, attention should be paid to what has been described as the 'autonomy paradox' – i.e. each policy initiative should be judged on the degree to which autonomy and welfare have been traded off against each other, and *perceived* autonomy should be regarded as a consideration equally as important as substantive freedoms. Third, although not inherently coercive, even soft forms of paternalism can be shaped by asymmetries of power. Inequalities in their application and adoption are thus important factors in comparing their potential consequences. Relatedly, there should be some analysis of the prevailing forms of citizenship evident within polities pursuing neuroliberal policies – are citizens historically conformist or dissenting? Are they supported in developing behavioural literacy in order to increase their autonomy or effective capabilities to make decisions for their own welfare, as judged by themselves? What conditions are required to ensure that this literacy can be put into action? Finally we would argue that a critical analysis of neuroliberalism should consider to what extent governments can be held to account in their use of behavioural insights to change citizens' decisions and actions. How much are behaviourally informed policies discussed, debated and modified informally in the public sphere and media, and more formally through representative democratic fora? It is in this last respect that the Netherlands has demonstrated a more tentative engagement with neuroliberalism than Singapore.

These discussions on the role of the state are picked up in the next chapter, where we move from considering the relationships between neuroliberalism and questions of freedom, character and autonomy, to considering the *impacts* that neuroliberalism is having on the state apparatus, and the role and form of government.

Notes

1 An ongoing issue for the Dutch state is when citizens in receipt of state-subsidised social housing start to earn more money, they are disinclined to leave housing that is relatively cheap to rent. This of course has implications for the state's welfarist commitment to low-income groups in need of social housing.

2 A Tip for Policy-Making – Nudge, Not Shove" | Challenge Online. Available at www. challenge.gov.sg/print/cover-story/a-tip-for-policy-making-nudge-not-shove.

6

THE NEUROLIBERAL STATE

Introduction

The key argument underpinning this chapter is that neuroliberalism has led to a reconfiguration of the state as a political organization. We showed in the previous chapter how states are increasingly interacting with and intervening in their subjects' lives in different ways as a result of insights emanating from the behavioural and psychological sciences. New conceptions of human decision making have led to the refashioning of public policies in the hope that they can be made more efficient and cost effective. If this were the end of the story, then there would be little need to include a chapter on the 'neuroliberal state' in this book. And yet the evidence that we have amassed over recent years shows clearly that the shift towards neuroliberalism is leading to a situation in which: (1) states are being organized in different ways; (2) state employees are changing the ways in which they think and work; (3) the relationship between the state and that which lies outside or beyond it – civil society, the economy, or the family for instance – is being recast. These changes have come about because of a growing belief that the state has not been particularly effective in discharging its duties, particularly in terms of its lack of response to the various challenges associated with neoliberalism. Moreover, the selfsame psychological and behavioural insights that have been used to develop purportedly more accurate understandings of subjects, freedom and decision making (the topic of discussion in Chapters 4–5) have often been turned inwards in order to comprehend better the failings and frailties of state employees and organizations, while, at the same time, using these insights to develop improved kinds of state forms and practices. In short, our contention is that states have become increasingly neuroliberalized in recent years, albeit to different degrees in different countries.

Our aims in this chapter are threefold. Our first, and primary, aim is to demonstrate the significant changes taking place to states around the world as they become more neuroliberal in outlook and form. States are beginning to think, act and organize themselves in different ways as a result of engaging in more sustained ways with insights from the behavioural and psychological sciences. One of the best recent examples of this change has been the creation of the Social and Behavioural Sciences Team (SBST) within the US Federal Government (SBST, 2015; 2016) (see Chapter 3 in this volume). As part of the creation of the SBST, all federal Agencies in the US were instructed by President Obama on 15 September 2015 as part of Executive Order 13707 to apply insights from the behavioural sciences to their various programmes and spheres of activity. This shift in mindset was to be accompanied by a change in state practices, with the order specifying the different mechanisms by which behavioural insights might be better incorporated into federal policy in the US. Individuals would be tasked with identifying potential policy areas that might benefit from behavioural insights. These interventions would then be implemented and rigorously tested. Behavioural experts would be recruited to work in various government departments and agencies, including the SBST, and there would be an attempt to foster closer relationships between the SBST and the behavioural science research community (SBST, 2015: 2–3). And of course, the shift to a more neuroliberally informed state also possessed an organizational aspect in the form of the SBST itself. Although possessing a modest staff, the SBST has grown in stature since its creation in 2014, and by 2016 it impacted on the development of alternative approaches in a range of policy arenas. It has also, significantly, turned its attention towards using behavioural insights as a way of securing improvements in government effectiveness and efficiency (SBST, 2016: 31–2).

In all this, we witness how states are thinking, doing and organizing things differently. But this is not to say that the shift to neuroliberal state forms and functions has been wholly straightforward or as far-reaching as it could have been. The emergence of the neuroliberal state has been characterized by contradictions and tensions, given the fact that it represents a clear departure from conventional state forms. Precisely because it valorizes different kinds of knowledge and expertise, different processes for developing public policy, different organizational arrangements to those that have been conventionally lauded by the state, the emergence of the neurological state has raised a series of fundamental questions about how to 'mainstream' neuroliberalism within the state or, at the very least, about how to ensure that those individuals and organizations in the neuroliberal 'avant garde' interact productively with those who are not. To speak of a neuroliberal state is, therefore, misleading. It might be more correct, though less succinct perhaps, to refer to the emergence of a state that is informed, to varying degrees, by neuroliberal ideas, and is interacting in sometimes uncomfortable ways with more conventional state practices and forms.

Our third and final aim in this chapter is to discuss how the emergence of neuroliberalist ideas and ideals is forcing us to reconsider the ways in which we theorize the state. We cannot provide a systematic account of the implications of neuroliberalism on theorizations of the state in the space available to us in this chapter. Theories of the state are, simply, too numerous for us to consider how they could be informed, amended and/or contradicted by neuroliberalism. Nor do we believe that we should formulate what might be termed a comprehensive theory of a neuroliberal state. Even if it were possible to do so, we argue that this would be premature, largely for the reasons outlined in the preceding paragraph: the state has not been wholly transformed, yet, as a result of neuroliberal thinking. It has merely experimented with aspects of neuroliberalism to date. As such, what we do aim to provide in this chapter are some reflections on how neuroliberalism is encouraging us to ask new questions of conventional theories of the state, while also allowing us to point out some of the gaps or weaknesses associated with newer ones.

The fact that we discuss how neuroliberalism is forcing us to rethink state theories of different kinds means that we should give the reader some idea, at the very beginning of this chapter, of how we conceptualize the state. In broad terms, we adhere to an anthropological viewpoint, which conceives of the state as an assemblage of individuals, ideas and things (e.g. Bratsis, 2006; Corbridge et al., 2005; Hansen and Stepputat, 2001; Jones, 2008). While the state possesses some organizational coherence, territorial expression and physical form, we need to remember that these various aspects of statehood – ones that we tend to take for granted – are always tentative, contradictory and variegated in character. To talk of 'the state' in the singular or as something that exists in isolation from civil society (Mitchell, 2006 [1999]) is, therefore, misleading. It is even more misleading to speak of a state as something that possesses a form of singular agency or, in other words, to think of it as an organization that can make things happen in isolation. Taken together, an anthropological view of the state sees it as something that is brought into being in and through discourses, mundane and prosaic practices (Painter, 2006) and a mixture of affects and things (Barry, 2013). How is neuroliberalism, as a new philosophy of government, helped or hindered by a state conceived of in such ways? By the same token, to what extent is neuroliberalism changing states that exist in such varied ways?

The chapter is structured as follows. In the first section we discuss the significant impact that neuroliberalism is having on state structures, with innovative and imaginative governmental 'skunkworks' now beginning to emerge in various national and local states. We then proceed in the second section to elaborate on how neuroliberalism is leading to the valorization of new kinds of practice and expertise among state employees of different kinds. The final substantive section then examines how neuroliberalism is leading to a reconsideration of the relationship between the state and civil society and, in particular, causing the emergence of new forms of political subjectivity. We conclude the chapter by providing a brief discussion of the implications of neuroliberalism for a selection of theories of the state.

Neuroliberal state structures

As we noted above, we adhere to a theoretical vision of the state that is largely anthropological in outlook: the state, ultimately, does not exist outside of the discourses and practices of the individuals working within it, as well as those individuals affected by it in their everyday lives. A state, therefore, is little more than a 'symbolic presence' (Painter 2006: 758) or, as Taussig (1997: 3) has put it, an 'invented whole of materialized artifice into whose woeful insufficiency of being we have placed soulstuff'. And yet, part of the significance of the state lies in the way in which these discourses, practices, material objects and institutions coalesce to give the impression of coherence, stability and materiality. Government departments publish state documents – policies, strategies and press releases – often with little indication of their authorship; here, the organization takes precedence over the state employee. Individual state employees work within particular departments, branches or agencies of the state. Collaboration, secondment or transfers may take place but these interactions between or movements of people do not fundamentally question the existence of a state, which is structured ultimately as a series of organizations. The state is also predicated on the existence of organizational hierarchies. Although the exact location of decision making is often the subject of political and popular debate, the premise that the state is a hierarchical political organization is rarely called into question; again, despite our knowledge that the state – or its many departments and ministries – does not possess any agency as such, our eyes are unfailingly drawn to its organizational make-up. State organizations or structures matter. How, therefore, is neuroliberalism becoming entwined with the state as viewed in these organizational or structural terms?

At a very basic level, there is clear evidence of an attempt to institutionalize neuroliberalism within the state. As noted earlier, the SBST has been constituted as a federal unit in the US and has been responsible for running a series of trials to test the effectiveness of behavioural insights in policy areas including health coverage, farm subsidies and retirement saving (SBST, 2015). Another notable example has been the creation of the Behavioural Insights Team (BIT) in the UK, otherwise referred to as the 'nudge unit' (see Chapter 3 in this volume). The history of BIT has been well documented, both in academic and more popular contexts (e.g. Halpern, 2015; Jones et al., 2013). The BIT was formed in 2010 following the election of the coalition government in the UK, and was housed within the Cabinet Office of the UK Government (the administrative body supporting the work of the UK Prime Minister). It comprises a mixture of civil servants and academics, and its aim has been to use insights from the behavioural and psychological sciences as a way of reframing public policy. It has been in the vanguard of public policy innovation in the UK most famously by: encouraging the Driver Vehicle Licensing Authority to mandate individuals registering for a driving licence to decide whether they would like to donate their organs in the event of their death (thus overcoming individuals' tendency to not make decisions about such issues); rephrasing tax reminder letters to emphasize the fact that the majority of individuals pay their taxes on time (thereby making the prompt payment of taxes the social norm that individuals should aspire to); and developing more innovative forms of text messaging as a means of improving the rates of collection of court fines (see Haynes et al., 2012).

While the SBST and the BIT in the UK represent, perhaps, the most notable examples of neuroliberalism taking institutional form within states, other instances exist in a range of different countries. A Behavioural Insights Unit was established in Australia in 2012 (as an offshoot of the BIT) and it has advised the New South Wales Government on the use of behavioural insights in relation to, inter alia, the use of text messages to encourage individuals to keep hospital appointments, as well as helping government departments to word their correspondence with state citizens more effectively (BIU 2016). Beyond Australia, other local states have established new units or organizations tasked with trialling innovative and behaviourally informed solutions to various social-economic and environmental ills. Examples include: the Fond d'expérimentation pour la jeunesse (Experimental fund for youth), based in Paris; the Barcelona Urban Lab, the unit created by Barcelona's municipality with a view to turning the city into an 'urban laboratory'; and the Centre for Public Service Innovation in South Africa, whose aim is to 'create an innovation culture across the South African government' (Pittick et al., 2014: 22) (for more on developments in the Dutch and Singaporean states see Chapter 5 in this volume).

At face value, one could argue that there was no necessity to create these new state organizations as a way of promoting a neuroliberal agenda. Neuroliberal ideas, after all, could have been implemented by existing governmental structures. And yet we maintain that part of the significance of the neuroliberal turn is its predicatation on a belief that new state structures or organizations have been needed in order to allow novel, innovative and neuroliberal ways of thinking to flourish. In this respect, much work has been expended in organizational theory in order to understand how to create the conditions within which organizations can innovate and experiment (Nooteboom, 2000; Kelman, 2005). The subtext here, of course, is that organizations are generally prone to promoting inertia and to resisting innovation and positive change. A number of reasons for this resistance have been outlined, including 'the power of routines, psychological factors and standard operation procedures, which tend to benefit those in power' (John, 2013: 9; World Bank, 2015). A recent report on governmental innovators – the so-called 'i-teams' – published jointly by NESTA (National Endowment for Science Technology and the Arts) and Bloomberg Philanthropies – makes the same point. The report maintains that '[b]ureaucracies exist to bring predictability and order' and, more problematically, that the 'natural stance of bureaucracies is to stifle ideas' (Pittick et al., 2014: 3).

If this is the 'natural' condition of governmental organizations, then new structures and practices would appear to be required in order to allow neuroliberal innovation to take place. Some of the key factors that enable neuroliberal innovation include the existence of a flatter hierarchy, forms of performance evaluation that extend beyond the short term, senior managers who can provide innovators with more intellectual freedom, and the existence of separate funding streams and separate physical spaces. A low turnover of staff also helps to engender a sense of loyalty and trust among individuals working within such organizations (John, 2013: 11). In many respects, such a blueprint for governmental innovation draws inspiration from various private corporations, in which innovation and experimentation is highly valued. One of the most famous instances of such innovative organizations was the so-called 'skunkworks', the nickname used for Lockheed Martin's Advanced Development Projects Division, which designed Lockheed's P-80 Shooting Star during the Second World War. Similar developments have taken place in other corporations, with Apple's Texaco Towers team being another notable example. Creative solutions to familiar problems have also been sought in the context of biotechnological companies and research centres. Attempts have been made in these latter contexts to promote creativity and innovation by intermixing individuals and disciplines within the same buildings and, indeed, floors, as well as ensuring that there are sufficient informal spaces to allow creative interactions to take place (Thrift, 2004). In all of this, we see how skunkworks and other kinds of innovative organizations can be created through the valorization of particular kinds of organizational structures, relationships, practices and spaces.

Given these kinds of sentiment, it is no surprise that advocates of neuroliberalism – a new and often counter-intuitive way of framing public policy, it must be remembered – have deemed it necessary to create new state structures. These new organizations – what we may term governmental skunkworks – have provided the more favourable conditions necessary for neuroliberalism to be able to take root within the state. We have already discussed the significance of the BIT as an archetypal example of a neuroliberal innovator. John (2013) has traced how the BIT's role in promoting neuroliberal practices in the UK state derives from its peculiar organizational status. For instance, during its early years of operation, the BIT was characterized by a relatively 'flat' management structure, with steering being 'light touch' (ibid.: 13). Similarly, the BIT was allowed a certain latitude in relation to the goals that it set for itself and was allowed by politicians to 'fail'. It also received backing from powerful patrons, including David Cameron, the former UK Prime Minister and Sir Gus O'Donnell, the erstwhile Cabinet Secretary (chief civil servant) of the UK Government. The BIT was not housed in a separate building, as have been many other skunkworks, but in most other respects it follows the norms associated with those units responsible for promoting innovation within organizations (John, 2013: 14–15).

As noted in the introduction to this chapter, one of the key challenges associated with promoting neuroliberalism within states is to ensure that the insights emanating from various innovation units interact effectively with the more 'traditional' forms of government being practised elsewhere within the state. Christiansen and Bunt (2012: 3) maintain that the 'emerging paradigm in public governance is still interacting uncomfortably with existing administrative systems'. An uncomfortable organizational interaction can exist, therefore, between governmental skunkworks and more conventional governmental structures (John, 2013: 5). There are different ways of addressing this particular challenge. The first option is to house innovators in a central and cross-cutting governmental department, in the hope that innovative solutions to old problems can be mainstreamed across all government departments. The BIT's status as part of the UK's Cabinet Office fits into this model and more recent examples include the coordinating role played by the SBST in the US

Federal Government, and the Department of the Premier and Cabinet in mainstreaming behavioural insights in different government departments in the state of New South Wales in Australia. The problem with such a structure, of course, is that it still depends on an appetite for novel solutions in other government departments and, as some of our interviewees in different states suggested to us, such an appetite is not always present.

A second option is to embed behavioural innovation units in different departments, so that more experimental attitudes are distributed more evenly across government. The Netherlands have considered developing such a structure. As an individual familiar with the growth of the use of behavioural insights and experimentation in the Netherlands put it: 'you saw many ministries thinking about these ideas and thinking about using it and setting up experiments. Thinking about, should we have nudge units?' (Government representative, Netherlands, interview, 2014). In positive terms, such an approach has the potential to create a situation in which ownership over neuroliberalism is dispersed throughout the state. Of course, there is an associated danger that it may lead to a relative lack of coordination of neuroliberal approaches across government.

A final option is to house neuroliberal forms of governmental innovation in institutions that lie – at least in technical and legal senses – outside of the state, at the same time as ensuring that there are close enough links between these institutions and state organizations to ensure that new behavioural insights are fed effectively into the policy-making process. The more recent history of the BIT adheres to this organizational arrangement. Since 2014, it has been reconstituted as a 'social purpose company', which is owned jointly by the UK Government, NESTA and its employees. Other instances of this kind of approach exist. One of the most striking examples is the UK's What Works Network. This Network – and specifically its constituent What Works Centres – represents the fruit of collaboration between the UK Government, the Economic and Social Research Council and the Big Lottery Fund. The overall aim of the What Works Network and Centres is to help 'government to make policy in a fundamentally different way: deliberately testing variations in approach, vigorously evaluating, and stopping things that don't work'.[1] The centres themselves focus on a range of different policy ills, including those associated with health and social care, educational achievement, crime reduction, early inventions, local economic growth, improved quality of life in older people and wellbeing (What Works Network, 2014). As the names suggest, part of the reasoning behind the formation of the Network and the various Centres is the fact that many policy initiatives have failed to date and that there is a need to: (1) incorporate new insights into the ways in which individuals behave and act, including those associated with neuroliberalism, into public policy; (2) rigorously test and evaluate policy inteventions in order to ensure that they are as effective as they can possibly be. In the context of the present discussion, what is most significant is the fact that it has been deemed necessary to locate these organizational drivers of neuroliberal innovation at a fair distance from formal governmental structures.

A similar situation has emerged in the US. While the SBST acts as the main clearinghouse of neuroliberal innovation within federal state structures, considerable use is made of the expertise of individuals associated with the National Academy of Sciences, the independent and not-for-profit organization set up in 1863 to provide 'scientific advice to the nation'.[2] Some of the individuals who had been providing guidance and advice to federal and state governments in the US drew attention to the value of their independence from the state: 'we're not a government agency by any means … but the thing is when we do a study, we bring in these volunteers. And you know volunteer scientists have a mind of their own' (National Academy of Sciences representative, US, interview, 2014). The same individual praised the independence and robustness that this kind of arm's length relationship afforded, maintaining that volunteer scientists would not say 'what the government wants to hear or what the administration wants' (ibid.). While this respondent might be propounding an overly rosy account of the relationship between the National Academy of Sciences and different kinds of states in the US, they still highlight an important aspect of this type of approach to promoting state engagements with neuroliberalism; namely that positioning neuroliberal expertise outside the formal structures of the state has the potential to create more intellectual space for innovative and neuroliberally informed solutions to various 'wicked problems' to emerge. Such an approach, of course, adds further grist to the mill of anthropological accounts of the state, in which the boundary between the state and civil society is deemed to be something that is constructed through political discourse and practice (Mitchell 2006 [1999]). Neuroliberalism, when thought of as a political project, is closely aligned with the state, but it is something that emerges and is practised both within and beyond the formal boundaries of the state.

Neuroliberalism, the state and civil society

Previous sections have started to touch on an important aspect of the growth of neuroliberalism, namely how these new ways of thinking about and doing public policy are also leading to different conceptions of the relationship between the state and civil society, the location of the boundary (if one can possible demarcate it) between the state and civil society and the changing character of state-derived forms of citizenship. This section examines these themes in a more systematic manner than the rather piecemeal way in which we have engaged with them to date in this chapter.

Rethinking the boundary between the state and civil society

As we noted in the introduction to this chapter, we espouse a broadly anthropological approach to the state, which maintains that what we think of as the state actually comprises a dispersed and sometimes contradictory set of institutions, people and things. Conceiving of the state in such ways has obvious implications for how we think about the boundary between the state and civil society. If the state is actually dispersed in different ways, it becomes difficult to view it as something that can be defined in precise fashion and especially as something that exists in isolation from an equally well-defined and coherent civil society. Mitchell (2006 [1999]: 176), for instance, has maintained that the legal system comprises:

> a complex system of rights, statutes, penalties, enforcement agencies, litigants, legal personnel, prisons, rehabilitation systems, psychiatrists, legal scholars, libraries, and law schools, in which the exact dividing line between the legal structure and the 'society' it structures is … very difficult to locate.

For Mitchell, therefore, the legal system – something that is often conceived as representing the essence of the state – actually comprises a mixture of civil society actors (e.g. NGOs working with young offenders and with individuals on parole) and private sector individuals and organizations (e.g. self-employed barristers and private companies running prisons and detention centres). A similar, albeit more focused, argument has been made by Painter (2006) in his discussion of the growth of Anti-Social Behaviour Orders (ASBOs) in the UK. While ASBOs have assumed an important role within the UK's legal system and, as such, might well be regarded as an example of the legal structure of the state in action, they actually represent an uneasy amalgam of different institutions and agents – 'partnerships, community organizations, and voluntary bodies' (ibid.: 767) – which 'confirms that it is impossible to draw a line between "state" and "(civil) society"' (ibid.). Following this line of argument encourages us to think of the boundary between the state and civil society as something that is blurred, illusory and constructed in nature.

We claim, in this respect, that the emergence of neuroliberalism as a new approach to governance has only served further to blur our conception of the boundary between the state and civil society as the state has been 'stretched' in different directions. This process has taken place in a range of different contexts in somewhere like the UK. First, a decentring has taken place in organizational contexts; witness, for instance, the designation since 2014 of the BIT as something that exists at arm's length from the UK state. Such a redesignation, indeed, has been viewed as an almost necessary precursor of the development of more innovative forms of neuroliberal approach to government. Attempts to further reinforce a decentred approach in the UK state's engagement with neuroliberalism have been made in the context of the What Works Centres, where leading academics and policy-makers have been brought together to discover novel solutions to age-old governmental problems in organizational contexts that are distant from, yet ultimately connected to, the state.

A second context for this decentring of the UK state's approach to neuroliberalism has arisen in relation to the emphasis that has been placed on the philosophical and methodological contributions of key academics. Perhaps as a result of the sometimes counter-intuitive nature of certain neuroliberal insights, it is significant that critical proponents of neuroliberal approaches have been invited to speak to groups of policy-makers and civil servants. We listed earlier the academics who have been involved in the popularization of neuroliberalism in the UK state and it is clear that similar processes are taking place in different states across the world. Organizations such as iNudgeyou, based in Denmark, have also begun to market themselves as global purveyors of neuroliberal expertise, and it is clear that the BIT is seeking to develop a similar reputation, albeit through more devolved or 'franchised' ways of operating.

Third, we should appreciate the extent to which think tanks have contributed to the popularization of behavioural insights. A series of think tank publications have appeared and seminars have taken place in the UK since 2004, for instance, which have been dedicated to behavioural insights. These have, as one interviewee from the Policy Exchange think tank put it, helped to give form to an ongoing 'cycle of trends of thought' surrounding behavioural insights and neuroliberalism (see NEF, 2005; Futerra, 2007; IPPR, 2007; Demos, 2008; the Kings Fund, 2008; London Collaborative, 2009) (see also Chapter 5 in this volume for discussion of the actions of think tanks in Singapore). These think tanks have not simply acted as intermediaries between more abstract academic ideas floating around civil society, and the generation of useful policy recommendations for the state, as is sometimes thought to be the case. They are themselves engaged in political manœuvring and agenda setting (see Stone and Denham, 2004), with much cross-fertilization of ideas. To a certain extent, it is therefore possible to identify an 'opinion-forming' sub-culture or epistemic community, peopled by think tanks, senior civil servants, journalists and so on, whose dialogue serves to 'talk up' the significance of neuroliberalism as a novel policy agenda. In all this, we witness how the boundary between what we consider as the state and what we consider to be part of civil society is being blurred. Ideas emanate from multiples sources, located in different organizations and sectors. They then circulate in complex ways as a result of the direct communication of ideas in expert seminars and meetings and through particular things, such as key articles and books. The political infrastructures of neuroliberalism are, thus, plural and extensive in character.

Neuroliberalism, experimentation and the recasting of state-subject relations

If the neuroliberal state is characterized by an intensified set of ties to various parts of civil society, other aspects of neuroliberal statehood appear to be changing the nature of the relations between the state and citizens. One notable aspect of the development of neuroliberalism across the world has been the emphasis that has been placed on testing interventions rigorously in order to ensure their effectiveness. The need to ensure that behavioural insights are tested and regularly adapted, for instance, is an intrinsic element in the EAST framework promoted by the BIT (Service et al., 2014: 47–8; see also Haynes et al., 2012). The promotion of experimental methodologies within government – particularly Randomized Controlled Trials (RCTs) – has stemmed from the sometimes controversial and counter-intuitive nature of many neuroliberal policies. It has ultimately seen the transferal of a preferred methodology of the behavioural sciences into the practices of statehood. What is clear is that these experimental methodologies raise important questions about the changing relationship between the state and its subjects.

First, there has been some discussion concerning the unfairness of dividing society into groups that receive a new intervention and those that do not, leading to the creation of control or placebo citizens who do not receive the same access to more effective policy interventions than their counterparts. Indeed, in Finland it was suggested that the desire to utilize RCTs would require a change in the state constitution, so as to allow the government to treat 'treatment' and 'control' groups in the population in different ways (Breckton, 2015).

A second issue arises in the context of how individuals are recruited into trials. While in the social and behavioural sciences people are recruited into experimental trials on a voluntary basis, it is less clear that this will be the case within public policy initiatives. At one level, concern has been raised about the fact that, in some cases, individuals are unaware that they are taking part in a state-sanctioned trial. There are obvious issues relating to the lack of informed consent associated with such experiments. But the issue of consent is only heightened when it comes to the potential use of social media platforms to conduct large-scale RCTs on unwitting participants (see Chapter 1 of this volume for discussion of Facebook's Voter Megaphone initiative). The lack of openness represented here, of course, echoes the much larger concerns voiced by many critics of neuroliberalism, particularly the arguments made in relation to its manipulation of subjects (Mettler, 2011).

A third concern centres around the coercive aspects of RCTs. In a much-discussed trial delivered by the BIT in the UK, various behavioural insights were used to support job seekers finding new employment. The scheme was, however, criticized on the basis that the job seekers involved in the trial felt that non-participation would result in a threat to their unemployment benefits (Sanders, 2014). In addition to the association between trial participation and *coercion through implication*, there is a danger than RCTs can consistently target the most vulnerable in society, as those with the least capacity to resist enrolment with state experiments. This raises the possibility that vulnerable segments of the population could end up being governed by the ongoing threat of non-participation in trials (see Jones and Whitehead, 2017). The work of Sunder-Rajan is particularly salient in this context (2007: 85). In her analysis of clinical drug trials in less economically developed countries, Sunder-Rajan argues that the voluntary consent that may be the precursor to being involved in experimental trials needs to be positioned and understood in the context of the broader socio-economic circumstances of the volunteer. It is in this context that we feel that the uneven application of RCTs on communities who are dependent on the state programme should be recognized, and the conditions under which their consent is achieved should be assessed from a more diverse set of ethical perspectives.

Taken together, therefore, research on the experimental aspects of neuroliberalism shows that there are potentially significant challenges associated with this new form of governance. New, experimental forms of subjectivity and citizenship are said to be brought into being by such state-sanctioned practices, ones that are at odds with conventional understandings of citizenship. Dobson (2014: n.p.) aptly characterizes the ethical challenges associated with these new kinds of state–subject relationships when he argues that:

> for nudgers, people are not citizens involved in the co-creation of policy, but experimental subjects to be prodded and poked in the petri dish of the behavioural economist's imagination.

But the idea of experimental citizenship also opens up the possibility for thinking about more progressive and potentially empowering ways that subjects can become active participants in public policy experiments. There is an emerging body of work devoted to analyzing the relationship between citizenship and scientific experimentation (see Pallet, 2012; Irwin, 2006; Sunder-Rajan, 2007, 2010, 2011). This body of work takes the constitutional and ethical challenges associated with emerging forms of experimental citizenship, and argues that it may be possible to imagine alternative and more empowering ways in which subjects can be involved in state-orchestrated experimentation (Pallet, 2012). At the heart of this project is a desire to challenge the notion that trial participants can ever be 'innocent citizens' who engage in experiments as impartial participants (Irwin, 2006), and to explore more engaging forms of trial participation.

These alternative visions of experimental citizenship are captured effectively in the following reflection on the use of RCTs in the analysis of international development policy:

> In the absence of political debate, this approach [experimental trials] can exacerbate the tendency to see people as subjects requiring treatment, rather than as citizens with a political voice. Power silences any challenges to the technical framing of 'the problem', foreclosing discussion of the structural causes and consequences of inequality and how these should be tackled.
>
> *(Eyben and Roche, 2013)*

The relationship between the state and its citizens posited in this context is far more progressive and radical, with participants taking part in trials, but also being active participants in their construction and evaluation (Jones and Whitehead, 2017). This approach to policy experimentation has three key aspects. First, it not only seeks to protect the rights of citizens (to be involved or not involved in trials), but it also emphasizes the responsibility of citizens to contribute insights into the efficacy of policies and behavioural government. Second, it openly embraces the value of the subjective perspective, explicitly acknowledges that reality cannot be adequately controlled or randomized, and suggests that valuable insights into reality can be cultivated when you don't even try to subject the world to formal experimental conditions. Third, it is based upon a vision of state–citizen relationships that is far more equal in nature. This repositioning of state and citizen is redolent of the co-production of public policy inherent in certain interpretations of neuroliberalism discussed elsewhere in this volume. While the notion of collective experiments may appear to be optimistic, if not utopic, we maintain that developing experiments that engage people could help address key ethical and intellectual critiques of neuroliberalism. It also, moreover, has the potential to lead to more progressive kinds of relationships between the state and those citizens who are enrolled in its neuroliberal experiments.

Neuroliberalism and the changing nature of state expertise

While the state is conventionally thought of as a series of organizations that seek to influence different aspects of our lives, one of the key tenets of an anthropological approach is that the state, to a large extent, is a product of the often mundane practices of state personnel of different kinds. While these practices may take place within particular organizational settings, as well as physical spaces, the state is ultimately a 'peopled organisation' (Jones, 2008) and, as such, attention needs to be directed towards the 'everyday life' of government employees of different kinds (Rhodes, 2011).

Fortunately, there has been a long, if somewhat intermittent, tradition of academic study of state personnel. The key academic figure, in this respect, is the political and social philosopher Max Weber. First, Weber has much to say concerning the general qualities of state personnel. He emphasizes, for instance, that the character of the state as an organization depends on such factors as the mode of administration, the extent of its jurisdiction, the objects that it controls and the character of state personnel (1947: 153–4; see also Giddens, 1985: 8). The state as a rational bureaucracy is, therefore, said to be peopled by a certain type of functionary, referred to as an 'administrative' or 'genuine' official (Weber, 1991: 95). The counterpoint of the faceless and uniform character of the modern state bureaucrat lies in Weber's discussion of the notion of charisma. Charismatic leaders display extraordinary personal qualities and it is these that are used to generate enthusiasm for particular state projects and strategies. Charisma, therefore, concerns the personal qualities of select leaders. It is something that is more an attribute of a second type of state functionary, namely that of the 'political' official (Weber, 1991: 90–5). Charisma, moreover, is cast as a rare occurrence, highlighting the broader significance of the more common rational and bureaucratic state actor (Weber, 1991: 79).

A second, associated, theme running through this literature relates to the kinds of expertise that are valued among state personnel. State functionaries are educated and trained to a certain level in order to deal with the technical rules and norms that undergird the state bureaucracy (Weber 1947: 331). One crucial, if generic, hallmark of administrative bureaucrats, according to Weber, is their use of rational knowledge as a means of discharging their duties. While many state functionaries learn and develop their rationality 'on the job', in other cases, individuals receive training through their formal education. The most notable examples, here, are the elite schools that play a key role in shaping the character and identities of the leaders of the French state and its related industries (Bourdieu 1996). But it is also clear that state bureaucracies have also valued more specialist skills or forms of expertise. From the nineteenth century onwards, states have increasingly valued forms of expert knowledge and have sought to incorporate these kinds of expertise into their public policy development (MacLeod 1988).

How has the notion of neuroliberalism interacted with the state, therefore, when viewed in these highly peopled ways? At a very basic level, one certainly sees the valuing of different kinds of expertise emerging in many states in recent years. Whereas the state under advanced neoliberalism may have valorized economic expertise above all else (Davies, 2014; Peck, 2010), there is considerable evidence to show that states are increasingly valuing the skills of the behavioural scientist or psychologist. Some of our interviewees, for instance, maintained that the civil services were actively seeking individuals with expertise in the behavioural and psychological sciences and that this shift was being facilitated by the growth in interest in such sciences in academia more generally. It is significant that some of the more enthusiastic advocates of neuroliberalism within the state are experts in these subject areas. David Halpern, head of the BIT and of the What Works Network, for instance, specialized in experimental psychology as part of his undergraduate degree. Rory Gallagher, who now leads the Behavioural Insights Unit in the Department of the Premier and Cabinet in New South Wales, Australia, completed a doctorate on HIV/AIDS and behaviour change. And the head of the SBST in the US, Maya Shankar, has a background in cognitive neuroscience at both undergraduate and postgraduate levels. This shift in expertise has not taken place only at a managerial level. Our interviewees in a number of states maintained that graduate entrants were bringing new – and more neuroliberally informed – skills into the civil service. In all this, we witness a shift in emphasis in relation to the kind of technical expertise that is increasingly being valued within the deep state, with neuroliberal experts coming to the fore at all levels.

There are other, more indirect ways of promoting neuroliberal expertise within the state. The growth of neuroliberal approaches within the state has been characterized by a series of expert seminars and workshops that have been delivered by key academic experts on behavioural science and different aspects of psychology. One civil servant in the UK, for instance, explained the significance of such personal interactions for the formation and genesis of policy ideas:

> I asked Danny Kahneman if he would drop by … about 2001–2 … So Danny came in, and we'd invited some people, just for a chat around the table, to talk about these things, because you know I think we should be really interested in this sort of new literature, and he comes in and he says … I've just been sent a draft of this paper, called libertarian paternalism … and he says it's really interesting, I think it's going to be a very important paper, and so that was the first time I came across it.
>
> *(UK Government representative, interview, 2009)*

The presence of Nobel prize-winning behavioural economist Daniel Kahneman (Kahneman et al., 1982) at a seminar held within the Cabinet Office, according to this highly placed individual, was crucial to the popularization of neuroliberal ideas within the British state. This is not an isolated example. Another civil servant in the UK noted how Robert Cialdini (see Cialdini, 2007 [1984]), from the University of Arizona, was asked to present a seminar to government ministers in 2006. It has also been argued (e.g. *Independent*, 2010) that Richard Thaler's visit to Britain in 2008 and his meeting with David Cameron helped to communicate the value of neuroliberal approaches to highly placed members of the Conservative Party. Prominent behavioural economists and psychologists from the USA also gave talks in the UK's Department for Work and Pensions between 2000 and 2004, including David Laibson, Sheena Iyengar and Shlomo Benartzi. British-based academics have also played their part, most notably Paul Dolan from the London School of Economics, who co-authored *Mindspace* (Dolan et al., 2010).

The nature of the individuals associated with the What Works Network – the network charged with providing independent and expert advice to the UK state on experimental and neuroliberally informed public policy development – is also significant. The head of the Network – the What Works National Adviser – is David Halpern, who is also head of the BIT. As we have seen, he has a strong academic background in neuroliberal approaches. The Network is also supported by a Cross-Government Trial Advice Panel, whose aim is to 'make sure we are using public money to maximum effect' (Cabinet Office, 2015: 1). The membership of the Advice Panel is wide-ranging but, significantly, includes a large number of academics and other external experts who are well versed in behavioural interventions and experimental methods.

But, of course, the introduction of new forms of neuroliberal expertise into the workings of the state – whether in direct or more indirect ways – raises its own series of challenges. Echoing the statements made in the previous section, one needs to consider how these new forms of expertise interact with the other, perhaps more traditional, kinds of skillsets or mentalities that exist among state personnel. Many of our interviewees, for instance, maintained that civil servants, on the whole, were not attuned to the kinds of experimental attitude that should be part and parcel of a behaviourally informed approach to government. Interestingly, this was a problem that was seen to characterize civil servants in all states. One interviewee from Denmark, for instance, noted that:

> Stuff has to be tested and tried and we're not very experimental. And in a state, it's probably one of the things that's hardest to implement. It's this experimental view about doing public policy. It's like it's so alien for most public servants. So it takes a lot of time, kind of like making people kind of understand the reasons behind it and how we do it.
>
> *(iNudgeyou representative, interview, 2014)*

In Singapore, too, there is a real sense that civil servants, as one highly placed individual put it, are struggling to grasp the value of the 'iterative process' associated with testing, learning and adapting behaviourally informed interventions (see

Chapter 5 in this volume). The same individual went on to comment on the need for civil servants to embrace 'the meta principle in behavioural economics, which is experiment and evaluate, experiment and evaluate'. Unfortunately for this individual, there was little evidence that this had been 'truly internalized' yet in Singapore.

One of the most sustained and imaginative engagements with these challenges appears in a document that focuses on using behavioural insights as a means of transforming the public service in Canada (Galley et al., 2013). The most relevant section of the report for the current discussion is the one that examines ways of 'incentivizing innovation' in relation to what we would term neuroliberalism (ibid.: 20–2). The authors discuss some of the challenges to innovation – some of which we have discussed earlier – including rigid organizational hierarchies and a public service culture that tends to be risk averse. Some of the solutions to these challenges involve redesigning governmental structures, in a way that echoes some of the themes discussed in the previous section (ibid.: 3). But there is also an emphasis on the need to cultivate particular kinds of attitudes or cultures among state personnel, ones that are attuned to innovation and experimentation:

> Innovation is characterized by a style of thinking that is unorthodox, creative and not overly determined by short-term, well-defined outputs. Studies of human cognition have found that, while some individuals may be more inclined to innovative thinking than others, there is also a relationship between creativity, mood, and environment. Positive, low-stress environments are conducive to more creativity.
>
> *(ibid.: 20)*

Overall, the above quote highlights the need for a creative state employee to be able to develop neuroliberally informed solutions to old problems. At the same time, the quote also suggests that the environments within which people work have an impact on their creativity and their ability and willingness to innovate and experiment. There is a recognition, here, at least implicitly, that it is possible for choice architects to design working environments within governments that will encourage and enable state employees to be more imaginative in the ways that they work. It is only by doing this, it is argued, that states can create 'work cultures that are more open to experimentation and more tolerant of risk' (ibid.; Thrift, 2004). The emerging attempts to instil cultures of experimental neuroliberalism within public policy-making communities reflects the state reflexively incorporating the very same behavioural insights it is using in policy design within its own working practices. The construction of favourable choice architectures in government to support more innovative policy practices also reveals that civil servants are susceptible to the same psychological nudges and prompts that have been used to change behaviours in civil society.

In broader terms, of course, such ideas raise important questions about academic theorizations on the nature of state employees. Weber (1947, 1991) saw two different kinds of state employee peopling the modern state: the nameless or faceless bureaucrat and the charismatic politician. And yet, the emphasis being placed on neuroliberal and experimental approaches to the practice of statehood does not necessarily fit into either conception. The neuroliberal state employee is not a bureaucratic pen-pusher but rather someone who is charged with seeking creative solutions to various social ills. Neither do they fit into the mould of the charismatic politician. Even though they should possess a creative spark that allows them to think differently about policy challenges, the solutions that they identify do not derive from the force of their character or their personality. Rather, it is said to derive from their methodological acuity and perseverance. What, therefore, should we call this new state bureaucrat? The scientist is perhaps one option here, but there is something about this new kind of state functionary that is also similar to an inventor; an individual who identifies a particular social, governmental or policy failing and tirelessly tinkers with different policy approaches before identifying the one solution that works best. Moreover, this is an inventor who appears in multiple locations, working in some cases at the heart of deep state bureaucracies and, in others, at arm's length from the state 'proper'. It is these individuals working in concert who represent the whole embodiment of neuroliberalism within what we describe as the state.

Conclusions: neuoliberalism and state theory

Our aims in this chapter have been to show how neuroliberalism is leading to the emergence of new state organizations, new pratices and attitudes among state personnel and new kinds of relationships between the state and civil society. There does seem to be something novel happening as states experiment with new forms of knowing and governing. At the same time, there is also a real sense in which these neuroliberal experiments are posing new questions of some familiar state theories, as well as opening up further conceptual lines of enquiry.

We have deployed a broadly anthropological perspective on the state in this chapter and it is evident that the growing significance of neuroliberal approaches is adding further grist to this particular conceptual mill. Anthropological perspectives, first, draw attention to the fact that the state is a highly peopled, embodied and practised political form. Such an approach to understanding the state, we contend, has become all the more relevant in the context of neuroliberalism. Under neuroliberalism, the role of state actors of different kinds in constantly experimenting, innovating and adapting in the light of evidence is lauded as a valued mode of governance. In many respects, such a vision of the state echoes recent work in geography that has promoted a notion of statehood as being something that is rehearsed. Even though this work has focused on the kinds of statehood emerging in the context of a Tibetan government in exile (McConnell, 2016) – a state that has been, doomed, potentially, to a perpetual state of rehearsal – it seems to us that such work possesses many parallels with the kinds of statehood being practised under neuroliberalism. The notion of rehearsal seems highly apposite in an age of constant experimentation, as state policies are tinkered with day-in, day-out by a series of 'inventors' adhering to a mantra of 'test, learn, adapt' (Haynes et al., 2012). States in this context are in a constant state of becoming. The actual performance, in which a completed neuroliberal state is finally unveiled to the public, almost never arrives.

Second, anthropological perspectives also highlight how problematic it is to draw a firm line between the state and civil society. We construct a firm boundary between the state and that which it seeks to govern but, in many respects, the line is imagined and is in a constant state of flux. Neuroliberalism has only served to heighten this indeterminacy, as academics and the public are enrolled into state experiments and as policy innovation is devolved to semi-independent organizations such as the BIT and SBST. Where does neuroliberalism as a state project begin and end in the context of such complex policy assemblages? Even though this chapter focuses on the link between neuroliberalism and the state, it is impossible to reduce one to the other. Neuroliberalism draws in a series of actors that are, at once, close to and distanciated from the state per se, but all contribute in subtle ways to the philosophies and methodologies that are fundamental to the operation of this new mode of government. Focusing on a neuroliberal state may be a useful heuristic device in the context of this chapter, therefore, but it would be unwise to think of neuroliberalism as a political project that derives its theoretical and methodological sustenance solely from the state.

Beyond these anthropological concerns, it is evident that the shift towards neuroliberalism also raises a series of broader conceptual questions. First of all, the emergence of neuroliberal forms of statehood poses some interesting questions for those academics placing emphasis on the need to chart the state's many infrastructural characteristics. Government offices are often housed in impressive buildings, thus contributing to the awe and majesty of the state. National infrastructures of roads, railways, dams, sewerage, schools, hospitals, power lines and boundary fences all reinforce the material qualities of the state (along, of course, with a perception that the state exists, primarily, in a collective, organizational sense) (Barry, 2013; Mukerji, 2015). And yet, to what extent has the shift towards neuroliberalism changed the infrastructural or material qualities of the state? Do neuroliberal states, arguably, possess fewer material and infrastructural qualities than some of its predecessors? Beyond CAT scanners, which have been in the vanguard of the development of neurologically informed understandings of the workings of the human brain (Abi-Rached and Rose, 2010), what is there, materially speaking, to mark the shift to more neuroliberally informed state forms? It may be that a state form that concerns itself with the workings of the brain – focusing on its biases, emotions and (ir)rationality – has less need for overt, tangible and material things. One might even suggest, on the basis of the specific context of the neuroliberal turn, that the significance of material things for states may well be becoming overstated, given that the neuroliberal state is able to survive, and even thrive, in their relative absence (although see Chapter 8 in this volume).

Second, there is a need to consider how the recent focus on more neuroliberal forms of statehood is problematizing the role played by the state in shaping emotions and affects. State organizations and performances elicit emotions and affects, for the performers (state personnel) and the audience (subjects in civil society) alike (Closs Stephens, 2016). States, moreover, have long exercised an ability to manipulate the affective capacities of their subjects (Thrift, 2004) and, indeed, this has been a feature of the whole neuroliberal agenda. One of the key aspects of the *Mindspace* primer for policy-makers keen on using behavioural insights was the need to use emotions and affects as a way of encouraging particular behaviours (Dolan et al., 2010) (see Chapter 2 in this volume). The shift to more experimental forms of statehood – ones that are instrumental to the whole neuroliberal agenda – is, however, possibly taking the state's cultivation of affect in new directions. In relation to state employees, we are, arguably, witnessing an attempt by the state to exclude all forms of affect and emotion from state bureaucracies. The limited space that was once occupied by the charismatic state employee is gradually being replaced by a more scientific, rational and dispassionate outlook; one whose logic derives from the quantifiable results of RCTs. Little room is left for interpretation, intuition and gut instinct in this new mode of government. Those that are subject to neuroliberal forms of governmental intervention may also be experiencing different kinds of affective experience to the ones posited, say, as part of the *Mindspace* document. Instead of the state promoting positive affective connections with particular kinds of behaviour, we may be witnessing – in the case of the insidious experimentation associated with more RCT-informed kinds of public policy – the emergence of a more disturbing and persistent form of state oppression, especially for marginalized individuals and groups.

Third, we should also remain cognisant of the fact that states' engagement with neuroliberalism has not been uniform and consistent. The implementation of neuroliberalism in various states has relied upon social and spatial 'translations', with neuroliberalism evolving into different forms (Freeman, 2009; Jones et al., 2014) (see Chapter 5 in this volume). Some of the pertinent translations of neuroliberalism, in this respect, have occurred from theory to practice and back again. The development of neuroliberalism has, therefore, been characterized by a two-way flow of ideas between academia and public policy. Neuroliberal ideas have also mutated as they have been adopted by different parties. There is also potential for behavioural insights to be adapted and translated as they are applied in different policy sectors or, alternatively, as they are targeted at different kinds of problematic behaviour. And, of course, we should be aware that while neuroliberalism has been used to inform public policy in different states across the world, there is also potential for its application to vary from one state to another as ideas become meshed with the political cultures that exist in different countries (see Chapter 5 in this volume). As we argue consistently in this volume, there are clearly multiple versions of neuroliberalism in different states, in different policy sectors and at different times. To speak of a 'neuroliberal state', therefore, may well be misleading. It may be more appropriate to refer to the existence of many neuroliberal states, even multiple states of neuroliberalism. What is clear is that neuroliberal ideas are reshaping state systems at multiple levels, while state cultures and practices are in turn leading to mutations in neuroliberalism.

Notes

1 See www.gov.uk/guidance/what-works-network, accessed on 10 January 2017.
2 See www.nasonline.org, accessed on 11 January 2017.

7

THE NEUROLIBERAL CORPORATION

Introduction: economic governance and corporate power

I (Mark) was in London to carry out one of the approximately one hundred interviews that have either directly or indirectly informed this book. Having made my way up a narrow flight of stairs from the street I found myself in an airy converted loft space with high ceilings and an art studio feel. While I waited for my interviewees to arrive I was invited to take a seat on a small sofa, which was situated next to a table football pitch and a small spotlight – the kind you might expect to find in a Hollywood studio (see Figure 7.1). On the sofa were two cushions, one with the image of a hare on it, the other with a tortoise. When I mentioned these cushions to my interviewees I was informed that this was a 'thinking fast/thinking slow' sofa, which was meant to remind people of System 1 and System 2 forms of human decision making. The sofa was essentially a representation of neuroliberalism in home furnishing form.

The neuroliberal sofa was actually in the office of a company called the Behavioural Architects. With offices in Shanghai and Sydney (as well as London), the Behavioural Architects is one of a series of new companies that have been formed to exploit the commercial opportunities that the sciences associated with neuroliberalism have generated. Formed in 2011, the Behavioural Architects' website claims:

> [n]ew insights from the behavioural sciences and from behavioural economics, in particular, have inspired us to develop powerful frameworks that fuel deeper understanding of consumer behaviour and ways to influence it.
>
> *(Behavioural Architects, 2016)*

Working with major international companies such as Pepsico, Disney, Virgin, Google, Unilever and Kelloggs, the company provides bespoke applications of

FIGURE 7.1   Neuroliberal sofa: Behavioural Architects' Offices, London, April 2014
Source: Authors' collection.

new behavioural insights to reveal how consumers think and act, to support the more effective design of brands and to encourage the development of more salient communication strategies. The neuroliberal couch, I was informed, provides a space that employees can go to when they want to reconnect with the behavioural DNA upon which the company is founded.

The Behavioural Architects is concerned primarily with the commercial application of behavioural insights in the marketing sector. Other companies, both established and new, are exploring the commercial application of behavioural insights in the fields of design, management and training. Others still, such as Fuller and Thaler Asset Management (a company on whose Board of Directors and Management Team sits behavioural economist and co-author of the book *Nudge* Richard Thaler), are using the insights of behavioural economics to enable investors to profit from the irrationality of the financial markets and mispriced stocks.

This chapter is concerned with emerging relations between neuroliberalism and the corporate world. In exploring these connections, however, we are interested in more than just the commercialization of neuroliberal insights. We explore the ways in which the creative adaptation of neuroliberal insights in the commercial sphere is changing emerging behaviour change strategies. At the same time we consider how new behavioural insights are changing the ways in which companies relate to their clients and workforces. Most importantly, we are interested in the ways in which neuroliberalism is defining novel arenas within which corporations reimagine their corporate social responsibility agendas and take a more active role in the processes of government. This is evident not least in the related development of the social enterprises, social innovation labs and public service design consultancies delivering on government contracts that we encountered in Chapter 5. For the purposes of this chapter, however, we argue that neuroliberalism is witnessing novel forms of corporate involvement in spheres of government that have conventionally been the preserve of public sector institutions.

Unlike previous chapters, this chapter is framed not through an overt theoretical lens but through an empirical focus on neuroliberal commercial activities. This is in part because there remains important groundwork to be done in setting out the novel intersections between neuroliberalism and the corporate world, while drawing on the insights of practitioners operating at these interfaces. Notwithstanding this, it is important to consider the established role of the corporation within market economies as a benchmark against which to think about how this role may, or may not, be changing under neuroliberalism. A core assumption of neoliberal government is that corporations and companies operate according to the same principles of rational action as the figure of homo economicus we have discussed at different points in this volume. Corporations are thus expected to act as self-interested profit maximizers who operate in isolation from the needs and interest of others, towards the goals of the long-term wellbeing of the company. Within neoliberal thinking, however, these forms of corporate behaviour are not just about serving the needs of corporations. Under the stimulation of the profit motive, it is anticipated that corporations will produce more efficiently the goods and services desired by consumers at the lowest price. Furthermore, by acting in isolation, it is expected that companies will not become involved in forms of collusion and monopoly formation that would be counter to the broader interests of consumers (see Davies, 2014). In the neoliberal universe, the assumed rational action of corporations is not just in the corporation's interests, it is also a key requisite of broader forms of social order. This is, of course, why neoliberalists argue against state intervention in corporate activities: state intervention could be seen to undermine the broader social purpose and benefits that self-interested corporations bring.

In Chapter 1 we briefly discussed how the financial crisis of 2008 undermined many of the neoliberal assumptions about corporate behaviour (Akerlof and Schiller, 2010). The short-term thinking, socially deleterious actions, skewed assessments of risk and pernicious collusions associated with the credit crunch served to demonstrate that financial corporations were subject to the same human psychological traits that behavioural economists had been studying in individuals for several decades (Thaler, 2016). In response to the 2008 financial crisis, neuroliberal insights have been used to regulate the conduct of financial corporations in new ways. In the UK, for example, the Financial Conduct Authority used a series of measures (including mandated information disclosure, the reframing of risk strategies and the deployment of cooling-off periods) to ensure that corporations use behavioural insights to support effective consumer choice, rather than exploiting related insights for corporate gain (Erta et al., 2013). In this chapter we are not primarily interested in the neuroliberal government of corporate activity. Instead we are interested in the ways in which corporations are themselves creatively engaging with neuroliberal insights in order to forge novel governmental relations between themselves and their clients. While the idea of an expanded governmental role for companies is not new (Schrauwers, 2011), it is important to note that the idea of *corporate governmentality* must be very much set in opposition to the neoliberal view of the company.

If, after Foucault, we interpret government as a disposition of power that is focused upon the ordering of social-economic life through a broad ethic of pastoral care, then there is no necessary reason that corporations cannot contribute to the governmental project (or indeed that we should limit our search of governmental practices within the institutions of the state) (Foucault, 2007 [2004]). However, while it is possible to conceive of a role for the corporation within the broad acts of social care associated with government, there are very specific reasons why corporations should not be involved in neoliberal systems of government. In *Capitalism and Freedom*, Milton Friedman reflects on precisely why corporations must limit their sense of social responsibility (2002 [1982]). According to Friedman:

> The view has been gaining widespread acceptance that corporate officials and labor leaders have a 'social responsibility' that goes beyond serving the interest of their stockholders or their members. This view shows a fundamental misconception of the character and nature of the free economy. In such an economy, there is one and only one social responsibility of business – to use its resources and engage in activities designed to increase its profits so long as it stays within the rules of the game.
>
> *(Friedman, 2002[2982]: 133)*

Friedman focuses his critique of social responsibility in the corporate sphere primarily on the potential role of business in maintaining low prices and supporting charitable giving (ibid.: 134–5). In this chapter we will be focusing on the social responsibility of corporations in supporting welfare-enhancing changes in the behaviours of consumers. But regardless of the nature of the social responsibilities of the corporation, there can be little doubt as to Friedman's position:

> Few trends could so thoroughly undermine the very foundations of our free society as the acceptance by corporate officials of a social responsibility other than to make as much money for their stockholders as possible. This is a fundamentally subversive doctrine. If businessmen [sic] do have a social responsibility other than making profits for stockholders, how are they to know what it is? Can self-elected private individuals decide what the social interest is?
>
> *(ibid.: 133)*

In the context of the neoliberal orthodoxies expressed by Friedman, this chapter considers the new governmental opportunities that neuroliberalism presents to corporations. Particular attention will be given to the new forms of social responsibility that emerge for corporations once it is acknowledged that their consumers do not interact with their products and services in rational and self-interested ways. Further consideration is given to the ways in which neuroliberal techniques of government enable corporations to circumvent the ethical and constitutional limits that have historically been placed on corporate involvement in government.

Commercializing neuroliberalism: 'behavioural impresarios' and creative start-ups

Before considering the purported emergence of systems of corporate governmentality associated with neuroliberalism, this section reflects upon the ways in which the corporate world has contributed to the evolution of neuroliberal practices. It is important to be clear about the precise nature of these relations. It is evident, for example, that the scientific insights associated with neuroliberalism have informed a range of developments in the activities of the corporate world. To speak of corporate neuroliberalism, however, is not to refer to the use of behavioural insights to enable corporations to exploit cognitive biases to sell products, or generate certain 'feelings' around brands in order to enhance consumption. Much has been written about neuromarketing and the search for the psychological and neurological basis of the so-called 'buy-button' (Lindstrom, 2008; du Plessis, 2011). While these developments are important and raise significant ethical issues, they are not the primary focus of discussion in this chapter. In this chapter we are interested primarily in the ways in which corporations are being drawn into acts of neuroliberal government that are based upon the use of behavioural insights, a commitment to liberal freedom and a broader project of social care. As we will see, separating out the use of new behavioural insights to support the goals of expanded consumption and neuroliberal government is not always easy or indeed possible. The motives of profit and government are deeply intertwined within varied practices of corporate neuroliberalism. In this section, however, we are more interested in the commercialization of the ideas associated with neuroliberalism, as opposed to the direct exploitation of these ideas within the selling of products.

In Chapter 2, we outlined the ways in which the corporate sector had contributed to the practical history of neuroliberalism (for example, the marketing industry and the Depth Boys). In addition to the historical relationship between corporate activity and neuroliberalism, the last five years have seen the rapid adaptation and commercialization of the behavioural insights associated with neuroliberalism within various corporate spheres. The commercialization of neuroliberalism has taken two main forms: (1) the emergence of consultancies that specialize in new behavioural insights and offer advice to corporations and public agencies on the new ways in which they can reach and relate to their clients; and (2) the rise of consultancies that utilize neuroliberal insights as a basis for reshaping the working practices and norms of corporations. These different modes of neuroliberal commercialization are not exclusive and many consultancies operate in both of them. What we do claim, however, is that relatively small, but numerous, consultancies (some of which are novel start-ups, others that are neuroliberal iterations of older enterprises) have played an important role in enabling the spread and adaptation of neuroliberalism within the corporate and wider world. There is significant diversity in the way in which these start-ups have developed neuroliberalism. We claim that this diversity challenges the notion that the commercialization of neuroliberalism has involved a rather narrow exploitation of new behavioural insights for commercial gain. Rather, it is a commercialization process that has involved the regular transfer of ideas, practices and values between the public and private sectors. It is also a commercialization process that has been based upon very different understandings of the nature of the human condition and how behaviours can most effectively be changed.

The remainder of this section explores the two forms of commercialization outlined above through the examples of two behavioural consultancies: Ogilvy Change and Corporate Culture. This section utilizes these agencies as exemplars for exploring some of the implications of corporately based neuroliberalism.

Entering the System 1 Software Studio: the case of Ogilvy Change

Ogilvy Change (or #ogilvychange, as it is also known) is a 'behavioural economics practice' that has emerged out of the Ogilvy & Mather Group.[1] Ogilvy Change was established in London in 2012 in order to develop an *expert centre* that was able to bring the insights of behavioural economics (and psychology) into the world of marketing and public relations. Since its inception it has expanded rapidly and now has offices in London, Paris, Madrid, Stockholm, Milan, Toronto, Cape Town, Johannesburg, Sydney, Singapore and Wellington. Their clients include British Airways, Coca Cola and American Express. One of the key features of Ogilvy Change is the way in which it seeks to bring academics working in the behavioural sciences, cognitive psychology and social psychology together with so-called 'creatives' from the marketing and advertising industry. As an organization, Ogilvy Change is predicated on a belief 'that combining a scientific understanding of behaviour with the power of creativity is the best way to solve real world problems' (2016). In the case of Ogilvy Change this statement would appear more than a platitude. Not only does the organization actively work with leading academics, it has also developed and promoted innovative, and often challenging, thinking on behavioural insights themselves. For example, at a workshop we organized,[2] one of the founders of Ogilvy Change spoke at length about the pejorative misuse of the terms rational and irrational, and argued the need to think about 'irrationality' as a form of rational response when understood from the long-term perspective of human evolution. Ultimately, Ogilvy Change sees itself as an organization of 'behavioural impresarios', that is blending and orchestrating behavioural science with marketing insight. Employees, who are generally psychology, behavioural science or sociology graduates, are referred to as *choice architects*, while the company directors are *chief architects*.[3]

In attempting to open up a more effective dialogue between the behavioural sciences and the creative industries, Ogilvy Change has devoted much of its time to thinking about the most effective ways in which emerging insights into human behaviour can be applied to real world situations. This is, of course, an agenda that scientists, and even policy-makers, are not always particularly skilled in pursuing. As one representative of Ogilvy Change observed:

> I'm bored of reading about studies in Princeton with 20 students. I'm really quite bored. I am bored about social marketing programmes in India to get people to wash their hands. What I am more interested in is seeing how communities and organizations are tackling problems utilizing this combination of psychological principles and applying [them] creatively … if you were to draw a parallel with Silicon Valley, it feels like we're beginning to understand what the code is. We now need to let people loose with the code.
>
> *(Ogilvy Change representative, interview, 2014)*

What animates much of the work of Ogilvy Change is a desire to share and adapt this behavioural code – to release it from its staid academic roots.

The ethos of the company appears to be about recognizing the scientific hardware with which the behavioural sciences have provided us (specifically in terms of understanding what humans are actually like), and then developing software for these insights, which means that they can more effectively interface with real world needs and problems. The idea of behavioural software appears to be the subject of everyday discourse in the Ogilvy Change's office:

> [w]e need to write more software for System One [thinking]. So whenever we're designing work … we talk about going to the System One Software Studio. That's where we deign our concepts.
>
> *(Ogilvy Change representative, interview, 2014)*

The notion of the *System 1 Software Studio* is emblematic of the work of Ogilvy Change to the extent that it suggests the development of a more creative (and perhaps less scientific) engagement with neuroliberal ideas. The conversations we have had with Ogilvy Change indicate their desire to shift behavioural economics and psychology from the rational spheres of science to more user-friendly and intuitive environments: to apply behavioural insights to neuroliberalism itself perhaps. At the centre of the project is a recognition that many of the scientists and public policy-makers who have been at the vanguard of neuroliberal innovation are not necessarily skilled in the creative adaptation of the ideas that they have developed and advocated. As a member of Ogilvy Change observed:

> When you take creative minds … more intuitive thinkers, people that create beautiful things – and this might be in language or sounds, or feelings or smell – when those two things come together, you do get magic. You really

get magic. And so what we are finding is that sometimes we might take some psychological principle and talk to more creatively minded people. Then they take that quite abstract concept and make it so simple and intuitive. And if we can get those ladies and those guys on board and get them thinking this way, which they do already, but you [get them] to think about it more predictably and systematically then that's where we start to apply creative and intellectual brands to solve some of the world's biggest problems.

(Ogilvy Change representative, interview, 2014)

The reference here to 'solving the world's biggest problems' begins to outline the governmental ambitions of these commercial enterprises.

To continue the software metaphor, it appears that Ogilvy Change embodies an attempt to develop a form of neuroliberalism 3.0. If neuroliberalism 1.0 is associated with the initial scientific breakthroughs that were forged in the behavioural and psychological sciences, and neuroliberalism 2.0 involved the application of those ideas within various public policy programmes, then neuroliberalism 3.0 reflects a more creative adaptation of these ideas commercially. Ogilvy Change argues that its existence as a relatively small, commercial start-up gives it advantages over both big science and governments, which have been associated most closely with neuroliberal practices. As the representative of Ogilvy Change we interviewed noted:

[There is] something very powerful about science and academia [but] there's also something fundamentally intellectual, based on sectoral snobbery … [there are also issues] around accessibility, around usability and around actionability.

(Ogilvy Change representative, interview, 2014)

In addition to being more action-oriented than academic, Ogilvy Change also claims that it is able to move much more quickly and engage more freely within the ideas of the behavioural sciences than those bound by the bureaucracies and oversights of the public sector.

However, there appear to be two main downsides to corporately based forms of neuroliberalism that are openly acknowledged by Ogilvy Change. At one level are questions of scientific rigour. Taken out of the conventions of scientific testing and peer review, it is acknowledged that adaptations of behavioural government in certain commercial contexts are not always subject to the same systems of evaluation and scrutiny:

[o]ne of the strengths that we [have] got is we can move quicker. But one of the weaknesses is that we could become not so robust in our methodology and our practice. So what we are trying to do is to ensure that we're maintaining the energy, momentum, and agility of a private sector organization, but we have public sector principles of robustness, without the bureaucracy.

(Ogilvy Change representative, interview, 2014)

In the case of Ogilvy Change and many of the other behaviour change consultancies we spoke to, *robustness without bureaucracy* is pursued by working closely with academic partners and advisors. Even with these safeguards in place, however, questions remain about the impacts of broader corporate cultures of profit making on the behavioural knowledge that is produced within neuroliberal interventions. From a neoliberal perspective, the assumption would be that the market would naturally weed out bad behavioural research and change strategies, but in the context of unreliable assessment it remains unclear how this purging process would operate.

The second set of issues relating to corporately based forms of neuroliberalism are those concerning ethics. The ethical challenges of corporate neuroliberalism can be discerned in two main ways. The first relates to the use of behavioural insights to assist the sale of products. Ogilvy Change argues that while their work does support sales growth for their clients, they are also attempting to make the consumption process less cognitively effortful and challenging for consumers (ultimately making things easier for consumers to get to the products they want within a complex marketplace). Ogilvy Change describes the ethical challenges associated with this area of their work on the following terms:

> you need to make it cognitively [easier], at least it shouldn't take people four weeks of their lives to work out what type of phone is right for them. And if you can use a heuristic to guide them – that most people go for this one – then that would help sell our products and services more easily than maybe a competitor ... So you give that treatment and we're happy to do that so long as we have the code, which is the brand, product, or service that normally doesn't harm. Then we're happy with that. And also [we need to] be transparent in the heuristics we're using. So you know I have no doubt that there is going to be some relevant uses in communications of [social] norms. [The danger is] misinformation you know, of specific information where the norm is bent or biased to try and change people's behaviour and actually that norm isn't prevalent there anyway.
>
> *(Ogilvy Change representative, interview, 2014)*

There are two interesting themes that emerge out of this statement. First is the notion of a revised 'harm to others principle', which suggests that the psychological facilitation of consumption is ethically acceptable so long as that product is not harmful to the consumers (as in the case of tobacco or alcohol, for example). This 'harm to consumers principle' could provide a useful ethical heuristic for corporate systems of neuroliberalism, although it does rely on a fairly narrowly defined notion of harm (what, for example, of the financial harm caused by general patterns of overconsumption?) Second is the notion of lying with heuristics! It appears that while it is one thing to exploit a cognitive bias to achieve a certain behavioural end, it is quite another to target a behavioural heuristic with misinformation.

The unethical exploitation of cognitive biases has recently been exposed by the action brought against the hotel booking company Booking.com by the Dutch

Advertising Standards Authority (Dutch News, 2014). The booking company, which originated in the Netherlands, now operates in fifty countries and books in excess of 625,000 hotel rooms a day (ibid.). The Booking.com site routinely exploits the so-called scarcity heuristic, a bias that leads us to value a good or service on the basis of how available it is. The bias works on the assumption that the scarcer a resource is the more valuable it is likely to be. Booking.com used to state things such as 'we only have one room left' in a given hotel, with an indication of how many other people were currently looking at the room you were viewing (ibid.). The assumption was that in the rush and confusion of booking a room, a quicker decision is likely to be made to purchase a particular product if that product is seen to be in short supply, and soon to be lost to another a competitor consumer. The Dutch Advertising Standards Authority claimed that such statements were misleading because they only related to the rooms that Booking.com were able to book, with other rooms in a given hotel potentially still being available in the hotel via other booking systems (ibid.). In response to the action of the Dutch Advertising Standards Authority the heuristic loophole exploited by Booking.com has now been closed: their website now makes statements such as 'Only two rooms left *on our site*'.

Ogilvy Change also acknowledged a second set of ethical challenges associated with their work. These ethical challenges relate to the evolving scope of the forms of behaviour change that their work is beginning to support. We will speak more about this governmentally oriented behaviour change mission, and what is contributing towards its emergence, later in this chapter. At this point, however, it is important to note that this work focuses less on the short-term behaviours associated with the sale of goods and services, and more on long-term shifts in habits and lifestyles. According to Ogilvy Change, this changing commercial focus from sales to lifestyles demands new levels of ethical scrutiny that are not yet a common part of commercial culture and practice:

> I said to some of the creative teams and people in agencies, 'I'm not going to do this work unless it goes through an ethics committee'. Because this isn't about selling a product or service, this is about changing the behaviour and perception of someone in terms of how it is going to impact upon their [the consumer's] life.
>
> *(Ogilvy Change representative, interview, 2014)*

Changing corporate cultures and the human operating system

The work of Corporate Culture provides a different set of insights into the corporate appropriation of neuroliberal practices. Corporate Culture is a communications consultancy that helps with strategic branding processes, but also offers support for corporations attempting to instigate transformational change in their operations. In this section we are going to focus primarily on the work that Corporate Culture is undertaking as they apply neuroliberal insights to the internal operations of corporations themselves.

Over recent years Corporate Culture has been involved in developing some innovative approaches to thinking about how organizations work and can be changed. The context for these innovations is described by Corporate Culture in the following terms:

> Success in business and government depends on an understanding of people. But what if our thinking is based on an incomplete understanding of people – of employees, customers, citizens? What if business leaders and political leaders are seeking results based on an outdated model of human nature? Now based on the most recent insight from neuroscience, psychology, and behaviour change, a new human operating system is beginning to emerge. It's not complete. But it's a step on from the beliefs that currently guide our actions to achieve social, business or political change.
>
> *(Corporate Culture 2015)*

The idea of a revised human operating system, which is being uncovered by the behavioural sciences, is now key to the emerging work of Corporate Culture. At the centre of Corporate Culture's vision of the human operating system are the key tenets of neuroliberalism: namely, recognition that humans make the vast majority of their decisions unconsciously; and that within this unconscious decision-making context our actions are shaped by unconscious biases. There are, however, two innovative aspects of Corporate Culture's vision that take it beyond many mainstream approaches to neuroliberalism (see Corporate Culture, 2015).

The first innovative aspect of Corporate Culture's vision of the human is the emphasis that it places on the necessary integration of conscious and unconscious drivers of actions. Thus in keeping with those who argue for a continued appreciation of the power of intent and neurological reflexivity (see Chapter 4), Corporate Culture emphasizes the complex interplay between the *conscious me* and *unconscious me* within human behaviour (ibid.). A representative of Corporate Culture we interviewed described this perspective in the following terms:

> The reality is that if you are looking at change in any area, the odds are it includes conscious and unconscious … [Antonio] Damasio, another influencer, is absolutely clear about this and it is pretty bloody obvious whether you're an academic or just a human. You can't divorce the head from the heart. You can't divorce the brain from the body. We learn lessons of principled thinking based upon our experience and our senses. And we experience things with our senses based on our thinking. So it's a single organism.
>
> *(Corporate Culture representative, interview, 2014)*

This call for a *single organism* vision of humanity, which recognizes conscious and unconscious actions, and rational and irrational motivations, as always already emerging conditions of each other, stands in partial contrast to certain interpretations of dual-system thinking, which understand behaviour through two integrated but ultimately separate systems of thought and action (see Chapters 3 and 4). The second innovative aspect of Corporate Culture's Human Operating System model is the emphasis that it places on the social dimensions of behaviour. We spoke in Chapter 4 about the role of social context in shaping unconscious aspects of our physical lives, but Corporate Culture's paradigm emphasizes the importance of considering both the *unconscious us* and the *conscious us* (ibid.). In behavioural terms the *unconscious us* reflects a view of humanity that is acknowledged within socially oriented nudges (particularly relating to herd instincts and social proofing) that are now being widely used in the public and private sectors. Acknowledging the notion of the *conscious us* though is more novel within the contemporary sphere of behavioural government. The notion of a conscious collective recognizes that our behaviours are not just individually reflexive, but are also based upon socially conditioned forms of behavioural awareness. In this way Corporate Culture's Human Operating System is based in part upon a realization that human behaviours are predicated upon forms of deliberation that recognize and reward the importance of collective action (ibid.). While these forms of collective intentionality may be a feature of evolutionary biology, in organizational terms they are now an established part of the discourses of management science (expressed in the mantras of teamwork, collaborative leadership and co-production).

Together the ideas of the *conscious* and *unconscious us* have led Corporate Culture to explore new ways in which behaviour change and government can be approached through social vectors. Corporate Culture has become particularly interested in the nature and scale of social networks and how they can be used to affect behaviour change. They recognize for example that most meaningful social networks have tended traditionally to be of around 150 people (this is the average size of many English villages; and the designed size of military units) (Corporate Culture, 2015: 19). While social networks can include over 150 people, 150 appears to be the anthropological limit to the amount of people we can have meaningful relations with (ibid.).[4] Recognizing that behavioural learning and change are connected directly to the quantity of contacts we have with a desired behaviour, Corporate Culture has sought to utilize meaningful social networks as key vectors for behavioural change. It has thus sought to mobilize established social networks for bringing people into contact with role models, and to generate tipping points in and through which *behavioural tribes* can co-generate social and organizational transformation. Corporate Cultures' sophisticated use of social networks could be interpreted as a form of exploitation of the unconscious influence of social forces. However, the emphasis that Corporate Culture places on the value of exposing employees and members of the public to a diverse range of ideas and influences suggests a commitment to behavioural reflexivity and empowerment that is reminiscent of the work of the Social Brain Centre (see Chapter 4).[5] It is here that we begin to see that Corporate Culture's approach to the *unconscious us* and the *conscious us* could have different forms of corporate value. While the notion of the *unconscious us* suggests ways of manipulating organizational behaviour change in subtle ways, the idea of a *conscious us* reflects a commitment to forms of behavioural learning that could result in less predictable, but potentially lucrative, forms of innovation.

The main insight associated with Corporate Culture's Human Operating System model is that successful behaviour change strategies must recognize that human decisions are influenced by the conscious and unconscious aspects of personal and social life. It is ultimately a holistic approach to behavioural government that stands in marked contrast to nudges. A representive of Corporate Culture we spoke with outlined this distinction with nudges in the following way:

> For me Nudge and Nudge Theory, and the work of the Behavioural Insights Team, are tactical rather than strategic. For me it is one of the tactics that can be used. It is very far from being the only way of achieving behaviour change at scale.
>
> *(Corporate Culture representative, interview, 2014)*

The distinction made here between a behavioural tactic and strategy is an important one, suggesting as it does a difference between a tool that can be used to address specific behavioural problems and a broader framework for thinking about the nature of human life and action.

An example of Corporate Cultures' application of their human operating system model is provided in their work with Unilever. As part of Unilever's attempts to free their employees from the constraints of complexity and bureaucracy, they have partnered with Corporate Culture to develop the 'Winning Together Initiative'.[6] At the heart of the Winning Together Initiative is an attempt to change the way in which people understand and relate to time in order to generate more effective forms of corporate action and decision making. At the heart of this scheme is the key behavioural insight that a shortage of time in the modern workplace tends to result in the use of unhelpful decision-making shortcuts (particularly in relation to the prevalence of status quo and sunk costs biases), and risk-averse behaviours. Rather than focusing on changing the behaviours that result from a lack of time, Corporate Culture decided to focus on the problems of constrained time itself. The scheme also involves a more subtle behavioural insight: that time as well as money can be thought of as a form of currency that can be used to motivate behavioural shifts and incentives.

The Winning Together Initiative was based upon a global engagement campaign, which involved thousands of Unilever's employees. The principle behind the campaign was to generate and share simple practical techniques that could be used in individual and collective contexts to save (and reallocate) time during the working day. The scheme involved the promotion of a series of simple timesaving habits (such as writing simple emails, declining to attend meetings that you do not need to attend, establishing new norms around the length of meetings). It also sought to generate timesaving techniques from employees themselves. The Winning Together Initiative embodies the principles of Corporate Culture's Human Operating System model in a series of ways. First of all, and in keeping with the broad principles of neuroliberalism, it is based upon the realization that financial incentives are not the only, or even the most important, way in which behaviour change can be pursued. The Winning Together Initiative thus recognizes the utilitarian and emotional value that is placed on time at different points in people's lives. It also draws particular attention to the fact that for busy professionals, time reflects a vital commodity, which is important not only for effective working, but also for personal wellbeing. The Winning Together Initiative emphasizes the unconscious relation between the individual employee and time (the *unconscious me*), as many people remain unaware of the impacts that time mismanagement has on their decision making and wellbeing. Perhaps the most radical aspects of this scheme, however, relate to how it addresses the conscious and unconscious relations people collectively have with time. The Initiative ultimately rests upon the realization that time-use behaviours cannot be determined and controlled by individual actors alone (as they would be in classic personal time management models, where time is seen as an economic utility that can be effectively traded and regulated by the rational actor), as they are also products of the social fields in which we live (the *conscious and unconscious us*). We thus have collective and unconscious relationships with time to the extent that we hold in common what we unthinkingly assume are good time-use behaviours (perhaps attending all meetings, working long hours, making snap decisions). Furthermore, it is to be expected that only through conscious collective action can we hope to change the ways in which organizations use and abuse time. Only by collectively acting on time use, and the associated establishment of new organizational norms concerning what reflects effective forms of time management can transformations in individual temporal behaviours be achieved. These insights have informed Corporate Culture's work with Unilever to generate collective action on the conscious and unconscious aspects of time management in the organization.

If the case of Ogilvy Change highlighted the creative ways in which corporations can adapt neuroliberalism into more user-friendly forms, the case of Corporate Culture highlights something else. In developing its human operating system model, Corporate Culture demonstrates that the commercialization of neuroliberalism need not involve either the mobilization of exploitative behavioural tactics, or a highly simplified vision of the human condition. The recent work of Corporate Culture reminds us that in the pursuit of profit from the behavioural sciences, the more holistic and complete the model of the human that is deployed the more commercially successful it is likely to be. Furthermore, the socially oriented model of behaviour change developed by Corporate Culture is an interesting antidote to some of the individualizing tendencies associated with neuroliberalism. Corporate Culture's emphasis on collective behavioural action also has the potential to be more empowering than many of the approaches to behavioural government that are emerging in the public sector (although we acknowledge that the initiative does not bring into question the rates of pay that people receive for their time at work, or the overall number of hours they are expected to work).

Behavioural government and the corporation

The previous section demonstrated some of the diverse ways in which neuroliberal ideas are being commercialized. Our discussion so far has focused on behaviour change in fairly narrowly constrained commercial contexts (the purchasing practices of consumers and the working practices of employees). In this section we extend our discussion of corporate neuroliberalism to consider the broader role of corporations in shaping public behaviours and the actions of private lives. Understanding government broadly as the ordering of social-economic life through a general ethic of care, this section argues that the combined development of the corporate social responsibility agenda and neuroliberal insights has paved the way for new forms of *corporately orchestrated neuroliberal governmentalities*. These forms of corporate neuroliberalism are associated with companies becoming increasingly engaged with public behaviours beyond acts of consumption. Related forms of behavioural government see energy companies promoting low-carbon household practices; car manufacturers supporting more energy-efficient driving habits; fast food retailers promoting the practices of healthy living; drinks manufacturers facilitating responsible alcohol consumption; and gaming outlets fostering more responsible financial behaviours. Although these emerging forms of behavioural government are often removed from purchasing practices, they are still strongly influenced by the profit motivations of corporations. Notwithstanding this, we claim that these behavioural initiatives reflect a subtle, but not insignificant shift in the behavioural thinking of corporations. As we will see, corporate strands of neuroliberalism appear to reflect a corporate pre-emption of the socio-economic and environmental externalities (including obesity, debt, climate change) that their activities have historically generated, and an extension of their zone of behavioural responsibility. Related initiatives seek both to regulate the forms of excessive consumption that have generated many existing socio-economic problems, and to instil forms of behaviour that can militate against ongoing excesses in consumption practices.

Corporate neuroliberalism in action: Unilever and sustainable living

Before reflecting critically upon corporate neuroliberal government, it is helpful to outline an example of related activities. In order to do this we return to the case of Unilever. In the previous section we considered how Unilever (with the support of Corporate Culture) uses neuroliberal insights to shape employee behaviour. In this section we focus on Unilever's Project Sunlight initiative. Initiated in 2013, Project Sunlight is a behaviour change campaign developed by Unilever in order to promote more sustainable patterns of development throughout the world. The project is governmental to the extent that in many of its modes of operation it is not directly about profit making (although see the next section for a critical discussion of profit making and corporate neuroliberalism). Project Sunlight is neuroliberal to the extent that it recognizes and exploits cognitive biases and the emotional aspects of human behaviour, and emphasizes the importance of unconscious habits in sustaining pro-environmental and pro-social behaviours (Unilever, n.d.: 3–4). Indeed, the project draws directly upon the insights of the behavioural sciences and behavioural consultancies such as Corporate Culture. Project Sunlight is also based upon Unilever's ongoing research and work promoting hygiene habits in less economically developed countries through brands such as Lifebuoy and Signal Toothpaste (ibid.: 1).

In its account of Project Sunlight, Unilever reveals the significant governmental potential of large multinational corporations. Unilever brands, which include Dove, Magnum, Persil, Surf, Lifebuoy, Ben & Jerry's, Signal and Omo, are used over two billion times every day by over half of the households on the planet (ibid.: 3). This level of brand penetration means that the potential governmental reach of Unilever's activities is far greater than that of many large nation states. Unilever describes its emerging governmental agenda as follows:

> The need for action has never been greater. Governments alone cannot provide solutions, so business and the public also have to rise to the challenge. We have a responsibility to take a leadership role in co-creating a world where everyone can live well and within the natural limits of our planet – what we call sustainable living.
>
> *(Unilever, n.d.: 4)*

A significant amount of Unilever's sustainable behaviour change work is channelled through its products. Through its advancements in washing powders, for example, Unilever claims that it is supporting the emergence of more *conscious consumers*, who can more easily reduce their household energy use by washing at lower temperatures (ibid.: 5). But Project Sunlight is broader than this, and partially divorces commercial sales from behavioural government.

Drawing on its 'Five Levers of Change' model, Unilever approaches sustainable behaviour change by considering key *barriers*, *motivators* and *triggers*. In relation to barriers, Unilever has grounded its work in the behavioural insight that inaction on major environmental issues is based on cognitive dissonance, which tends to emerge when issues appear to be both geographically distant to the subject, but are still a significant threat to the subject's long-term wellbeing. The motivational focus of Project Sunlight is more original. Drawing on its work on hygiene habits with young children, it recognizes that children can play a significant role in promoting sustainable behaviours among their parents. Project Sunlight is based upon the realization that simply having children tends to make parents more sensitive to questions of sustainability and more likely to reassess their values (ibid.: 6). Unilever suggests that children can transmit sustainable behaviours to their parents, and instil more optimistic attitudes concerning what sustainable behaviours can achieve (ibid.). Within Project Sunlight children are thus seen as important agents in the promotion of long-term shifts in household behaviours. In relation to behavioural triggers, Project Sunlight attempts to promote sustainable behaviours by focusing on important life stages (including having a child, starting a career, seeing your child go to school, buying your first home, and leaving school and university) (ibid.: 7). These so-called 'transition zones' are seen to be critical moments when sustainable lifestyles can become a conscious part of a person's life choices, and subsequently become embedded within a person's habitual behaviours (ibid.).

Drawing on these behavioural insights, the Project Sunlight initiative was initially introduced in five countries (Brazil, UK, USA, India and Indonesia) with the aim of generating a social movement for significant forms of sustainable lifestyle changes. While the notion of a social movement seems grandiose, for us Project Sunlight, and Unilever's subsequent sustainable lifestyle initiatives, are emblematic of corporate neuroliberal government. Fusing as they do behavioural insights with a renewed governmental zeal within the corporate world, they appear to reflect more than just the use of psychology to sell more products or services. To draw on the language of Michel Foucault, these initiatives reflect corporations becoming more involved in the administration of life understood both as a set of behaviours and a condition of wellbeing. As corporations become more involved in the ordering of present and future life it is necessary to think critically about what may be driving this process and what its likely consequences may be.

'Corporate social responsibility on steroids': neuroliberalism in the shadow of regulation

In this section we consider the different explanations that can be used to interpret the emerging practices of corporate neuroliberalism. In order to excavate these different modes of explanation we reflect upon the interviews we conducted with representatives of Ogilvy Change and Corporate Culture.

One explanation of the emergence of corporate neuroliberalism relates to a reorientation of the relations between companies and the socio-economic environments in which they operate. Following what has happened to companies like Enron and Lehman Brothers, and the broader impacts of the 2008 credit crunch, companies appear to have been forced into a partial rethinking of their operating principles. We interviewed a representative of Corporate Culture, who explained these changes in the following terms:

> existing business models have been challenged. They've been challenged by an assumption that the recognition that the whole economic system is just wrong. It doesn't work. Practice has been challenged by the idea that businesses that focus purely on the short-term financial gain actually risk their survival and go out of business. And so there is something wrong with their business models, that they're short-termist. And their risk thinking is primarily around financial risk. And as soon as you start thinking about new business models to achieve long-term success, you're forced to start looking outside of the organization. And that leads you into an understanding of context: what is it that I need to be in place in order to be financially successful in the long term? And the issues are the same whatever organizations

you are talking to: I need a sustainable supply of energy; I need a sustainable supply of water. I need sustainable resources; I need it all!

(Corporate Culture representative, interview, 2014)

This purported shift in corporate worldviews is significant because it reflects the kinds of psychological insights – particularly the challenges of acknowledging and confronting long-term risk – upon which neuroliberalism is based. It is also significant to the extent that it embodies an active attempt by corporations to manage the broader socio-economic environments in which they work. This desire to control the broader conditions of life is a hallmark of a governmental project (Foucault, 2007 [2004]). The corporate concern for longer-term forms of risk does not necessarily denote a shift from an underlying profit motivation, but it does suggest a recognition that corporate interests may be well served by understanding and anticipating where long-term risks may lie.

Some industry insiders suggest that there is something more transformative going on in the shift towards corporate neuroliberalism. They claim that the corporate adoption of neuroliberal techniques reflects a shift in the underlying rationality of companies. Reflecting on emerging forms of corporate-instigated behaviour change initiatives, the representative of Ogilvy Change we spoke to suggested that:

> [it] doesn't mean offsetting. That doesn't mean doing bad things on one side and offsetting it with good. And so you know I think as we're finding that a lot of businesses and organizations are trying to find this higher role or purpose that their contribution to society has got to transcend making a profit.
>
> *(Ogilvy Change representative, interview, 2014)*

The suggestion here is that corporate neuroliberalism may reflect more than a profit-oriented corporate social responsibility exercise. CSR initiatives often involve companies offsetting the harm they cause in the pursuit of profits through acts of social beneficence, while enhancing profits and still causing harm. The argument here claims that corporate neuroliberalism reflects the emergence of a new form of business logic. While we are more suspicious of this form of explanation, it is supported by the not unreasonable assertion that those working in the corporate world often share the same social goals that we might expect of the public sector. Our interviewee went on to reflect:

> I don't have a problem with a gaming company creating an app that has got some psychological principles baked in that makes it particularly attractive to play and have fun. And if it's such that what they are trying to do is get people to play 24 hours a week then there's something wrong. And I think [there is] something fundamentally wrong if an organization like that doesn't contribute to how they might use their skills to [think about] how you can get children or adults to go out and get some fresh air and do some exercise

> ... because you know the guys in the gaming industry don't want our children to be fat and unhealthy. They really don't. They want our children to be happy.
>
> *(Ogilvy Change representative, interview, 2014)*

The most compelling argument we found for the emergence of corporate neuroliberalism came in the context of the work of energy companies and their promotion of energy-saving behaviours in the home. It was observed:

> Well, you see, what's interesting is there's a difference between ... what people say is the reason why they are doing it, and why they are actually doing it. And the leaders would say the reason they are doing it is ... so it's primarily you know building strong relations is the lead thing. And then, there's all these other things about competitive advantage. And they say, but that's not a real driver. To save money is a real driver. The motive, often, is ... at the moment in practical terms for the private sector, is circumstance. In other words, in energy the regulator is seen to [be challenging] your ability to create sustainable energy supply. In order to do that, there's a need for an investment according to OFGEM of £200 billion by 2020. In order to do that you've got to raise your bills. And the politicians are saying this is a big issue. And it's about affordability. And they start finger pointing at the energy companies. Then in order to help [customers] manage bills, they're looking at helping people save energy, then its pragmatism.
>
> *(Corporate Culture representative, interview, 2014)*

The argument being suggested here is that in the context of the regulatory need to produce sustainable energy (while remaining competitive) it is necessary for energy companies to find ways to enable people to reduce energy costs effectively. Here it is clear that the profit motivation (to supply competitively priced domestic energy, while making significant investments in sustainable energy futures) is aligned with behavioural government (reducing household energy use and thus maintaining the overall cost of bills). What is most intriguing in relation to this rationalization is to think about neuroliberalism emerging out of broader regulatory pressures. Throughout this book we have depicted neuroliberalism as a form of non-regulatory response to some of the challenges of twenty-first-century government. It may, however, be more helpful to think of corporate forms of neuroliberalism as acting in the *shadow of regulatory hierarchy* (see Whitehead, 2003). To these ends, many forms of corporate behavioural government, within and beyond the energy sector, can be understood as a response to regulatory pressures. Similar regulatory pressures to reduce personal debt and irresponsible lending can be seen in the financial sector. So too, regulatory pressures are informing healthy lifestyles initiatives in the food and drinks industry. In the awarding of commercial licences and the enforcement of government codes of conduct, the state can still generate regulatory regimes that can drive corporate neuroliberal initiatives.

The implications and consequences of corporate governmentalities

Whatever may be driving corporate neuroliberalism it is important to reflect critically upon what the implications of related processes are. We recognize that beneath the discussion of corporate social responsibility and the higher calling for corporations, the profit motivation may still be the driving force for the forms of corporate governmentality we have described in this chapter. If this is the case it is important to recognize the dangers that are associated with profit-oriented systems of government. Such systems of government are able to reach into the spheres of everyday life and practices that are far beyond the points of consumption that have marked the traditional limits of corporate activity. Under the legitimizing guise of governmental care, corporations could be able to establish (often unconscious) habits that may support their own profits more than social wellbeing. Furthermore, as a form of government that operates largely outside the democratic checks and balances of the public sector, corporate governmentality raises questions of precisely how companies' actions can be scrutinized and held to account.

Another, perhaps less troubling, aspect of corporate neuroliberalism concerns behavioural knowledge sharing. Within the conventional governmental practices associated with neuroliberalism there is a strong emphasis on sharing practical knowledge that can contribute towards behaviour change. Within the corporate sphere, however, the profit motivation can drive the commercial protection of behavioural insights. Small behavioural consultancies and large firms alike may want to protect their 'psychological assets' and the details of their behaviour change programmes. We found direct evidence of the 'pay-walling' of behavioural insights in the example of one small behavioural consultancy that we spoke and worked with. In some of its work with larger companies this consultancy had been required to sign a non-disclosure clause within its contract, which stated that it would not share the behavioural insights that had been developed out of the projects on which it had worked. While protecting behavioural insights in this way may be an important factor in driving creative innovation, it does run counter to the more openly sourced origins of neuroliberalism within science and government. In extreme cases, this commercial partitioning of behavioural insights could result in certain portions of the population being subject to more or less effective forms of behaviour change, depending on what particular company is being used to promote its behavioural insights. Neoliberalists would, we suspect, claim that this situation is unproblematic to the extent that the most effective companies in the field of corporate neuroliberalism will succeed while others fail, thus meaning that all will have the opportunity to benefit from the most effective behaviour change regimes. But what this hypothetical situation does highlight is the fact that whatever its underlying motivations, corporate neuroliberalism is likely to have a much more uneven impact upon the public than state policies, and is thus likely to result in the emergence of inequalities in behavioural capacities (even if only over a relatively short term).

Of course, these concerns over corporate neuroliberalism are partly allayed if neuroliberalism is interpreted as a response to state regulations. In this situation, concerns over both the accountability and unevenness of corporate neuroliberalism are mitigated by the fact that related initiatives are framed ultimately within the broader mandates of the state. As a form of displaced governmentality, however, it is clear that corporate neuroliberalism will continue to raise practical and ethical questions as it develops and evolves.

Conclusion

In this chapter we have considered the emerging relations that are being forged between neuroliberalism and the corporate world. In many ways, of course, it is erroneous to speak of neuroliberalism and corporate activity as separate fields. Since the very inception of neuroliberal ideas, corporate activity has been a central part of the project (see Chapter 2). In this chapter, however, we have seen the particular ways in which neuroliberal insights are shaping corporate activity – from the formation/reformation of behavioural start-ups to the impacts that the commercialization of these insights is having on the neuroliberal project more broadly. Ultimately we have claimed that the commercialization of neuroliberalism has run parallel to the emergence of new forms of corporate neuroliberal government. These novel forms of corporate governmentality are being driven by a diverse set of forces (including profit making, regulatory necessity and rethinking of corporate purpose). Ultimately, these developments raise interesting ethical questions for neuroliberalism, as well as presenting novel governmental pratices that appear to span the profit motive and the securing of social stability. In the chapter that follows, we will continue to explore the relations between neuroliberalism and corporate activity in the context of the world of product design.

Notes

1 The Ogilvy & Mather Group is an international advertising, marketing and public relations organization.
2 This workshop explored ethical dilemmas to applying behavioural insights, and was held on 11 May 2015 at the RSA in London.
3 These titles were revealed to us in a conversation we held with one of the directors of Ogilvy Change in May 2014.
4 While social media have clearly extended the scales of our social networks (up to around 500 people on average), they have not changed the number of meaningful relations we can sustain (Corporate Culture, 2015: 19).
5 It is important to note, however, that Corporate Culture proposes a narrower conception of 'social' than the Social Brain Centre, focusing on social networks rather than the social forces that shape inequality and difference.
6 This section draws on material concerning the Winning Together Initiative that is publicly available here: www.corporateculture.co.uk/case-studies/unilever (accessed 7 April 2017).

8

NEUROLIBERAL ENVIRONMENTS

Design, context and materiality

Introduction: neuroliberal's environmental assumptions

Neuroliberalism is nothing if it is not an environmental project. From its deployment of the popular concept of *choice architecture*, to the insistent focus on reshaping contexts as opposed to changing people, neuroliberalism is, at its core, a project of environmental government. While the idea of the choice architect was, perhaps, initially only a playful allusion to neuroliberalism's broader environmental potential (with early iterations of such architects limiting their ambitions to rearranging fruit in school canteens and implementing alcohol-only check-outs in supermarkets), the full environmental implications of neuroliberal government are now starting to hove into view. Neuroliberalism is now shaping the everyday environments of the home (particularly in the form of smart devices); buildings (expressed in the emergence of neuro-architecture); and broader geographical features (such as the street, neighbourhood and even cities). The environmental ambitions of the neuroliberal project can perhaps be seen most directly in the work of the UK's BIT, which has partnered with Bloomberg Philanthropies to support the delivery of a new (US)$42 million project entitled What Works Cities, which seeks to apply neuroliberal insights on pan-urban scales.

This chapter considers the relationship between neuroliberalism and the everyday environments in which we live. In exploring this relationship this chapter is in part interested in how neuroliberalism seeks to govern through the production and redesigning of environments. In addition to considering the practices of governing through environments, this chapter also problematizes the neuroliberal appropriation of the environment itself. We claim that neuroliberal understandings of the environment are marked by two limitations. First, they tend to overestimate the extent that environments, on a range of scales, can be adapted to serve the needs of behavioural government (or to put things another way, they fail to account for the obstinate nature of environmental legacies and the agency of the material world). Second, they misconceive the ways in which material environments shape and are enrolled within human behaviour and habits. In this context, we are particularly interested in exploring the extent to which the constraints that environments place on human behaviour can be overcome creatively as part of more empowering forms of neuroliberal environmental strategies – and how these strategies require us to think beyond narrowly defined material definitions of environments. In exploring these issues we also consider the more or less empowering ways in which environments can be transformed in the pursuit of behavioural government. Throughout the different sections of this chapter we return to consider the themes of subjectivity, autonomy and freedom that have run through various chapters in this volume. In this chapter, however, we consider how these issues – which have continually haunted neuroliberalism – are expressed, made problematic and resolved within the realms of design and the material environment.

Neuroliberal designs and redesigning neuroliberalism

The material environment (including everyday objects, buildings and spaces) is an important target of neuroliberalism (see Chapters 2 and 3 in this volume). The material environment is central to the neuroliberal project because it is connected to both the behavioural and liberal goals of this system of government. Behaviourally, the environment is recognized within neuroliberalism as a key source of the more-than-rational factors that shape our decisions and behaviours. The material environment is a key part of the 'push of the world' from which emotions are generated, optimal decision-making options are hidden and bad habits inevitably evolve (Anderson, 2014). This is not to say that our rationality is not cognitively bounded, but that the environments in which we live often provide a kid of double-bounding for our behavioural capacities (see Chapter 3). But neuroliberal interventions in the material environment are also what enable the project to preserve its liberal pretensions: personal character is not changed, just the choice architectures within which we live. On these terms then the material environment is both the stimulus of, and vector for, neuroliberalism.

It is in the context of the crucial connections that bind neuroliberalism and the material environment that design professionals have played an important role in the emergence of neuroliberal styles of government. The relationship between design professionals and neuroliberalism is, however, complex. As we discussed in Chapter 3 of this volume, prominent cognitive designers such as Donald Norman have clearly played a role in shaping the ideas and practices that are associated with neuroliberalism. Norman was a leading figure in the emergence of user-centred design, and was concerned with ensuring that the 20,000 objects on average that we surround ourselves with on a daily basis were constructed in ways that made life easier to live. Despite the popular assumption that design thinking has had a significant role in shaping neuroliberalism, psychological insights (particularly those associated with behavioural economics) have also clearly had an impact on the design sector (see Wendel, 2013). As one cognitive designer we interviewed reflected:

> I think probably, design really isn't actually much of a subject. I mean it's very much, you know, there isn't actually that much theory in design that isn't related to something else. It's always drawing on sort of practical applications. So I feel this … I mean … I think there's a bit of both, both ways with that. I think it is much more design drawing on other disciplines than other disciplines being informed by design, you know. I mean it would be nice to say that, of course, design is having a big influence on economics or sort of behavioural economics, but I don't think it is really.
>
> *(Cognitive designer Dan Lockton, interview, 2014)*

Regardless of the dominant direction in which the arrow of influence is pointing in relation to design and neuroliberalism, it appears clear that over the last thirty years the design sector and neuroliberal government have been through an intensive co-evolutionary phase.

The nature of the relationship between neuroliberalism and the design sector has taken two forms. The first relates to the physical design of objects and environments. In this instance the design sector has played an important role in materializing the neuroliberal project. At the centre of this materialization project has been the design communities' ongoing attempts to relocate emerging understanding of human irrationality and automaticity partially, from the cognitive sphere of the laboratory and into the messiness of everyday life. Materializing neuroliberalism has, in large part, been about recognizing that bounded rationality is not simply a function of our human internal psychology, but is also a product of the irrational push of the world around us. A cognitive designer we spoke to summarized the situation as follows:

> But people looking at things like heuristics and how people actually make situating decisions in real life, you know. But then trying to look at that even more broadly about the social context or the actual physical environment. So it's not just about presenting people options in a list and, you know, which one is, which one is most salient, but actually how does the environment around, how do the people who are with them how do they, how does everything affect those.
>
> *(Cognitive designer Dan Lockton, interview, 2014)*

The broader significance of the design communities' materialization of neuroliberalism is, perhaps, captured most effectively in the pioneering work of Donald Norman. In his now classic 1988 book *The Psychology of Everyday Things* (now available under the title *The Design of Everyday Things*) Norman (2002) explores how human error is often the simultaneous outcome of cognitive bias and the design inadequacies of the everyday environments we inhabit. According to Norman, while the mental models (or heuristics) that we construct to help us to navigate our lives are in part a product of limited cognitive capacity, they are also co-produced by the objects and environments we encounter. Consequently, just as our cognitive models lead to bias Norman claims that the design form of the world around us can also produce false mental models that can lead to consistent errors and more general patterns of undesired behaviour. According to Norman, the problem with many of the objects and environments we encounter in everyday life is that they provide limited clues as to how they actually work. In the absence of visual or ergonomic clues about how things work, Norman argues that humans construct explanatory shortcuts, which in turn contribute to false mental models (or 'naïve psychologies', to use Norman's vocabulary) and error-prone and inefficient behaviours.

In order to explain his design philosophy Norman reflects on two everyday objects: the floppy disk and the central heating thermostat (see Norman, 2002: 34–80). According to Norman the floppy disk is a very well-designed object, to the extent that in spite of the eight different ways it is possible to insert it into a disk drive it is (was) very easy to ascertain and then remember how to use it (this was achieved by the use of visual clues and physical barriers to prevent it being inserted in the wrong way). In this way the floppy disk made it easy for people not only to carry out an action with effective precision, but also reduced the cognitive capacity that was needed to conduct the task (because the clues needed to carry out the behaviour were stored in the world and not in the mind of the user) (ibid.).

Thermostats that are used on central heating systems, however, provide no real clue as to how they actually work. Norman observes that there are two commonly held folk theories concerning how thermostats operate (ibid.: 39). The first is the *timer theory*, which suggests that the thermostat controls the amount of time a heating system stays on (set the thermostat higher and the systems stays on longer, set it lower, it turns off more quickly) (ibid.). The second popular understanding is the *valve theory*. The theory suggests that the thermostat controls the amount of heat a system releases (the higher the setting of a thermostat the more heat it gives out and the more quickly a room will heat up) (ibid.). The thing is that these theories are both wrong: the thermostat is simply an on–off switch that turns on the heat in a system (to the maximum until a certain desired ambient temperature is reached). Our naïve psychology of thermostats is a product of the lack of available evidence that the device gives us about how it works and our desire to form a shortcut explanation. Such erroneous understandings can, of course, lead to a wasteful use of energy (as thermostats are set higher than they need to be). Norman ultimately reflects:

> The real point of the [thermostat] example is not that some people have erroneous theories; it is that everyone forms theories (mental models) to explain what they have observed. In the case of the thermostat, the design gives absolutely no hint as to the correct answer. In the absence of external information, people are free to let their imaginations run free as long as the mental models they develop account for the facts as they perceive them.
>
> *(ibid.: 39)*

FIGURE 8.1   The naïve psychology of the home heating thermostat
Source: Authors' collection.

On the basis of these insights into design psychology, user-centred cognitive designers and engineers like Donald Norman have been attempting to transform the material environments we inhabit. Redesigning our behavioural environments involves both making desired behaviours easier to practice, and encouraging changes in behaviours that we may be more reluctant to alter. Making desired behaviours easier to achieve can be seen in various newly designed objects ranging from in-house display energy use meters (which make it simpler to observe energy use and set energy use budgets in order to reduce consumption) (see Figure 8.2), to novel urinals replete with a fly to aim at (which have been shown to reduce toilet-based accidents and cleaning bills by tapping into a human desire for target practice) (see Figure 8.3). Attempts to change more recalcitrant behaviours can be seen in recent attempts to provide environmental cues to drivers to reduce their speed. In many UK villages road designers now have started to add bucolic-looking picket fences at key entry points to communities (see Figure 8.4). These fences have no practical purpose, but are instead designed to signal to drivers that they are entering a distinct place that is different from the open road that they have been travelling on. It appears that the contrast between the non-space of the open road and lived-in space of a community is an important prompt to reduce driving speed.

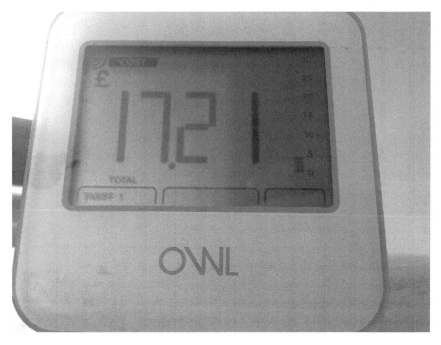

FIGURE 8.2   In-home energy display (note the energy budget target on the right hand
side of the digit display)
Source: Authors' collection.

What unites all of these neuroliberal design initiatives is a desire to ensure that not
only do environments no longer contribute to the bounding of human rationality,
but they actively ease our collective cognitive burden. The neuroliberal design of
the material world thus focuses on embedding the code for correct conduct within
the world around us so that humans do not have constantly to remember what that
code is. In the words of Donald Norman, it is about embedding the procedural
knowledge we need to bring healthy, environmentally friendly, and financially
responsible behaviours into the world around us, so that our subconscious can
work to our behavioural advantage rather than to its detriment (ibid.).

The second way in which neuroliberalism connects with the design community
is in relation to design thinking. When we speak of design thinking we are referring
specifically to the emerging approaches to design problems that have become popular
within user-centred design and the service's design professionals. These forms of
design thinking emphasize the importance of approaching issues from the perspective
of everyday human use (as opposed to prioritizing aesthetics or functionality), and of
developing iterative prototypes. In Chapter 6 we described the connections that exist
between neuroliberalism, experimentalism and RCTs. While neuroliberalism has
strong connections with the formal experimental methodologies of RCTs, the design
sciences have also infused them with a commitment to design trials that are more

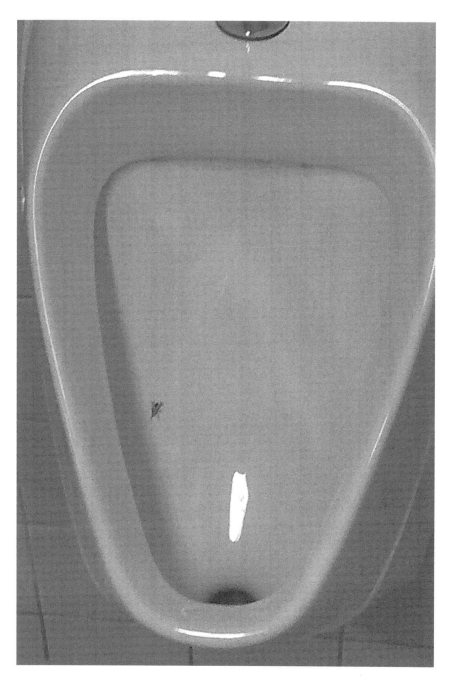

FIGURE 8.3 Neuroliberal urinal, Schiphol Airport
Source: Authors' collection.

FIGURE 8.4 Psychologically demarcating places on British roads
Source: Authors' collection.

qualitatively oriented. These trials place less emphasis on controlled experimentation and more on up-close, ethnographic observations of end-users by policy designers. The cognitive designer we interviewed reflected that:

> you have to do some ethnographic work even if … I know the sample sizes would be too small for that, you know, for their kind of RCT approach, but I would suggest that their design process for the trials and for the approaches they take ought to start with observation, ought to start with contextual insight around, you know, the realities of what it's like to, I don't know, to go to a Job Centre everyday, or what it's like to be trying to make a decision about pension options, or those kind of things. To understand the context in which people are making the decisions rather than starting from the point of view saying, 'Well, studies with undergraduate psychology students in the US show that people are bias in this way or that way, so we need to assume that that applies to the public as a whole.' … that would be my main criticism.
>
> *(Cognitive designer Dan Lockton, interview, 2014)*

In a sense the ethnographic sensibilities of design thinking are the methodological route through which designers have sought to provide a more rigorous materialist contextualization for neuroliberalism.

While RCTs are now seen as the dominant methodological trope of neuroliberalism, it is important to note that design thinking remains a strong influence of neuroliberal approaches to public policy development. In his account of the early months of the UK government's BIT, for example, Steve Hilton reflects upon how the founders of the team engaged widely with the design profession, and sought to use human-centred design and prototyping as strategies to avoid forms of self-referential biases emerging within the team itself (Hilton, 2015: 44–6). We also note that in its recent promotion of neuroliberalism the World Bank has advocated the use of key design thinking methodologies within development policy and evaluation (World Bank, 2015).

Interestingly, the design sciences' materialization of neuroliberalism reflects the broader emphasis of critical social sciences on the significance of materialism in everyday life (see Latour, 1993, 2005). This neo-materialism is, in part, a reaction against the emphasis that was placed on discursive power and Kantian notions of social perception in the social sciences in the later part of twentieth century. But this neo-materialistic turn in the critical social sciences also offers a platform for critiques of neuroliberalism as an emerging materialist project. What is immediately apparent when viewing neuroliberalism through a critical neo-materialist lens is that it exhibits a form of naïve materialism. This naïve materialism assumes that the problems of behavioural government can be displaced successfully into the material realm of the objects of everyday life. But this displacement activity fails to understand that the agency of objects is not only found in the object itself, but is also part of the wider network of practices that the object facilitates and is in turn animated by (see Shove, 2010). Well-designed objects can solve behavioural problems, but only the ones that revolve around fairly simple technical issues. Reconfigured objects alone cannot be relied upon to solve more complex long-term behavioural issues (this will be discussed at greater length below). The naïve materialism of neuroliberalism also rests upon its assumption that not only can the material world provide an effective zone for behavioural government, but that material environments are malleable to government desires. One of the key insights of neo-materialist studies has been to recognize the enduring influence and obduracy of objects, infrastructures and environments. The effective transformation of behavioural environments is thus far more challenging than simply prototyping a new device in a design workshop. It must take into account the challenging material legacy of historical objects and infrastructures, not to mention the invested economic, political and cultural interests that reside in these environments.

Neuroliberalism's material project is also marked by a narrow ontology. This narrow ontology tends to reduce reality to the measurable qualities of the physical environment. We have witnessed this narrow ontology in relation to the forms of experimental statehood discussed in Chapter 6. But in relation to design thinking, it manifests itself in an often implicit belief that all there is to know of a situation is to be found in the realm of tangible materiality. It is this narrow ontology that tends to result in the belief that a behavioural problem can be solved through the more careful cognitive and ergonomic alignment of the user and the objects of everyday life. The limitations of this perspective are captured expertly by Harman when, reflecting on Heidegger's phenomenology, he states:

> We must avoid any theory that converts things into nothing but visible objects. Since this only strips away the full reality of things and reduces them to caricatures. Things are not objects: instead, they have significance, which means they belong to a system of relations with other things in the environment. We encounter everything only from in the midst of life.
>
> *(Harman, 2011: 29)*

The challenge for neuroliberalism then becomes how it can account for a material universe that escapes our sensual grasp. This is a vision of the behavioural environment within which behaviours are understood as the outcome of changing relations between subjects and objects, in contexts determined by socio-economic relations that exceed the immediate space of design. The challenge of taking up this more holistic material approach to behavioural government is something that emerging strands of neuroliberalism are now grappling with. It is to these forms of neuroliberalism that we now turn our attention.

Rematerialising neuroliberalism: social practice theory and the Consensus programme

As we have seen throughout this volume, it is unwise to attempt to caricature neuroliberalism too narrowly. While it may have dominant tropes, which, for example, focus on nudge technologies and product redesign, neuroliberalism remains an emergent and open area of experimentation. In this context, it should come as little surprise that there are strands of neuroliberalism that have sought to respond to the naïve materialism and narrow ontologies that we outlined in the previous section. In this section we consider two approaches to behavioural government, which, while exhibiting many of the qualities of neuroliberalism, have sought to challenge and redefine its materialist and ultimately behavioural assumptions. These approaches find their points of origin in two areas: (1) emerging realizations of the practical limitations in the capacity of systems of neuroliberal design to enact significant forms of long-term behaviour change; (2) intellectual challenges to the theories of behaviour change upon which neuroliberalism is often predicated.

The intellectual challenges to the design orthodoxies of neuroliberalism have come from different analytical traditions. What appears to unite these traditions, however, is that they assert the limited potential of product innovation or environmental redesign strategies to achieve significant and sustained social change (see Davies and Doyle, 2015: 427). Transition management theorists have been particularly critical of narrowly defined solutions to complex social problems (Rip and Kemp, 1998). Transition management theorists are concerned primarily with what they see as 'large-scale transformations in socio-technical regimes' ranging from the transition from coal fires to central heating, and horse power to motor cars

(Davies and Doyle, 2015: 427). Critically, and in contrast to more product-oriented design perspectives, notions of transition management actively avoid the externalization of context when trying to understand previous regimes of social change, and when seeking to instigate future regimes of transition (Shove, 2010: 1278). In order to account for broader forms of socio-material context, theories of transition management draw on multilevel perspectives in order to understand better 'how innovations (mainly technological) come to be adopted, upscaled, and ultimately mainstreamed through system transition' (Davies and Doyle, 2015: 427). While drawing attention to forms of *system transition* (perhaps in home energy use, or modal forms of transport), transition theories seek to avoid deterministic readings of systems as forms of inevitable structure. Transition management is thus concerned with understating how systems are the product of co-evolving events, technologies and habits (see Shove, 2010: 1278). If, for example, we take the case of suburbs. As a system of living the suburbs started to emerge in the main during the twentieth century. They were the product of both the desire to escape the overcrowded city and the emergence of flexible forms of personal transport in the form of the motorcar. But the suburbs are not merely the product of one technological change: namely the development of the motorcar. They are also the product of land speculation, the financialization of mortgage-backed securities, changing urban planning regimes, cultural expectations around house and garden size and the ability to mass-produce affordable housing at scale (Molotch, 1976). Suburbs are, however, also the co-evolved product of the rise of supermarkets, refrigerators and microwaves and fast food, which all emerged as part of independent socio-technological transitions, but also in response to the living demands associated with commuting. The suburbs are essentially the product of a co-evolving system of technological and social forces, and transition managers would suggest that any attempt to change patterns of consumer behaviour must recognize this.

A second group of interconnected theories that have challenged the design-based behavioural assumptions of neuroliberalism are those of social practice theory (see Shove, 2003; Davies and Doyle, 2015). As with notions of transition management, social practice theorists emphasize the broader technical and material factors that frame the cognitive behavioural system. Theories of social practice claim, however, that in abstracting from the immediate material context of behaviour, transition management perspectives tend to underplay the role of power and politics and the importance of the direct relations between humans and technological/design objects (Davies and Doyle, 2015). Prominent practice theorist Elizabeth Shove has suggested that behavioural shifts thus need to be positioned within the complex and ever-evolving interplay between *stuff* (material objects, technologies and infrastructures), *skills* (the knowledge and ability to do certain things in certain ways) and *understandings* (which pertain to social norms and expectations) (ibid.: 427). In these contexts, the notion of social practice attempts to position behavioural changes and transitions within a complex web of micro and macro material forces, but also, crucially, the habits and procedures that emerge when these forces interact with human perceptions, capacities and understandings.

One much-discussed example of a social practice is that of the daily shower (see Davies and Doyle, 2015). The routine of taking a daily shower is clearly the product of the invention of the modern shower, and the greater ease with which it enables people to cleanse themselves. However, as a social practice the daily shower is not something that is determined by technology alone. The daily shower is a product of the establishment of a habit, which is itself an outcome of the observed behaviours of others, and the benefits that are perceived to come from showering first thing in the morning (benefits that are particularly connected to the sensations of warmth, comfort and waking up). But the daily shower is not merely a product of personal habit and pleasure, it has established itself more broadly because of emerging social expectations that have developed around cleanliness, body odour and the presentation oneself in public (see Shove, 2003). These social norms have in turn played an important role in driving the broader provision of showering facilities in hotels, service stations and increasingly in workplaces. Understood on these terms, the daily shower routine is a practice that has emerged at the interface of co-evolving technological, infrastructural, social and personal systems. Crucially, theorists of social practice would argue that any attempt to transform showering practices (perhaps in an effort to reduce domestic energy consumption or water use) must consider the broader social and material contexts from which the practice has evolved.

It is instructive at this point to reflect upon the connections between social practice theory and neuroliberalism. It is possible to think of social practice theory in critical opposition to the nuroliberalism, suggesting as it does that social transformation can only be achieved on scales that exceed the localized behavioural contexts characterizing many forms of neuroliberal government. For us this perspective is too simplistic and fails to recognize the significant parallels that exist between social practice theory and neuroliberalism. In this context, it is particularly important to recognize that social practice theory and neuroliberalism are premised upon the assumption that social transformation and/or behaviour change are not driven predominantly by rationally motivated, autonomous human action, but instead by the habits, norms and affects that flow from the unconscious interaction between people and their social and material environments. If not a direct critique then, it is tempting to think of social practice theory operating someone in the zone between the hard materialism of transition management approaches and the localized psychologies of neuroliberalism. For us, social practice theory reflects both a critical challenge to neuroliberal thought and action, but increasingly an adaptive context within which neuroliberalism can evolve and adapt. As one social practice advocate we spoke to explained:

> Because it (social practice theory) is the most all-encompassing and kind of nuanced theory, I feel. And then also, it very much matches our social science and geographical perspective. A lot of the literature, you know, comes from, you know, the behavioural economics and psychology side of things. And I do feel that those theories can be absorbed to a degree within

the social practice theory but for me, it's the context that's within the social practice theory. It kind of ... it's the *zoomed out picture*, which looks at the context also married with the *zoomed in picture*, which allows you to kind of deconstruct the practices. So I feel like it's got this good mix of the macro situation with the micro situation because you need to understand the micro to actually transform the practices. And also, the fact that it doesn't sort of promote disjointed interventions which is ... how everything else has failed at ...

> *(Consensus representative (and behaviour change researcher),*
> *interview, 2014, emphasis added)*

In the following section we consider one attempt to fuse the *zoomed-in* insights of neuroliberalism adaptively with the *zoomed-out* perspectives of social practice theory.

Putting social practice theory into practice

In this section we consider a practical attempt that has been made to combine the psychological and design insights of neuroliberalism with the sociological insights of social practice theory. Consensus is an action-oriented research collaboration based in the Republic of Ireland. The title *Consensus* is as actually a contracted acronym, which stands for *Con*sumption *En*vironment and *Su*stainability. The project 'uses innovative social science and collaborative research methods to explore trends and solutions for sustainable household consumption' (Consensus, 2017). Consensus is a research partnership of the Irish government's Environment Protection Agency and academics from Trinity College Dublin and NUI Galway (OÉ Gaillimh). Focusing, among other things, on the drivers and incentives of sustainable household behaviours, the project explores strategies for changing domestic practices associated with transport, energy and water.

In its attempts to deploy social practice theory within applied contexts Consensus has been constructed consciously as a critical response to many of the product design forms that neuroliberalism takes. As one Consensus representative we spoke to reflected:

> everyone's going on about behaviour change and, you know, they're writing all these articles on FAS Company and Guardian Business, sustainable business and they're all just ... they're not really picking up on a more contextual approach and I think that's because a lot of them are written by consultancies who are working with the corporate sector and the corporate sector want to know how they can do things within the limits of their agenda which is, you know, sell the products or sell services. So I think they're writing for an audience, I guess. And that audience wants to be told that things are going to be easily changed with [a] single activity and it can also make money.

> *(Consensus representative, interview, 2014)*

It is interesting to reflect here on whether the simplifying and decontextualized design logics of neuroliberalism are as much a product of corporate need as they are a reflection on epistemological logics of the project itself (see Chapter 7 in this volume). What is clear is that in its attempts to mobilize social practice theory, Consensus was keen to ensure that this approach was seen as a realistic strategy that could be used within the public and private sectors:

> So I think that's the issue but I kind of wanted to get that across. Maybe it's not … maybe it isn't so difficult to work with practice theory. You know, maybe it does require some collaboration but collaboration and transparency is kind of where things are going now.
>
> *(Consensus representative, interview, 2014)*

A key dimension of the Consensus project's attempts to implement a practice-based approach to behaviour change was the process of practice-oriented participatory (or POP) *backcasting*. According to Davies and Doyle (2015: 428):

> Backcasting describes an overarching, multiphase process involving the cocreation of desirable future vision(s), following by working back (or backcasting) from that future alternative to the present to design sequential steps for its achievement.

While backcasting need not necessarily be deployed in social practice theory approaches to change, it appears to have the advantage of breaking down the complex network of multi-scalar systems of change associated with practice theory into a series of incremental stages. The Consensus team described the benefits of backcasting to us in even broader terms:

> [the] backcasting approach has benefits, you know, it liberates you from the present, it brings people together. It provides more of a creative space for breaking through these wicked problems. So, but to do it, it involves collaborating with industry and with public sector and non-governmental actors.
>
> *(Consensus representative, interview, 2014)*

There are two things of note within this reflection. First is the emphasis it places on the creative value of shifting the focus of behavioural government from current conduct to desired future states. In addition to capturing the imaginative potential of participants, a concern with future visions appears to shift attention immediately away from localized behaviours to the broader worlds, in which desired behaviours will be a part. Second, focusing on broader visions of the future requires engagement with a diverse range of actors with power to shape that future. Inevitably, this field of actors extends well beyond the product designers and architects conventionally associated with neuroliberalism.

The POP backcasting methodology deployed by the Consensus project was based around a series of workshops. These workshops brought together stakeholders from civil society, government and commercial bodies, including designers and communication specialists. The immediate impact of the make-up of these workshops was to decentre the notion of expertise. In keeping with social practice theory, expertise in these workshops resided in a range of interconnected sectors as opposed to a more narrowly defined 'behavioural expert'. The operation of the backcasting workshops was described to us as follows:

> So we held a range of visiting workshops with these people. So we have to sort of teach them the practice approach for those workshops. So, we took the three dimensions of practices and I know they're called different labels and different names by various other people but, you know, being in scales, norms, tools and then context. So we sort of had those labels in our workshops and we got them to imagine new tools. We got them to imagine new motivations. We got them to imagine new infrastructures of provision. So we deconstructed wider practice … in a workshop, when we got them to work with this structure and to re-imagine it in the future. And we did do a lot of evaluation on that … some of the participants, architects, some of the designers didn't think it was that unusual an approach and didn't benefit from it hugely whereas some of the public officials and maybe more engineering types, find it … most of them find it really useful …
>
> *(Consensus representative, interview, 2014)*

It appears that the POP backcasting workshops provided a context within which to think creatively about both the micro and macro processes associated with social transformations, as well as engaging actors from a series of sectors that could contribute to change management. As the consensus team reflected:

> The visioning brainstorming thus drew on microconceptualizations of social practice theory while also considering the sociotechnical regimes (energy, water, and food) within which these practices were situated and are areas of typical concern in transitions visioning studies. Attention was paid to the role of commercial and governmental forces in shaping market conditions, infrastructures, and rules of access to resources that simultaneously influence socially constructed and contextually dependent expectations, norms, and needs of home energy, water, and food consumption.
>
> *(Davies and Doyle: 2015: 429)*

The fact that Consensus continually emphasizes the *microconceptualization* of social practice, and remain concerned with emotional needs as well as functional ones, is what marks the approach out as an adaptive form of neuroliberalism (and not just another version of transition management). In broader terms, it is also clear that in the project's belief that change can be managed (albeit in vary complex scalar contexts), Consensus works by the same operating principles as neuroliberalism.[1]

The final aspsect of the Consensus approach to behavioural government is the use of Homelabs. Homelabs form living laboratories within which Consensus tests the practice-based approaches to change that are developed through POP backcasting in Irish households. One example of the operation of Homelabs is provided by Consensus' work with Irish Water. In the context of Irish Water's roll-out of water meters throughout Ireland, Consensus has been working with affected households to explore the potential of this broader infrastructural transformation to provide a context for generating changes in socio-technical practices. The Homelabs water use trials involved a mixed approach to stimulate behaviour change with specific regard to body washing. First, conscious targets were set for households to try to reduce their weekly water usage (Davies et al., 2015). These targets were supported by the installations of technological devices such as shower litre meters and timers to provide new insights into rates of water use (ibid.). These technological devices were complemented by the provision of softer products that would reduce the need for daily showers and baths, such as low-foam shampoo (which takes less time to rinse), leave-in conditioner, and hair and body washes that do not require water (ibid.). In addition to products, households were also provided with skills-based information concerning how shower pausing and flow adjustment could be enacted, and splash washing techniques (ibid.). The Homelabs trials (which have also been used by Consensus in relation to eating practices) ran for five weeks with different households, and involved regular visits by the research team in order to ensure that the interventions were adapted to suit the needs and insights of the participating families. The overall philosophy of the trials was described to us in the following terms:

> So we'll be doing co-design processes with the householders over the course of five weeks. So this implementation phase is really what we're … We're trying to bridge the abstractness of, I guess, the social practice visiting research and see how we could actually transform practices within the home based on, you know, we have done four years research …
>
> *(Consensus representative, interview, 2014)*

An important part of the co-design process associated with the Homelabs initiative appears to have been a desire to instigate collective social reflections on washing practices:

> And it was all around creating social conversations on … and bringing something like such a private activity, bring it into a public space and getting people to debate around them. I think that's the issue with … especially when it comes to water use and washing, then, it is so private that people don't really … they don't discuss it. And also, there's a cultural thing like, you know, Ireland and probably Britain are … they're quite prudish and washing is so privatized and it's never a subject of debate.
>
> *(Consensus representative, interview, 2014)*

The familial discussions prompted within the Homelabs trials were an important way of attempting to shift established norms about washing and gaining social acceptance of alternative approaches. But beyond this there appears to be a deeper concern with the self-authoring of behavioural change. As a representive from Consensus stated:

> So I think you can disrupt people's thinking around this. Like when it comes to washing, we were saying that we have to promote more adaptive washing practices but to adapt your washing, you have to reflect on when you need to wash and you have to understand that you do not need to wash every single day for 10 minutes in the shower. And I think people are reasonable, they understand that. But they have to be disrupted or given an opportunity or prompted to think about that …
>
> *(Consensus representative, interview, 2014)*

Consensus' approach to adaptive washing behaviour appears to challenge established neuroliberal approaches to design-led behaviour change on two levels. First it asserts a more complex understanding of the material design environment that shapes conduct. Second, it encourages forms of neurological reflexivity that, rather than simply seeking to nudge people in new behavioural directions, involves the activation of more autonomous forms of volition (see Chapter 4 in this volume), which might ultimately morph into embedded habits. Significantly, the emphasis that Consensus places upon self-authored adaptive washing responds to some of the critiques of social practice theory, which suggest that in focusing on practices the agency of the human can be underplayed (see Groves et al., 2016).

Analysis of the Homelabs washing trials revealed some positive results, with declining showering and bathing frequency and a quarter of respondents reporting an increase in the sustainability of their washing practices (Davies et al., 2015: 4).[2] Given the relatively small scale of the trials, however, the likely long-term success associated with Consensus' behavioural methodology is hard to assess. In its focus on households, the Homelabs trials do, perhaps, indicate one of the problems of testing social practice theory approaches to behaviour change. While it may be possible to gain multi-scalar insights into the nature of the practices that need to be changed in order to promote more sustainable lifestyles, it is hard within a trial environment to activate, coordinate and measure transformations at multiple scales and across different sectors. While the Homelabs washing trials did capitalize on the infrastructural provision of water meters in Irish households, beyond that the project had to work within the relatively narrow confines of the individual home. At this scale it becomes difficult to understand how local shifts in washing practices can contribute to broader changes in social norms, and how more distant changes in water provision systems and regulation are translated into home environments. This appears to reflect the hermeneutic challenge of social practice theory: how to hold the study of micro-scale shifts alongside the analysis of more systemic forms of change.

Democratizing behavioural designs: hacking neuroliberalism

Consensus reflects an adaptive challenge to many of the materialist assumptions of neuroliberalism. The particular form of participatory practice theory adopted by Consensus also embodies a response to the potentially disempowering dynamics of neuroliberalism's engagement in the material world. In this section we consider the issues of design, disempowerment and participation in greater detail. What is obvious from our discussions so far in this chapter is that in redesigning the material environments in which we live, neuroliberal systems of government have the capacity both to enable citizens to become more aware of their behaviours (through feedback technologies), and to manipulate conduct (through the use of ambient design features that deliberately target our unconscious systems). Of course, these issues speak directly to the themes of subjectivity, autonomy and freedom that have run through different sections of this volume (see Chapters 4 and 5). In this section we reflect upon the pioneering work of the designer and researcher Dan Lockton. Dan Lockton is now based at the Carnegie Mellon University Design School in Pittsburgh, PA, USA, and before that worked at the Royal College of Art in London. His work is of interest to us because of the creative ways in which it has fused design thinking and methodologies with the behavioural insights upon which neuroliberalism rests.

Dan Lockton summarized the philosophy of his work to us in the following terms:

> Well, I suppose there are two angles where I think I've come to it from. One of them is that element of democratising design or making it more about involving people in the process by which their lives are configured, if you like. Because inevitably, you know, everything that you use, in some way, is configuring your everyday life. And if you don't have a way of questioning that, or have a way of understanding the reasoning behind it ... we think it's possibly unethical or, at least, in some circumstances it is. So there's that element. And I'm very much into the ... make a movement type approach where ... I suppose people have the knowledge and the tools to understand and change the world around them.
>
> *(Dan Lockton, interview, 2014)*

The idea of *democratizing design* echoes certain aspects of the participatory backcasting approach deployed by Consensus (see previous section). However, while Consensus engaged a wide variety of groups (including design experts and end-users) in order to ensure that behavioural initiatives were more effective, something else appears to be going on within Lockton's work. His assertion that 'people have the knowledge and the tools to understand and change the world around them' suggests something more than merely pre-design consultation; or even post-design consultation retrofitting. As Lockton states, he is trying to develop:

> a more nuanced approach to designing around people's behaviour, based on designing and researching *with* people rather than 'for' them, learning from

people's understanding of the world, and embracing the complexities of everyday human experience. As I said last year, I'm increasingly uncomfortable with how I see 'design for behaviour change', and the 'behaviour change agenda', being applied in practice, with simplistic, deterministic and individualist approaches which often seem to be about treating humans as defective components that need to be constrained or tricked, denying variety, complexity, culture and social context.

(Dan Lockton, interview, 2014)

Lockton's work emphasizes the importance of enabling people to understand better the psychological and material components of the behavioural environments that surround them, so that they can adapt to that environment. It is clear in this context that Lockton's work strives for the same forms of neurological reflectivity and empowerment that we discussed in Chapter 4. His work is different, however, to the extent that he seeks to produce adaptive design environments within which neurological reflexivity can take material form.

In this first instance Lockton's work suggests that designing with people has to be more than just a consultation exercise: it needs to be about developing design on the basis of the adaptive realities of people's everyday lives. Lockton observes:

I'm interested in that perspective of saying, well, you know, actually people are probably quite good at those things. And, you know, it … So, start from the point of view of understanding what people do well and why they do it well, and how people, you know, how people actually make, how people get by in everyday life and trying to build on that rather than seeing humanity as a problem to be sort of fixed is … I don't know. I suppose it's a more optimistic perspective maybe. But I think also it's more realistic. It's … you know, because it builds on real life rather than just looking at sort of … I think it's … I think it possibly is the recognition that people are actually quite good at doing things, I think.

(Dan Lockton, interview, 2014)

The idea of designing around existing observed behaviours is not new. The Dutch architect Rem Koolhas famously deployed this method in his design of the McCormick Tribune Campus Center at the Illinois Institute of Technology in Chicago. Before designing the Campus Centre, which connected a series of existing buildings at the Institute, Koolhaas observed the unplanned paths (or 'cow lines') that had been worn into the ground by students over the years. Koolhaas used the direction and relative width of these paths to determine the size and course of the hallways in the new Campus Section (see Muschamp, 1998). The utilization of existing desire lines is one way of democratizing design and simultaneously valuing the adaptive behaviours of those you are designing for. But Lockton's design philosophy goes further than merely learning from established behaviour patterns.

FIGURE 8.5   Following desire lines
Source: Authors' collection.

The broader significance of Lockton's design philosophy is captured in the following reflection:

> So that it's not about experts doing it, or deciding years in advance what, you know, what the setting should be on this, or whether you're allowed to unscrew the back of your phone without invalidating the warranty, those kind of things. So there's that element much more sort of almost a hacker kind of culture. And it's also that the … the bit around the public understanding of everyday systems … Well, some of the current projects I'm working on and previous ones, it's become clear that one of the main reasons that people don't just magically change their behaviour when they're given information about, you know, their energy use or the carbon footprint of their lunch, or, you know, all these things, is that people don't understand the systems that they're part of, you know. They may understand it … they often understand it on two levels. They have a general picture of how they think overall the system works, and they have a very local, localised sort of often seeing the heuristic space picture of 'Well, I know we need to do this' or 'I know we shouldn't have the window open when the air-conditioning is on but I don't know why, really'.
>
> *(Dan Lockton, interview, 2014)*

In his desire to make the operation of design environments more transparent to users, Lockton's work clearly echoes Donald Norman's crusade for user-centred design. Lockton's invocation of a form of designer *hacking culture* does, however, distinguish his work from both that of Norman and the practice-oriented approaches of Consensus. The notion that design environments should be designed in ways that facilitate future hacking asserts implicitly that not only should people be able to comprehend how the material environments around them work, but also they should be able to use this knowledge to reshape these environments creatively. According to Gladwell, hackers don't simply want the operating manual: they seek to subvert secrecy through craftiness and guile (2016: 124). For the hacker, secrecy and obscuring how things work are arbitrary conditions that need to be both brought to light and challenged (ibid.).[3]

While seemingly utopian in some regards, Lockton's vision of an open source design environments reflects an important material implication of more progressive versions of neuroliberalism. If, following the work of Gigerenzer, it is asserted that people can creatively control and adapt their automaticity then it would appear important that this adaptive potential be facilitated in the material environment around them. We assert that the cultivation of adaptive behavioural capacity will be difficult to maintain if this trait is constrained by the closed systems and technological lock-ins of past designers. Lockton reflects:

> I mean, it's obvious but it's quite profound in a way that we're often being asked to change our behaviour around things that we can't, that we're not, they're not visible to us, they're not tangible. So I'm … and I'm intrigued as to … I mean I started looking at this from a sort of energy point of view, but I suppose I'm interested in a long-term way of seeing, well, how does that relate to society on a big-scale.
>
> *(Dan Lockton, interview, 2014)*

Lockton's invocation of the need for big-scale change suggests that the idea of hacking could be extended to the immediate material environment of everyday life, to include increased transparency of the multi-scale forces that shape our material and psychological worlds. It is here that Lockton's hacking culture perhaps comes closest to the goals of social practice theory. This is also the context within which neuroliberal hacking culture moves between material design and the design of political systems. Lockton suggests that his ideas could be extended to designing new systems for democratic engagement, so that people can find out more easily:

> who to talk to, you know. So, who in the council, or which council … You know, those kind of things. So even … so by everyday systems, I suppose I mean kind of all of these invisible structures that we're part of and affect our lives. But how can we help people have a better understanding of what they can do within them? So it's not just how the systems are, but how can we change it.
>
> *(Dan Lockton, interview, 2014)*

The practical aspects of Lockton's design philosophy are captured in his *Design with Intent* methodology (Lockton, 2017). This methodology draws on the insights that Lockton has developed working on a series of collaborative design projects spanning different aspects of sustainable behaviour change and community engagement. These projects range from those that are focused on community design projects engaging members of the local community in redesigning their neighbourhood, to those concerned with addressing household energy use. The hacking ethos of Lockton's behavioural design approaches is expressed perhaps most clearly in his work as part of the European Sus Lab programme. The Sus Lab programme is an international research collaboration that uses living lab technologies to design and evaluate sustainable living technologies. As part of this programme, Lockton was involved in the development of a series of 'hackathons' (see also Chapter 5 in this volume). Within these hackathons, participants are not asked to test new products and designs but invited to experiment creatively and adapt new technologies and systems. As an enactment of Lockton's hacking culture, hackathons not only lead to the development of new prototypes that are hardwired with user insight, but also provide participants with the opportunity to understand better how products and systems work and can be adapted in the future (SuslabNWE, 2014).

While Lockton's hackathons remain fairly small-scale interventions within the world of neuroliberal design, they do indicate a potentially productive way of developing more progressive and empowering approaches to behavioural government. Hackathons do, of course, reveal only part of the broader promise of neuroliberal hacking. Hacking neuroliberalism could involve a constant ability to adapt and change products, technologies and spaces. The open sourcing of design environments in this way seeks to address directly the inertia and resistance that historical design environments place on behaviour change. In addition to being confronted with significant practical challenges, a broader culture of hacking must, however, contend with the economic imperatives and health and safety practices that currently appear to necessitate obscuring the internal workings of the infrastructures and products that surround us in our everyday lives. But in the very challenge it presents to proprietorial claims and risk aversion, Lockton's invocation of a hacking culture is suggestive of a more radically oriented political project that could be designed around neuroliberalism. Indeed the political proclivities of the hacker for transparency and change could provide creative contexts within which the liberal goals of behavioural government are challenged and progressively extended.

Conclusions

This chapter has explored the ways in which neuroliberalism is engaged in changing the behavioural environments in which we live. This chapter has demonstrated that, as a system of government, neuroliberalism is an inherently environmental project. The environmental focus of neuroliberalism reflects the project's concern with the irrational push of the world around us and its liberal sensitivities to changing things rather than transforming people. While acknowledging the environmental aspects of the neuroliberal project, this chapter has explored the limitations of many assumptions concerning the material environment that characterize neuroliberal government. Analysis has thus discussed both the naïve materiality and narrow ontology of many forms of neuroliberalism – which tend to assume that changes in the environment can be translated easily into behavioural shifts.

In light of the critiques of neuroliberalism's underlying environmental assumptions, this chapter has explored two adaptive forms of neuroliberalism that appear to address these limitations directly. The work of Consensus demonstrated the importance of thinking about behaviour change in relation to the practices that connect local design environments with broader infrastructures of provision and cultures of everyday life. If the work of Consensus demonstrated the importance of thinking about behavioural government beyond the scale of the immediate behavioural environment, Dan Lockton's work emphasized the different ways in which neuroliberal designs could be democratized. Lockton's *Design with Intent* methodology and design-hacking culture promote the idea that in building new behavioural environments more attention should be paid to existing cultures of adaptive behaviour that people deploy, and more opportunity should be provided for people to adapt their design environments to meet their behavioural needs. As neuroliberalism continues to evolve it will be interesting to see the extent to which it seeks to approach behavioural government through the context of more complex systems of environmental transformation, and whether it is willing/able to facilitate forms of behavioural freedom that are based upon our capacity to actively shape our lived environments.

Notes

1 It is worth reiterating here that it is this assumption of the inherent manageability of change that distinguishes neuroliberalism most strongly from neoliberal orthodoxy (where change is unpredictable, organic and the spontaneous outcome of market forces).
2 The Consensus Homelab trials report here involved five household and nineteen individuals (Davies, 2015).
3 Gladwell's discussion of the connection between hacking and the arbitrary nature of secrecy is derived from his reflection on the writings of the anthropologist Gabriella Coleman.

9

PRACTICAL INTERVENTIONS IN NEUROLIBERALISM

Mindfulness and behaviour change

Introduction: the Mindfulness and Behaviour Change programme

Throughout this volume we have developed a critical, but not unsympathetic, academic analysis of neuroliberalism and associated behaviour change strategies. In this chapter we attempt to do something that is less common within an academic volume of this kind. We offer an account of our own practical intervention within the sphere of neuroliberal government. Since 2013 we have developed a bespoke behaviour change training programme, which combines mindfulness practices with behavioural insights. Part of the inspiration for this programme is our interest in the potential of neuroliberal insights to support the development of behavioural capacity and psychological empowerment (see Chapter 4). The second driving force is increasingly valid evidence that mindfulness offers one way to achieve some degree of integration between the conscious and non-conscious aspects of decision making. One of the most novel aspects of this programme is that we have used it to provide training to those involved directly in the development and application of neuroliberal policies. We have utilized the programme in an attempt to influence the agencies and organizations that we have been describing and analysing within this volume. To these ends, if neuroliberalism is understood as a product of the varied government and non-governmental organizations that adapt and apply it, our programme embodies a deliberate attempt to engage and change emerging forms of neuroliberalism.

We have so far delivered and evaluated six full Mindfulness and Behaviour Change programmes. These programmes have been delivered to behaviour change practitioners in the public, private and third sectors. The organizations had all been influenced to varying degrees by neuroliberalism. At the heart of our programme is a desire to explore the impact that learning about behavioural insights through the practices of mindfulness has on participants' understanding of their own behaviours, and how this might translate into the future design and delivery of their behaviour change programmes.

Mindfulness is rooted in practices that date back some 2,500 years. Mindfulness originates within Buddhist traditions, although related contemplative and reflective practices are found in many religions. It has been adapted more recently within a range of secular contexts (including stress and pain relief, education, prisons and the workplace). While there is much discussion around what mindfulness is, it is commonly characterized as a capacity or state of *present-centred non-judgemental awareness*. It involves participants becoming more able to notice and direct their attention, and to shift the relationship between their attention and their experiences. Initial practices often involve an object of attention (such as the breath, body, sounds and thoughts), associated with the cultivation of a greater awareness of the mental, embodied and environmental processes that press in upon our existence. The non-judgemental aspect of mindfulness relates to developing the capacity to notice the role of thoughts, feelings and environmental prompts to action in our lives, without becoming caught up in responses to such impulses.

Given its relationship with the cultivation of both embodied attention and reflexivity, it has been suggested that mindfulness could be an interesting behaviour change strategy in and of itself, understood in relation to the notion of *neurological reflexivity* we encountered in Chapter 4 (see Rowson, 2011). We were, however, interested primarily in what happens when mindfulness was combined with learning about emerging behavioural insights (particularly those concerned with the power of emotions and unconscious biases within human behaviour). As a broad working hypothesis we wanted to test the extent to which mindfulness could provide not only an alternative way of learning about the scientific insights upon which neuroliberalism has been based, but also a set of techniques for actively noticing and experiencing them. We were further interested to explore the extent to which developing a mindful relationship with embodied emotions and biases could support the development of behavioural capacities through which individuals would not only be more aware of their behavioural proclivities, but also more able to reshape them. In testing out these ideas on behavioural policy-makers we also became concerned with the extent to which more mindfully oriented forms of behavioural government could both optimize learning and facilitate more ethical and empowering policy regimes.

This chapter begins with a detailed introduction to mindfulness and behaviour change. We give particular attention to the recent emergence of more transformatively oriented and deconstructive mindfulness practices and their potential relationships with behavioural government. In the second section we outline the content and operation of the Mindfulness and Behaviour Change programme that we devised and delivered. The third section of this chapter outlines the main results that emerged from our mindfulness and behaviour change trials.

Mindfulness and behavioural insights

> We're blind to our blindness. We have very little idea of how little we
> know. We're not designed to know how little we know.
>
> *(Kahneman, 2011)*

It is our contention that mindfulness and neuroliberalism offer frames through which we can reconsider how humans meet and respond to their experience in its broadest sense. Buddhist thinking suggests that our everyday consciousness is 'deluded' and mindfulness offers a capacity to help us wake up to and enquire into that delusion. It is sometimes seen as one wing of the bird that 'liberates' our view: the other wing being practices of compassion. One of the key figures of neuroliberalism, Daniel Kahneman, suggests that we are deluded in the sense that we are more Homer Simpson than homo economicus, and furthermore that *we don't know how little we know*. As we discussed in Chapter 3, Kahneman (and other neuroliberalists) offers a theoretical framework drawn from psychology, behavioural economics and neuroscience (among other social sciences) to help us navigate this delusion. Crucially while Kahneman's framework can be used in self-enquiry it has largely been directed at decoding the behaviour of others. Both mindfulness and neuroliberalism are thus interested in how we as humans attend to and process information, and the delusions and cognitive shortcomings that emerge from these processes. Both mindfulness and neuroliberalism are also sensitive to the fact that our behaviours are not 'rational' (as assumed by classical economics), but instead emerge from a complex interaction of internal states (emotions, thoughts, feelings) and external factors (including our social and physical context).

Mindfulness is a practice of turning towards our experience, when much of our instinct is to avoid it through strategies of aversion and craving. Mindfulness courses start to explore how we pay attention, and how doing so affects our mental state. It has become popularized through two 'standard' secular mindfulness courses, MBSR (Mindfulness Based Stress Relief) and MBCT (Mindfulness Based Cognitive Therapy). They are rooted in approaches developed by clinician and meditator Jon Kabat-Zinn in the 1960s and 1970s (see Williams and Kabat-Zinn, 2013). Kabat-Zinn innovated by bringing his Buddhist mindfulness practice to the clinical challenge of patients in chronic pain. He tailored the mindfulness practices of awareness, attention and acceptance, and reduced patients' tendency to resist pain, mentally or physically. This was the first time that mindfulness had been used in a clinical, secular setting. Kabat-Zinn's work was followed, a number of years later, by a further significant development when Mark Williams, John Teasdale and Zindal Segal adapted the stress based course using cognitive behavioural therapy to target people with depression (see Williams, Teasdale, Segal and Kabat-Zinn, 2007).[1] This new mindfulness adaptation proved successful in treating repeat episodes of depression and, after trials, experimentation and adaptations, the newly developed MBCT programme started to supersede the original MBSR course.

Given that mindfulness has been formally linked – both through course developments and professional enquiry – to the behavioural model of cognitive behavioural therapy (CBT), it is no surprise that other practitioners have started to explore its links with the models and theories of behaviour found within neuroliberalism. If we can make unconscious processes more conscious through enquiry and reflection for individual therapeutic aims (such as mindfulness and depression) or spiritual liberation (mindfulness and Buddhism), could related techniques be oriented towards other positive social aims (mindfulness and behaviour change)? Our argument is that mindfulness and neuroliberalism, like mindfulness and CBT, offer a potentially productive combination of capacities and understandings to start to overcome our lack of awareness, unconscious biases and cognitive blind-spots which prevent us making progress with some of the most challenging behavioural problems of our time. We further assert that a lack of reflective skill and knowledge in individuals, teams, organizations and societies is contributing to an unhelpful status quo and a lack of progress on social and environmental issues.

Our research has considered how a process of mindful enquiry can be used to increase practical awareness of both System 1 and System 2 thinking. As we have discussed elsewhere in this volume. As we have previously discussed, System 1 thinking relies on 'rules of thumb' (patterns of thinking often termed cognitive biases) to inform our decisions and behaviours. System 2 thinking, on the other hand, is slower, more reflective, and more able to consider new and novel information. System 1 thinking enables us to operate effectively in the world, but it can also limit what we see and how we interpret our experience and information. As discussed previously, many neuroliberal interventions attempt to understand how behavioural biases are operating in any particular situation and then they work with these to design communications or systems that will in turn shift behaviours. In our interventions we used the embodied attention-based practice of mindfulness as part of a process of making conscious the biased mind (and its embodied forms), and thus making us less subject to it. To these ends, our interventions were concerned with how mindfulness and behavioural insights could be combined in order to support the development of forms of character, autonomy and psychological capacity that certain strands of neuroliberalism have been seen to erode (see Chapters 3–5 in this volume).

While neuroliberalism and mindfulness both explore perception, what is real, what is subjective and what is objective, they are also marked by key differences of approach. Mindfulness is personal, it is understood within the 'I' and starts to put a question mark over what and who the 'I' is. Mindfulness 'is associated with a greater capacity to see relationships between thoughts, feelings and actions and to discern meanings and causes of experience and behaviour' (Bishop et al., 2004: 234). Neuroliberalism, on the other hand, explores ways of rethinking human relations with our behaviours in quite general ways. To put things another way, neuroliberalism is based upon a fairly universal account of the human condition (and its flaws), whereas mindfulness seeks highly personal forms of enquiry into behavioural experience. Our research interventions were thus designed, in part, to explore the extent to which mindfulness could enable the general theories of neuroliberalism to become part of a more personally grounded experience of behavioural reality.

Mindfulness, biases and behavioural transformations

We are not alone in starting to explore mindfulness in relation to behaviours other than those in clinical settings and related to depression, stress and anxiety. Work is emerging to support the positive development of mental insight and awareness to optimize the mind's capacity within a number of contexts. This includes work with mindfulness and specific cognitive biases (see, for example, Hafenbrack et al's 2014 work on mindfulness and status quo bias); mindfulness and unconscious bias to support inclusion, equality and diversity at work (see the work of Rhondda McGee (n.d.) on colour insight and Byron Lee (2016) on cultural wisdom); mindfulness and decision making (see Good et al. (2015) for a review on workplace mindfulness); and mindfulness in relation to behaviour change and environmental sustainability (Rowson, 2011; Ericssson et al., 2014). In this section we outline briefly some of these developments as a way of situating the significance and potential of the research we describe later in this chapter.

Our research sits alongside this work in considering how mindfulness and contemporary understandings and applications of behavioural economics can influence policy and change-making processes. One key focus of our work has been cognitive biases. In 2004, Bishop et al. measured mindfulness by its potential to increase our ability to meet our experience without preconceptions interfering:

> [t]he prediction is that mindfulness practice should facilitate the identification of objects in unexpected contexts because one would not bring pre-conceived beliefs about what should or should not be present.
>
> *(Bishop et al., 2004: 233)*

Bishop et al. argue that someone who practises mindfulness should be less subject to habitual thinking, have more capacity to see how their attention is being appropriated, and make conscious the unconscious factors involved in decisions (ibid.). Bishop et al.'s work suggests that mindfulness provides a valuable practical context in and through which subjects can militate against the forces of cognitive bias. In a related experiment by Hafenbrack et al. (2014), subjects were exposed to short practices of mindfulness before then being exposed to a 'status quo bias'-based problem. Those who had practised mindfulness were less subject to the bias and more able to make an informed decision.

Evidence to support the insights of Bishop et al. and Hafenbrack emerged in our research interventions (see Pykett et al., 2016). The subjects within our trials became more aware of confirmation biases playing out in their lives, which gave them insight into their unconscious behaviours and created opportunities to do things differently.

Our interventions also explored other biases such as optimism bias, sunk-cost bias and loss aversion. Participants, through processes of reflection and mindful enquiry, started to see the impacts of these mental shortcuts in their lives. A particularly important mental bias we started to explore in our interventions was that of scarcity thinking. This bias tends to make our mind obsess about that which we perceive as limited. As with many biases this makes sound evolutionary sense (obsessing about food when we have none will motivate us to find some), but in contemporary society, where problems are less linear and more complex it can also limit our capacity for more creative, long-term resolutions to the challenges we face. Scarcity bias often results in very short-term thinking. For people with little money that might mean taking out a pay-day loan; for busy people, where time is limited, it can mean over-simplifying or ignoring complex problems in favour of easy wins. Our participants started to see the effects of scarcity on their thinking and our research was interested in how raising and enquiring into cognitive scarcity might improve our capacity for better decisions when, as is often the case, time or money resources are limited.

Mindfulness is also being combined with unconscious bias training to address social prejudices, by reframing prejudice in behavioural terms. Previously, prejudice has been seen largely as an individual's responsibility (or irresponsibility), but unconscious bias work acknowledges that prejudice is partly based on experience and rooted in the unconscious. Rhonda McGee, a US based lawyer, combines theoretical training on the psychological roots of prejudice with an enquiry practice using mindfulness. McGee (n.d.) observes:

> I think there is a specific need to incorporate mindfulness in a way that moves from colour-blindness to what I call 'colour insight', which is an ongoing awareness of the many ways that race, colour, and culture impact us in our interactions with others.

(See also Lueke and Gibson, 2015.) In the UK, Byron Lee (2016) has developed a broader approach to mindfulness-based behaviour change and prejudice. He uses understandings of our cognitive shortcuts together with mindfulness to bring about what he terms 'cultural wisdom': a way of knowing that is different from either intelligence (content) or competence (skills). For Lee, mindfulness offers an important means by which to develop this wisdom as it is a 'chance to stimulate the kind of reflexive and emotionally engaged approach to diversity, inclusion and intercultural practice that is sorely needed' (ibid., 2016). He uses practices that enable people to deal with the difficulty of both speaking and being open to hearing the truth of discrimination in action. As we will see later in this chapter, Lee's work supports our research, which has shown that after a training intervention incorporating mindfulness practice and understanding of cognitive bias, people were far more open to seeing their own prejudice without judgement.

Beyond the issues of biases and prejudice, mindfulness is also being combined with broader behaviour change models in order to develop ways of addressing more complex problems of behavioural government, such as climate change mitigation and adaptation. Often termed a 'wicked problem' (characterized by complexity, uncertainty and ambiguity) it is increasingly being recognized that climate change needs to be addressed with creative and innovative mindsets (Marshall, 2014). It is also being acknowledged that mindfulness and behaviour change offer more informed understandings of how behaviour emerges and how, if appropriated effectively by individuals, teams and organizations, they can support more effective shifts at both the micro level of our daily habits and the macro level of designing and delivering services and interventions. In his influential report 'Transforming behaviour change: beyond nudge and neuromania', Rowson (2011) cites Kegan and Lahey's work on complexity thinking and ways of knowing as being key to understanding how both mindfulness and behavioural insights could shift 'how' we know our world. Rowson suggests that behaviour change, together with mindfulness, are empowering, and that they create a reflective practice which builds the mental capacity that might be effective in designing and implementing effective climate change interventions. He terms this process 'self-awareness in action' and relates it to what Kegan terms 'fourth-order thinking' (Rowson 2011). In a related experiment with taxi drivers in London, Rowson utilizes co-design, behavioural theory and mindful pauses as an approach to help them design systems to create efficient, low-carbon driving behaviours (see Chapter 4 this volume).

The varied body of work outlined in this section demonstrates the growing interest in the connections that exist between mindfulness and the forms of behavioural government associated with neuroliberalism. Ultimately our research is not concerned only with the extent to which mindfulness can facilitate effective forms of neuroliberal government, but the degree to which it can foster forms of neuroliberalism that support the development of psychological capacity and behavioural empowerment at both individual and collective levels.

The mindfulness, decision making and behaviour change intervention (MDBI)

Since 2013, and working with a range of partner organizations including the Welsh government, Ogilvy Mather, WWF and Global Action Plan, our experimental trial of workplace-based mindfulness, behaviour change and decision making training has been designed, refined and delivered. It was developed iteratively in response to feedback and research interviews with participants, and to suit the requirements and timescales of participating organizations.

The number and variety of workplace mindfulness courses is growing. Research studies on mindfulness in the workplace have primarily emphasized the role of mindfulness programmes on staff wellbeing, mental health and stress reduction: tackling problems of sickness absence, 'presenteeism', high staff turnover, depression, and anxiety. Largely, these therapeutic initiatives build in some way on the established status of the aforementioned MBCT and MBSR programmes, which by now have amassed convincing scientific evidence of their effectiveness. The non-therapeutic courses that are gradually being offered in the workplace vary dramatically, with some overlapping in content or orientation with the MBCT/MBSR courses and others that are more 'mindful light'. A standard MBSR course might ask a participant to practise for 45 minutes six times a week, whereas a mindfulness light course may simply ask people to integrate pauses, noticing practices and three-minute breathing spaces into their day. Some are heavily oriented towards increased productivity and effectiveness, others more towards leadership, or (in line with the more 'classic' interventions) wellbeing and stress management. At a recent event to launch the Business Case for Mindfulness at Work, General Electric suggested that their intervention was aimed at making their workforce more 'brain aware'.

The intervention delivered as part of this research was grounded in an understanding of MBSR and MBCT but adapted to include teaching and exploration of behaviour change theory. Both MBCT/SR and MDBI (Mindfulness, Decision Making and Behaviour Change Intervention) begin with an understanding and enquiry into the automatic 'unconscious' mind and its influence on how we interpret and behave in the world. However in the MDBI adaptation the understanding of the unconscious and automatic mind is more directed towards how heuristics affect work-based decision making, team working, organizational behaviours, stakeholder engagement, inclusion and project design and delivery. Both the MBCT and the MDBI include the teaching of formal mindfulness practices such as the body scan and the breath and body meditations. The MDBI follows the guidelines suggested in the programme developed by Mark Williams and Danny Penman in *Finding Peace in a Frantic World* (Williams and Penman, 2011), with participants doing formal practices of 15–20 minutes of meditation five to six times a week while integrating informal mindfulness practices into their everyday life. In MBCT and MBSR the theoretical element is focused implicitly and explicitly on stress and anxiety. This includes developing understandings of the processes and effects of the ruminating mind on mood and an exploration of which experiences improve our wellbeing positively and which ones detract from it. In our adapted MDBI course the frame of understanding is (broadly) on the effects of biases, social norms and context on behaviours and decision making in the participant's specific workplace. In the area of public service delivery, we identified confirmation, optimism, status quo and sunk-cost biases as particular barriers to effective working. The course content was, however, designed to have particular relevance to people who are designing interventions to facilitate behavioural shifts in others. The MDBI also considered how emotions affect our behaviours and decisions. This is a crucial part of understanding how many of our decisions are oriented less by mental rationality and more because they 'feel' right. The course uses mindful awareness in order to increase consciousness of emotional states, and also introduces relevant theories in order to enquire into our understanding of how emotional states affect engagement and decision making.

As the interventions developed they included more one-to-one coaching sessions as well as group teaching. Each group session lasted between one-and-a-half and two hours and included:

- a group check-in (reflecting on experiences of personal practices);
- a mindfulness practice (e.g. body scan, sitting, walking meditation, breath, body, sounds and thoughts meditations);

- pair and group reflection on the practice;
- interactive group learning on relevant behaviour change theory (e.g. exploring habit formation, the nature of System 1 and System 2 thinking and heuristics/biases).

Between sessions, participants were given interactive course material. This included recommendations for practice and reflection at home and work. It also included links to online video and written resources on the neuroliberal topics being covered in the programme. The individual coaching sessions at the beginning, middle and end of the programme helped accelerate learning and ensured its applicability to the working context.

Table 9.1 provides a brief overview of the final version of the programme (delivered at Ogilvy and Mather in the autumn of 2015), showing how the group and individual sessions were structured.

Mindfulness, decision making and behaviour change intervention

In this section we provide an overview of some of the key results and insights that emerged from the different mindfulness and behaviour change interventions that we ran between 2013 and 2015. Given the number of the interventions that we ran, and the fact that these interventions involved over one hundred participants, we are unable to provide a comprehensive account of our results in this chapter. More detailed accounts of our results are, however, available in a series of online reports that we have produced.[2]

Re-inhabiting behaviour: mindfulness, awareness, and behavioural insights

One of the central goals of our interventions was to explore the extent to which mindfulness could provide a practical route to facilitating greater personal awareness of the forms of habitual, unconscious and emotional drivers of behaviour that are the targets of neuroliberal government (see Lilley, 2014; Pykett et al., 2017; Karelaia and Reb, 2014). We surveyed participants at the beginning and end of our programmes in order to consider the impacts that the course had on their awareness of key behavioural insights including habit formation and change, the autopilot functions of the brain, the effects of the surrounding environments on behaviour, the role of emotions in shaping behaviour, mental shortcuts and biases, the impacts of values and belief systems on behaviour and the behavioural impacts of social norms (see Pykett et al., 2016). Our surveys revealed statistically significant increases (at the 95 per cent confidence level) in participants' awareness of key neuroliberal insights between when they commenced the programme and when they completed it. What this survey was unable to show was the extent to which increased awareness of behavioural insights was specifically affected by mindfulness practices.

TABLE 9.1 The MDBI Programme

Lesson	Format	Mindfulness	Behaviour change
Taster	Raisin practice,[a] reflection, questions	Overview of mindfulness	Overview of behaviour change
Coaching	Check-in one-to-one	Introduction of format, expected commitment, and rationale and understanding of ethical standards	Check-in regarding current participant's understanding of behaviour change and relevance to areas of work
Group sessions 1–3	Interactive informal training sessions utilising direct teaching, practices and inquiry	Introduction to basic mindfulness practices	System 1 and 2 thinking, reflective vs automatic response; Introduction to cognitive biases and effects; Introduction to role of emotions in decision making
Individual coaching session and 1-hour group session	Coaching/mentoring style discussion; developing practice. Extending practice into dealing with difficulty in practice	Check-in with experience and progress regarding practices and theoretical understandings of mindfulness; additional tailored coaching to support learning	Tailored support to help apply learning in individual contexts; Consideration of constraints on practice and learning and co-design of on-going practice
Group sessions 5–7	Interactive informal training sessions utilizing direct teaching, practices and inquiry	Development of practices; Mindfulness of body, breath, sound and thought; Mindfulness in movement; Extending length of practice to incorporate breath/body/thoughts	Considering social norms; Choice architectures; Soft infrastructures; Explore relevance to pro-social/environmental behaviours
Individual coaching sessions	Coaching/mentoring-style discussion; Embedding practice; Consolidating new perspective and insight	Co-designing on-going practice plan; Creating commitment devices	Reviewing learning; Identifying ongoing learning; Clarify future goals and support needs

Note:
a This practice involved eating a raisin (or chocolate) mindfully.

In order to assess more directly the impacts of mindfulness training on behavioural learning we conducted a series of in-depth, semi-structured interviews with selected participants on the course. The interviews were concerned not only with the extent to which mindfulness facilitated a greater awareness of behavioural insights, but the particular qualities that were associated with observed forms of new behavioural awareness. In general there was a strong sense that learning and experiencing behavioural insights through mindfulness practices had enhanced participants' awareness of their behavioural tendencies. As one policy-maker in the Welsh Government observed:

> [the course] raises your own awareness of perhaps your own personal prejudices and reactions when dealing with others ... but the thing with civil servants – this is a cliché – is that we are not really supposed to have opinions. But of course we do. We have to have professional opinions, which might not necessarily align with our personal opinions. But I think that [the course] facilitates the ability to do that. Because you have to engage in a form of double-think at times. And a course like this facilitates the ability to be able to think along a different line than the one you might be automatically inclined to fall into. At times, obviously what I am thinking is the obstacle to being able to pursue policy effectively.
>
> *(Welsh Government participant 1, interview, 2014)*

Here we see evidence that combining mindfulness practice with behavioural learning enabled this policy-maker to better acknowledge their prejudices, reactive states and automatic responses. Significantly, it appears that this awareness of both their professional and personal biases enabled them to think about policy situations in new and creative ways.

Another policy-maker in the Welsh Government observed:

> I think there was a logical link there [between mindfulness and neuroliberal insights] in the sense that very often the mindfulness was enabling us as individuals to sort of get a better understanding of the way that all this sort of extra thought, or all these extra thoughts and biases etc. would come into the mind. So I think mindfulness was excellent in almost putting us in a position where we could actually reflect and see what they would be thinking and then it would allow us to understand, to get an understanding about behaviour and so on ...
>
> *(Welsh Government participant 2, interview, 2015)*

The suggestion here is that mindfulness practices facilitated the opportunity to open up a space for neurological reflexivity, or enquiry, into the cognitive and more intuitive drivers of human behaviour (see Chapter 4 in this volume). It appears that mindfulness not only enabled a kind of *bare awareness* of the mental and felt senses of behavioural motivation, but also offered a space of reflection within which lessons could be learned about decision making and how it could be changed. Here mindfulness appeared to function not only as a transitory basis for experiencing behavioural motivation and response more deeply, but also as a context for behavioural enquiry and understanding. This quote reminds us that although mindfulness is often defined as a form of present-centred, non-judgemental awareness, this does not mean that (behavioural) judgement cannot be part of the broader practice of mindfulness. The non-judgemental aspect of mindfulness appears to be an important way of cultivating awareness of cognitive and embodied sensations moment by moment, without being drawn into their direct behavioural influence. This does not, however, mean that mindfulness cannot support more critical thinking about the need for behavioural change outside of the immediate meditative context.

A consistent theme in the interviews we conducted was the assertion that learning about neuroliberal insights in the context of mindfulness tended to move the exercise from being a theoretical endeavour into an experiential activity. Two participants on the programmes offered the following observations:

> What I would say I've personally taken directly from the course … is that they [academics and behaviour change experts] lack the experience of how difficult it is to change behaviour … I think that the mindfulness aspect of the course has perhaps given me more of an insight into behaviour change than the theoretical aspects of it.
>
> *(Welsh Government participant 1, interview, 2014)*

> I think that irrespective of the depth of your understanding or the breadth of your knowledge of behaviour change … there is a tendency if you know it in your head it is very easy to know it in your head and think that it is someone else. Whereas what mindfulness does it forces you to not just know it in your head but to feel it in your gut, and then you go you know actually it is me, if I keep behaving like that this will happen.
>
> *(Welsh Government participant 2, interview, 2015)*

It appears that mindfulness gave behavioural insights a form of personal saliency for the policy-makers we worked with. As a result of actually experiencing the operation of certain behavioural tendencies it also seems that policy-makers were more likely to develop systems of behavioural government that displayed compassion with end-users, and greater sophistication in their approach to judgement and decision making.

Our evidence suggests that mindfulness provides a supportive context for raising awareness of, and enquiry into, the forms of behavioural processes associated with neuroliberalism at a general level. Participants on our programmes suggested, however, that mindfulness could – in contrast to nudges – support a more nuanced and contextually situated framework within which to approach behaviour change. One participant, for example, made the following observation:

> I guess it looks at how you can, both meet in the middle so that you understand how your emotions will guide your decision-making and that we have emotional biases that exist, kind of, permanently and behavioural science shows what general biases we have but mindfulness is strongest in looking at the context and the moods that you're in and so a particular state that you're in.
>
> *(Ogilvy participant 1, interview, 2015)*

The suggestion here appears to be that while the behavioural sciences provide us with generic guidelines that we can use to identify key behavioural biases and tendencies (such as confirmation bias and hyperbolic discounting), mindfulness can enable us to become more aware of how these behaviours are connected to broader emotional states. Mindfulness appears to offer both a context to become more aware of general behavioural inclinations (exhibited by others, but recognized in the self), and the more bespoke, *in situ* moods that may activate or militate against such behavioural patterns. The same participant suggested that the kind of personally calibrated learning associated with mindfulness was like learning your own behavioural language:

> I don't think I've quite got there yet, I think in the last session I tried to explain that my understanding that it's like learning a language, you learn the language about yourself which is helpful so at least you then have a language or an understanding of your own felt senses, which you can then supplant onto other people, so at least you have a language to use, at the moment I don't think I have a language!
>
> *(Ogilvy participant 1, interview, 2015)*

Mindfulness is often associated with the development of states of meta-awareness. But it is interesting to consider the extent to which, when combined with behavioural insights training, it can both enhance awareness of general behavioural traits, while situating the activation and deactivation of such traits within an individual's behavioural tendencies.

What our programme, and related analysis, did not explore was the extent to which mindfulness training could facilitate forms of behaviour change that could actively subvert behavioural biases through forms of behavioural meta-consciousness. Such questions speak directly to debates over the extent to which more-than-rational forms of behaviour are actually 'baked' into the human condition and inevitably escape our regulatory grasp, or whether meaningful neurological reflexivity and self-regulation are possible (see Chapters 1, 3 and 4 in this volume). While our studies do not suggest a definitive answer to these broad questions, our research does indicate that mindfulness-based behavioural learning generates new ways for people to relate to their behaviours. Furthermore, it appears that these new relations offer the opportunity for building more empowering systems of neuroliberal government, which take seriously the suggestion that people have the capacity (if not necessarily the psychological capital) to shape their own behavioural destinies more effectively. As we discuss in greater detail below, it is unlikely that such behavioural capacities will be developed in the absence of broader forms of social transformation, which may themselves be reliant on more mindfully aware ways of being (see Forbes, 2016a).

Behavioural empathy and the relational state

A key aim of our interventions was to consider the impacts that combining mindfulness training with behavioural insights learning had on the ways in which policy-makers actually approached the *delivery* of behavioural initiatives. To these ends we were particularly interested to consider how the framing of neuroliberal insights through mindfulness practice affected how policy-makers sought to change the behaviour of others. While it is clear that embracing more nuanced understanding of the human subject will have an impact on the forms of policy one might design and deliver, it is less obvious how these insights will actually affect the ways in which policy-makers relate to those whose behaviours they wish to change. In the case of the nudge-type policies we have discussed previously in this volume, it appears that understanding the behavioural flaws and emotionally based decision-making vectors of humans has changed the policies that governments deliver, but not necessarily how governments relate to the public. While behaviourally nuanced, many nudge-type policies embody the forms of top-down, expert-driven policies that have been typical of centralized state bureaucracies the world over (although see Hilton, 2015: 41–6 for a discussion of the changing forms of governmental practices that could be associated with nudge policies; also see Chapter 6 in this volume).

Following our interventions it appears that learning about behavioural insights through mindfulness practices tends to stimulate a desire for a more radical change in the nature of behavioural government. One participant expressed this more radical version of change in the following terms:

> [w]e get told that we should act in this way, we should strive for excellence, we should be efficient. You know all of those kinds of mantras come out in terms of a corporate sort of approach. And I just, I do not think people connect with them at all. And I have made myself connect with them … but they want us all to be close, and us all to do x, y and z the same. And it always feels like that. But I just think that as a way of connecting with the vision of an organization, I think there is a lot more in the mindfulness theory that can help us to be better and more sensitive and listen more and be better connected to stakeholders[.]
>
> *[Welsh Government participant 3, interview, 2014]*

It appears that the combination of mindfulness and behavioural insights generated a desire in this participant to both enquire more deeply, and relate more meaningfully with those who are likely to be affected by behavioural government.

This emerging desire to connect to stakeholders in new ways could be related to the forms of acceptance and compassion for self and others that are often seen to emerge around mindfulness practices. It could also, however, be associated with the deeper understanding of the behavioural constraints experienced by humans that are encoded within neuroliberalism. What appears to be clear, however, is that the combination of mindfulness and behavioural insights could be utilized to support the emergence of a new way of approaching behavioural government. This new approach to behavioural government appears to have much in common with Rifkin's (2010) call for a more empathic civilization, in which the human capacity to feel the experiences of others is utilized to shape our moral codes and civil institutions. Our research would indicate that mindfully oriented behavioural insights could provide an important context within which to establish a more general ethos of empathy within systems of neuroliberal government. Furthermore, it could offer a practical route for the reorientation of the bureaucratic self that a more empathetic government would appear to require. Crucially, this is more than just a methodological shift in government (see Hilton, 2015), it is about changing the systems of awareness on which policy-makers rely.

Through interviews with participants on our interventions we were able to get an insight into the way in which the programme had begun to reorient how they related to stakeholders and the public. At one level it appears that the combined training in mindfulness and behavioural insights experienced by participants enabled them to recognize the cognitive barriers that existed to change in their organizations. It also, however, appeared to reorient people in relation to processes of change. As one participant observed:

> We are, you know, as a government bureaucracy we do what we've done all the time, we have reinforcement biases, we put a lot of money into things and then we will stick by them 'til the end and beyond because that's how it was done in the past so that's how we're doing it in the future and a lot of the people at the top of the tree have been there a long time and aren't possibly the most open-minded people when it comes to different ways of doing things.
>
> *(Welsh Government participant 4, interview, 2015)*

Here we see clear recognition emerging of the role of both status quo and sunk-cost biases within the spheres of government. Such biases can, of course, make it very difficult to respond to the behavioural needs and insights that the public may display. The reference made here to the closed-minded nature of government culture is also important, however. This reference is suggestive of a broader mindset towards change, which transcends specific cognitive states. This mindset is, perhaps, indicative of a general sense of unease, fear or habitual suspicion of the new insights into how people and systems operate that new forms of engagement are likely to generate.

Our research suggests that mindfulness provides the opportunity not only to recognize the short-term cognitive biases that may inhibit openness to change, but also to become more aware of individual and institutional reactions to change. Increased awareness of how we relate to new insights (including intrigue, suspicion and/or lack of understanding), and the implications they carry (including existential threats, time and workload increases and a sense of disempowerment), appear to be crucial steps in beginning to reorient our relation to change. It is not that a more mindfully oriented approach to behaviour change would make these forms of negative disposition to the spectre of change disappear. Rather, our work demonstrates that mindfulness may enable us to acknowledge these responses while not allowing them to engulf the valuable perspectives that exposure to new knowledge might generate. More empathetic forms of government would thus appear to rely as much on the mindsets that policy-makers take into processes of engagement as they do on appreciating why bureaucracies find changing course so difficult. This perspective was supported by one civil servant, who observed:

> [y]ou feel 'oh hang on a minute' you know, 'I'm here to, I wanted to do a public service. This is what I want to do'. And I don't think we are sensitive enough to the public and the public's need … What we should be doing is investing in relationships and we should be talking to people, and we should be out there really getting to grips and understanding what people are going through. They are not tangible things that you can put on a desk and show them [managers] what you have done.
>
> *(Welsh Government participant 1, interview, 2014)*

Investing in meaningful relationships with those whose behaviours you hope to change appears to be particularly important to civil servants, who will often be working in policy areas where direct forms of empathy are difficult to generate. As one policy-maker stated:

> It [mindfulness and behaviour change training] enables [you] to be quite flexible and adaptable day-to-day … you do have to turn your hand to a frightening number of types of task, and also I suppose because we are generalists, we move from subject area to subject area, so tomorrow I could in theory be advising on writing a curricula for 14 year olds, apart from having been a 14 year old, what qualifies me to do that, and maybe just being able to use both the mindfulness and behaviour change aspects to approach any subject would be helpful irrespective of the subject you are trying to tackle.
>
> *(Welsh Government participant 4, interview, 2014)*

The implication here is not that mindfulness and behaviour change training can somehow close the empathy gap that may exist between a middle-aged civil servant and a fourteen-year-old school-student. Rather the suggestion is that the combination of mindfulness and behavioural insights training can provide a more open framework of enquiry within which educational policy could be developed.

Changing the ways in which government relates to people's behaviours has significant implications for how we understand the subject positions of civil servants themselves. Talking specifically about the expectations of rationality and objectivity that surround public policy-makers, one civil servant observed:

> Our Permanent Secretary talks about the need for evidence-based decision making, the need to be actually more rational and objective in our decision making is a requirement in the civil service code, we are supposed to be honest, we are supposed to be objective, and actually you can't do that without understanding the emotions and the biases and all that as part of the picture, if you haven't got that feel for the other things you are working in a very narrow zone, which looks terribly logical and actually isn't at all rational … so [this programme is] a means of helping the civil servant to become more objective in the way they are giving advice and as a means of improving our relations with stakeholders as a way of understanding where we are and where they are.
> *(Welsh Government participant 2, interview, 2015)*

Two key points can be derived from these reflections. The first is the tension between attempting to achieve a form of objectivity in policy making when behavioural insights highlight the inherent subjectivity of so much of our everyday lives. The suggestion here is that by mindfully surfacing their biases and subjectivities it may be possible for civil servants to achieve more meaningful and effective forms of objectivity which, rather than denying subjectivity, seek to acknowledge and, potentially, regulate it. The second point relates to how establishing meaningful relationships with stakeholders involves recognizing the varied behavioural motivations and priorities of all groups involved.

Our interviews with participants highlighted consistently the impact that our programme had on their desire to build new types of relationship with stakeholders and the public. This echoes the broader vision of the relational state that was articulated by the Institute for Public Policy Research (see Cooke and Muir, 2012). The relational state is, in part, a response to the New Public Management (hereafter NPM) approaches to government, which have dominated the public sector in states like the UK and USA over the last thirty-five years. NPM is characterized by a command and control approach in the public sector (to be achieved through more rigorous procedures and a pervasive monitoring and audit culture), and the promotion of greater choice and competition in the delivery of public services (achieved largely through market mechanisms and the rise of league tables). Despite making public services more accountable to the people they serve, NPM processes have been heavily criticized for promoting cultures of homogeneity in the policy-making process, a narrow focus on measurable outcomes and a neglect of the importance of human relations (ibid.: 7). According to Cooke and Muir the NPM approach:

> risks reducing the complexity and texture of human experience to a simple number, leading to policies and services that do not address the core of a

problem. Targeting only the outcome forgets that the way people are treated matters too – it underplays the role of relationships in improving people's lives. A purely outcomes-focused mode also involves certain people – invariably elites of various forms – deciding for others what they should choose to value.

(ibid.: 7)

It appears that the combination of mindfulness and neuroliberal insights training surfaced participants' concerns with the NPM system they operate within. While we would expect greater knowledge of behavioural insights to generate critical thinking about the simplistic vision of human behaviour that runs through NPM discourses (which appears to rest upon assumptions of rationality and individualism), it appears that mindfulness has cultivated concern for the treatment of others in the policy-making process.

While there are different visions of the relational state, the Institute for Public Policy Research suggest the need to generate a form of statecraft that rejects dehumanizing traits of NPM (ibid.: 8). At its core the relational state:

is one that sees its role as being less about delivering services to the public and more about working with people to solve shared problems. This means rewiring the state to improve relationships, but particularly the relationship between the state and the people.

(ibid.: 10)

The relational state is characterized by new forms of relations that are open-ended and focus much more on process than on predetermined outcomes. But the relational state is also about facilitating relationship building between citizens. Thus its role is also to protect the time, the places and the institutions that enable people to engage in relational activity (ibid.: 10).

The vision of the relational state embodies many of the core characteristics we would associate with a more progressive, and effective, system of neuroliberal government. It is our contention that a combination of mindfulness and behavioural insight training could offer a practical challenge to the cultures of NPM. As a more relational approach to statecraft, it provides a route to: (1) generating greater awareness and acknowledgement of the limitations of current governmental systems; and (2) developing systems of behavioural government that are more sensitive to contemporary understanding about the nature of human life and relations.

Mindfulness, ethics and neuroliberalism

A final goal of our trial was to explore the extent to which mindfully framed behaviour change learning could support the development of more ethically sensitive and empowering behaviour change policies. A recurrent theme throughout this volume has been to consider the ethical implications that are associated with neuroliberal systems of government. These ethical debates tend to centre on the extent to which related systems of government undermine the autonomy and dignity of those who are subject to its techniques (see Sunstein, 2016). As various chapters in this volume have demonstrated, the ethical implications of neuroliberalism tend to depend on the particular brand of neuroliberalism that is being practised, with some systems exhibiting more manipulative tendencies than others, and some strategies supporting behavioural empowerment more than others. One of our working hypotheses when designing and delivering our intervention was an assumption that mindfulness would support behavioural policy making that was more transparent (and one would assume less manipulative) and more empowering to those who are subject to said policies.

One of the things that we noticed when analyzing the impacts of our trial was that the intervention certainly appeared to raise awareness among participants of the ethical contrast that exists between nudge and mindfulness-based approaches to behaviour change:

> You can obviously help people to change by using the dark arts of persuasion science, where they don't actually know that you are doing anything, or nudge ... [but] you are not being completely honest with people ... whereas mindfulness and linking it with values more I think gives it a more potentially ethical approach.
>
> *(Global Action Plan participant, interview, 2015)*

While mindfulness is linked here to the potential of a more ethical approach to behavioural government, it is instructive to consider what is meant by the term 'ethical'. Many advocates of nudge-based approaches to behaviour change would claim to be ethical to the extent that they are making it easier for people to behave in ways that are in their own best interests and bring clear welfare benefits (Sunstein, 2014; Thaler and Sunstein, 2008). Mindfulness-based behaviour change learning is associated with a different kind of ethical value. It is an ethics that values the ability of people to recognize and determine their own behavioural trajectories and to generate new reflexive capacities. It is, however, important to qualify the ethical potential of mindfulness where its goal is behavioural change. While it may be that mindfulness can support the development of a more liberated and liberating consciousness, it does not necessarily address the structures and system of material and ideological injustice that might limit behavioural capacities, agency and learning in the first place (Forbes, 2016a; 2016b) (see Chapters 4, 5 and 8 in this volume).

Those who participated in the interventions we ran reflected on what they saw as the ethical benefits of a more mindfully oriented approach to behaviour change. One participant for example observed that:

> We could call ourselves post-nudge. So we realize that there are issues of practicality and ethics with nudge and so therefore we are looking at the different things we can do hence obviously then the connections with

mindfulness is a fairly straightforward next step because that gives the possibility of building resilience.

(Welsh Government participant 2, interview, 2015)

But if mindfulness could encourage a kind of post-nudge behaviour change agenda that builds greater personal resilience, certain questions remain. One of the enduring critiques of the contemporary rise of mindfulness is that 'its therapeutic foundation is to comfort, adjust, and accommodate the self within the neoliberal, corporatized, militarized, and individualistic society' (Forbes, 2016a: 2). Care must thus be taken to ensure that mindfully oriented behaviour change initiatives do not simply become therapeutic forms of neuroliberalism, which obfuscate the broader processes and structures that shape and limit human behavioural possibilities (see Chapters 4, 5 and 6 in this volume). The fact that our trials have demonstrated that mindfulness-based behavioural change learning can stimulate a desire to change the ways in which government actually operates and relates to people (see previous section), means that we remain optimistic that mindfulness can offer much more than a therapeutic brand of neuroliberalism which might risk perpetuating individualized notions of neurosis and anxiety. In this vein, David Forbes has recently called for radically oriented ways to 'occupy mindfulness' (2016b). According to Forbes, despite its recent co-option within military, commercial and conformist contexts, mindfulness can be about occupying the self in ways that promote personal development and a more consistent desire to question shared systems of understandings and the structures they promote (ibid.). The results of our mindfulness and behavioural learning interventions indicate that this combination of ideas and practices could help both to facilitate a shift of mindfulness out of narrow therapeutic contexts, and to produce an enhanced ability to situate behaviours within the broader systems from which they emanate.

Beyond these larger ethical debates, a more practical question concerns precisely how mindfulness could provide a more ethically oriented system of behavioural government. It is clear that participants on our behaviour change programmes identified the role that mindfulness played in facilitating personal behavioural empowerment:

> It helps you to understand parts of your mind that you wouldn't otherwise be thinking about, and understanding can't be unethical. It is also very empowering, because it encourages control and calmness. I have certainly found it to be personally very empowering.

(Welsh Government participant 4, interview, 2015)

But the important practical question remains as to precisely how such behavioural capacity building can be delivered at scale. To be behaviourally empowering in any universal way it would appear that large numbers of people would need to be subjected to mindfulness training and behavioural education. We acknowledge that this would be a time-consuming, resource intensive and ultimately unrealistic way of generating widespread behavioural empowerment. Nevertheless we note the existing calls to instigate forms of behavioural learning in schools and the rise of mindfulness within education systems around the world. Furthermore, the particular fusion of mindfulness-based behavioural learning we have outlined in this book could be just one of a series of broader strategies that could contribute to the development of ethically imbued and empowering neuroliberal movements.

Conclusion

In this chapter we have outlined our own practical engagement in emerging neuroliberal practices. The MDBI outlined in this chapter speaks directly to two central themes that have run through this volume. The first is the extent to which neuroliberal insights are necessarily coupled to an understanding of human action that it based on a diminished sense of human character and agency. The second is the question of what types of government are emerging in response to the behavioural insights that are associated with neuroliberalism. In relation to this first question, our research has shown that combining training in neuroliberal insights with mindfulness practices appears to support an enhanced awareness of, and ability to self-regulate, automatic forms of behaviour. This insight validates the work of the Self-Regulation Lab and the Social Brain Centre (see Chapter 4), as well as notions of neuroliberal hacking cultures (see Chapter 8), in their quest to explore ways in which an appreciation of the more-than-rational drivers of human action can provide a basis for human empowerment and neurological reflexivity. The MDBI initiative, does, however, appear to offer a more personalized form of enquiry into the neuroliberal self than is envisaged in the work of the Self-Regulation Lab and the Social Brain Centre. Ultimately, our research reveals that more mindfully oriented approaches to neuroliberalism open up interesting opportunities for conceiving more empowering and ethically sensitive approaches to behavioural government. It appears that the practices of personal enquiry associated with mindfulness can support the development of systems of personal and collective government that seek to deliver enhanced, rather than degraded, forms of human agency. The idea of supporting the development of more empowering forms of behavioural government does, of course, take us back to the discussion of liberalism and freedom addressed in Chapters 4 and 5. It is our contention in this context that it is possible to develop approaches to neuroliberal government that are grounded on notions of liberalism that go far beyond negative understandings of freedom.

In relation to the second question, the MDBI programme has demonstrated that neuroliberal insights are not necessarily tied to the emerging forms of post-bureaucratic, expert-oriented government with which they have become associated (see Chapter 6 in this volume). When framed within the reflexive context of mindfulness meditation, it appears that neuroliberal insights can inspire at least the desire for more empathic styles of government. These empathic styles of behavioural government emphasize forms of enquiry into human behaviour that are based upon new relationships with those subject to neuroliberal interventions. These visions of behavioural government are very different to strands of neuroliberalism that focus on restructuring the architecture of the state: emphasizing as they do the importance of the processes associated with, as opposed to structures of, behavioural government.

The MDBI progamme appears to support the call for more progressively oriented, ethically sensitive and empowering forms of neuroliberalism that we have made consistently throughout this volume. Notwithstanding this, we must acknowledge the limitations of more mindfully oriented approaches to behavioural government. As Forbes (2016a) has pointed out (admittedly in a different context), mindfulness does not necessarily challenge the systems that produce behavioural or social problems in the first place. This limitation is in part a product of the fact that while mindfulness may enhance behavioural awareness it tends to do so in the context of the immediate behavioural environment, and not at the levels of broader social systems and structures (see Whitehead et al., 2016). This speaks directly to our analysis of social practice theory and the broader social and material factors that contribute to behavioural transformation (see Chapter 8). While we acknowledge openly these limitations with the MDBI approach, we remain interested in the potential of more mindfully oriented forms of behavioural enquiry into what it may take to transform the broader behavioural worlds we inhabit.

Notes

1 This mindfulness adaptation is of particular interest to our research as it was viewed with scepticism at the time. Kabat Zinn's MBSR course had begun to develop a significant evidence base and questions were raised whether it should, or could, be changed effectively.

2 See https://changingbehaviours.wordpress.com/2016/02/10/mindfulness-and-decision-making/; https://changingbehaviours.files.wordpress.com/2014/10/mbceppreport-1.pdf; https://changingbehaviours.wordpress.com/2016/01/20/mind-the-gap/; https://changing behaviours.wordpress.com/2016/06/10/mindfulness-and-behaviour-change-exploring-the-connections/ [accessed 15 April 2017].

BIBLIOGRAPHY

Abi-Rached, J. M. and Rose, N. (2010) 'The birth of the neuromolecular gaze', *History of the Human Sciences* 23(1): 11–36.

Adriaanse, M. A., Weijers, J., De Ridder, D. T. D., De Witt Huberts, J. and Evers, C. (2014) 'Confabulating reasons for behaving bad: the psychological consequences of unconsciously activated behaviour that violates one's standards', *European Journal of Social Psychology* 44(3): 255–66.

Akerlof, G. A. and Schiller, R. J. (2009) *Animal Spirits: How Human Psychology Drives the Economy and Why It Matters for Global Capitalism*. Princeton, NJ, Princeton University Press.

Allen, J. (2006) 'Ambient power: Berlin's Potsdamer Platz and the seductive logic of public spaces', *Urban Studies* 43(2): 441–55.

Amin, A. and Thrift, N. (2013) *The Arts of the Political: New Openings for the Left*. London, Duke University Press.

Anderson, B. (2014) *Encountering Affect: Capacities, Apparatuses, Conditions*. Farnham, Ashgate.

Barry, A. (2013) *Material Politics: Disputes Along the Pipeline*. Oxford, Blackwell.

Bason, C. (2014) *Design for Policy*. Farnham, Gower Publishing.

Becker, G. (1962) 'Irrational behavior and economic theory', *Journal of Political Economy* LXX: 1–13.

Behavioural Architects, The (2016) *Our Mission*, www.thebearchitects.com/who-are-we/our-mission/ [accessed 20 February 2017].

Behavioural Insights Team (2012) *Applying Behavioural Insights to Reduce Fraud, Error and Debt*. London, Cabinet Office.

Berlin, I. (1958) *Two Concepts of Liberty*. Oxford, Clarendon Press.

Bishop, S. R., Lau, M., Shapiro, S., Carlson, L., Anderson, N. D., Carmody, J. and Segal, Z. V. (2004) 'Mindfulness: a proposed operational definition', *Clinical Psychology: Science and Practice* 11(3): 230–41.

Biswas, A. K. and Hartley, K. (2015) 'The rise of Asia's think-tanks', *Straits Times*, 28 September, www.straitstimes.com/opinion/the-rise-of-asias-think-tanks [accessed 23 February 2017].

BIU (2016) *Behavioural Insights Unit: Update Report 2016*. Sydney, New South Wales Government.

Bourdieu, P. (1996) *The State Nobility: Elite Schools in the Field of Power.* Oxford, Polity Press.

Bratsis, P. (2006) *Everyday Life and the State.* Boulder, CO, Paradigm.

Breckton, J. (2015) 'Finland's political parties embrace experimentalism', *Nesta,* www.nesta. org.uk/blog/finlands-political-parties-embrace-experimentalism [accessed 19 July 2016].

Brenner, N. (2009) 'What is critical urban theory?' *City* 13(2–3): 198–208.

Burgin, A. (2012) *The Great Persuasion: Reinventing Free Markets Since the Depression.* Cambridge, MA, Harvard University Press.

Cabinet Office (2015) *The Cross-Government Trial Advice Panel.* London, Cabinet Office.

Camerer, C. F. (2007) 'Neuroeconomics: using neuroscience to make economic predictions', *Economic Journal* 117: 26–42.

Chandy, K. T., Balakrishman, T. R., Kantawalla, J. M., Mohan, K., Sen, N. P., Gupta, S. S. and Srivastva, S. (1965) 'Proposals for family planning promotion: a marketing plan', *Studies in Family Planning* 1(6): 7–12.

Christiansen, J. and Bunt, L. (2012) *Innovation in Policy: Allowing for Creativity, Social Complexity and Uncertainty in Public Governance.* London, Nesta.

Cialdini, R. B. (2007) [1984] *Influence. The Psychology of Persuasion.* New York, NY, HarperCollins Publishers.

Clarke, J. (2008) 'Living with/in and without neo-liberalism', *Focaal* 51: 135–47.

Closs Stephens, A. (2016) 'The affective atmospheres of nationalism', *Cultural Geographies* 23(2): 181–98.

Cohen, D. (2014) *Homo Economicus: The (Lost) Prophet of Modern Times.* Cambridge, Polity Press.

Conly, S. (2012) *Against Autonomy: Justifying Coercive Paternalism.* Cambridge, Cambridge University Press.

Consensus (2017) *Overview and Aims,* www.consensus.ie/wp/overview-aims/ [accessed 23 February 2017].

Cooke, G. and Muir, R. (2012) *The Relational State: How Recognizing the Importance of Human Relations Could Revolutionize the Role of the State.* London, IPPR.

Corbridge, S., Williams, G., Srivastava, M. and Véron, R. (2005) *Seeing the State: Governance and Governmentality in India.* Cambridge, Cambridge University Press.

Corporate Culture (2015) *Human: New Insights into the Human Operating System.* London, Corporate Culture.

Council for the Environment and Infrastructure (2014) *Influencing Behaviour: More Effective Environmental Policy through Insight into Human Behaviour,* http://en.rli.nl/sites/default/ files/rli201402influencingbehaviour.pdf [accessed 9 June 2015].

Damasio, A. (1994) *Descartes' Error: Emotion, Reason, and the Human Brain.* London, Picador.

Darnton, A. and Evans, D. (2013) *Influencing Behaviours: A Technical Guide to the ISM Tool.* Edinburgh, Scottish Government.

Davies, W. (2014) *The Limits of Neoliberalism: Authority, Sovereignty and the Logic of Competition.* London, Sage.

Davies, A. and Doyle, R. (2015) 'Transforming household consumption: from backcasting to Homelabs experiment', *Annals of the Association of American Geographers* 105 (2): 425–36.

Davies, A., Lavelle, M. J. and Doyle, R. (2015) *Washing Homelabs: Longitudinal Impact Study High Level Findings.* Dublin, Consensus, www.consensus.ie/wp/wpcontent/uploads/2013/10/ Washing-Labs-report_Nov_4_2015.pdf [accessed 18 January 2017].

Davies, W. (2014) *The Limits of Neoliberalism: Authority, Sovereignty, and the Logics of Competition.* London, Sage.

Demos (2008) *The Politics of Public Behaviour.* London, Demos.

De Ridder, D. T. D., De Vet, E., Stok, F. M., Adriaanse, M. A. and De Wit, J. B. F. (2013) 'Obesity, overconsumption and self-regulation failure: the unsung role of eating appropriateness standards', *Health Psychology Review,* 7(2): 146–65.

De Tocqueville, A. (2002 [1835]) *Democracy in America*, edited and translated by H. Mansfield and D. Winthrop. Chicago, Chicago University Press.

Deutsche Bank Research (2010) *Homo economicus – or more like Homer Simpson*. Frankfurt, Deutsche Bank.

Dobson, A. (2014) 'Nudging is anti-democratic and anti-political', *The Guardian*, 2 May, www.theguardian.com/politics/2014/may/02/nudging-anti-democratic-anti-political?CMP=twt_gu [accessed 12 September 2014].

Dolan, A., Hallsworth, M., Halpern, D., King, D. and Vlaev, I. (2010) *Mindspace: Influencing Behaviour through Public Policy*. London, Cabinet Office and Institute for Government.

Domehl, L. (2014) *The Formula: How Algorithms Solve All Our Problems… and Create More*. London, W.H. Allen.

Du Plessis, E. (2011) *The Branded Mind: What Neuroscience Really Tells Us about the Puzzle of the Brain and the Brand*. London, Kogan Page.

Dutch News (2014) '"Booking.com does mislead with 'one room left' claims", ad body says', www.dutchnews.nl/news/archives/2014/07/bookingcom_does_mislead_with_o/ [accessed 12 September 2016].

Dworkin, G. (1988) *The Theory and Practice of Autonomy*. Cambridge, Cambridge University Press.

Economist, The (2009) 'Herbert Simon', *The Economist*, 20 March, www.economist.com/node/13350892 [accessed 15 April 2017].

Economist, The (2011) 'The thinking capital', Bagehot Blog, *The Economist*, 8 April, www.economist.com/node/18618772 [accessed 29 April 2011].

Erta, K., Hunt, S., Iscenko, Z. and Brambley, W. (2013) *Applying Behavioural Economics at the Financial Conduct Authority*. London, Financial Conduct Authority.

Eyben, R. and Roche, C. (2013) 'The political implications of evidence-based approaches', http://blogs.worldbank.org/publicsphere/political-implications-evidence-based-approaches-aka-start-week-s-wonkwar-results-agenda [accessed 4 January 2017]

Fitzgerald, D. and Callard, F. (2015) 'Social science and neuroscience beyond interdisciplinarity: experimental entanglement', *Theory, Culture & Society* 31(1): 3–32.

Forbes, D. (2016a) 'Modes of mindfulness: prophetic critique and integral emergence', *Mindfulness* 7(6): 1256.

Forbes, D. (2016b) 'Occupy mindfulness', http://beamsandstruts.com/articles/item/982-occupy-mindfulness [accessed 9 November 2016].

Foucault, M. (2008 [2004]) *The Birth of Biopolitics: Lectures at the Collège de France 1978–79*, transl. G. Burchell. Basingstoke, Palgrave Macmillan.

Foucault, M. (2007 [2004]) *Security, Territory, Population – Lectures at the Collège De France 1977–1978*, transl. G. Burchell. New York, Palgrave Macmillan.

Freeman, R. (2009) 'What is translation?' *Evidence and Policy* 5(4): 429–47.

Friedman, M. (2002 [1982]) *Capitalism and Freedom*. Chicago, University of Chicago Press.

Furedi, F. (2011) *On Tolerance: A Defence of Moral Independence*. London, Continuum.

Futerra (2007) *Words That Sell: How the Public Talks about Sustainability*. London, Futerra.

Galley, A., Gold, J. and Johal, S. (2013) *Public Service Transformed: Harnessing the Power of Behavioural Insights*. Toronto, University of Toronto Press.

Giddens, A. (1985) *A Contemporary Critique of Historical Materialism vol. 2, The Nation-state and Violence*. Cambridge, Polity Press.

Giddens, A. (1998) *The Third Way: The Renewal of Social Democracy*. Cambridge, Polity Press.

Gigerenzer, G. (2000) *Adaptive Thinking: Rationality in the Real World*. New York, Oxford University Press.

Gladwell, M. (2016) 'Daniel Ellsberg, Edward Snowden, and the modern whistle-blower', *New Yorker*, www.newyorker.com/magazine/2016/12/19/daniel-ellsberg-edward-snowden-and-the-modern-whistle-blower [accessed 24 February 2017].

Good, D. J., Lyddy, C. J., Glomb, T. M., Bono, J. E., Brown, K. W., Duffy, M. K., Baer, R. A., Brewer, J. A. and Lazar, S. W. (2015) 'Contemplating mindfulness at work: an integrative review', *Journal of Management* 42(1): 114–42.

Grist, M. (2010) *Changing the Subject: How New Ways of Thinking about Human Behaviour Might Change Politics, Policy and Practice.* London, RSA.

Grist, M. (2011) *Steer: Mastering Our Behaviour Through Instinct, Environment and Reason* London, RSA.

Groves, C., Henwood, K., Shirani, F., Butler, C., Parkhill, K. and Pidgeon, N. (2016) 'Invested in unsustainability? On the psychosocial patterning of engagement in practices', *Environmental Values* 25(3): 309–28.

Guardian, The (2009) 'Tory-controlled borough of Barnet adopts budget airline model', *Guardian*, 27 August, www.theguardian.com/politics/2009/aug/27/tory-borough-barnet-budget-airline [accessed 7 July 2015].

Hafenbrack, A. C., Kinias, Z. and Barsade, S. G. (2014) 'Debiasing the mind through meditation mindfulness and the sunk-cost bias', *Psychological Science* 25(2): 369–76.

Halpern, D., Bates, C., Beales, G. and Heathfield, A. (2004) *Personal Responsibility and Changing Behaviour: The State of Knowledge and Its Implications for Public Policy.* London, Cabinet Office.

Halpern, D., Bates, C., Mulgan, G., Aldridge, S., Beales, G., and Heathfield, A. (2004) *Personal Responsibility and Changing Behaviour: The State of Knowledge and Its Implications for Public Policy.* London, Cabinet Office.

Halpern, D. (2015) *Inside the Nudge Unit: How Small Changes and Make a Big Difference.* London, W.H. Allen.

Hansen, T. B. and Stepputat, F. (eds) (2001) *States of Imagination: Ethnographic Explorations of the Postcolonial State.* Durham, NC, Duke University Press.

Harman, G. (2011) *Heidegger Explained: From Phenomenology to Thing.* Chicago, Open Court.

Harvey, D. (2005) *A Brief History of Neoliberalism.* Oxford, Oxford University Press.

Hayek, F. A. (1944) *The Road to Serfdom.* London, Routledge.

Haynes, L., Service, O., Goldacre, B. and Torgerson, D. (2012) *Test, Learn, Adapt: Developing Public Policy with Randomized Controlled Trials.* London, Behavioural Insights Team/Cabinet Office.

Hilton, S. (with Bade, S. and Bade, J.) (2015) *More Human: Designing a World Where People Come First.* London, W. H. Allen.

Huxley, M. (2006) 'Spatial rationalities: order, environment, evolution and government', *Social and Cultural Geography* 7(5): 771–87.

Independent (2010) 'First Obama, now Cameron embraces "nudge theory"', 12 August.

IPPR (2007) *States of Reason: Freedom, Responsibility and the Governing of Behaviour Change.* London, Institute of Public and Policy Research.

Irwin, A. (2006) 'The politics of talk coming to terms with the "new" scientific governance', *Social Studies of Science* 36(2): 299–320.

ISS (Council for Social Development) (2014) 'Resisting temptation: limits to the government's influence on behaviour', The Hague, ISS (council for Social Development), www.iss.nl/news_events/iss_news/detail/article/61233-irene-van-staveren-presents-council-for-social-development-report-to-minister-schippers/ [accessed 9 June 2015].

John, P. (2013) 'Policy entrepreneurship in UK central government: the behavioural insights team and the use of randomized controlled trials', *Public Policy and Administration* 29(3): 257–67.

John, P., Cotterill, S., Moseley, A., Richardson, L., Smith, G., Stoker, G. and Wales, C. (2011) *Nudge, Nudge, Think, Think.* London, Bloomsbury.

Joint Research Centre, European Union (2016) *Behavioural Insights Applied to Policy: The Netherlands Country Overview*, https://ec.europa.eu/jrc/sites/jrcsh/files/jrc-biap2016-netherlands_en.pdf [accessed 5 January 2017].

Jones, R. (2008) *People/States/Territories: The Political Geographies of British State Transformation*. Oxford, Blackwell.

Jones, R. and Whitehead, M. (2017) 'Politics done like science: critical perspectives on psychological governance and the experimental state', Mimeograph.

Jones, R., Pykett, J. and Whitehead, M. (2011) 'Governing temptation: changing behaviour in an age of libertarian paternalism', *Progress in Human Geography* 35(4): 483–501.

Jones, R., Pykett, J. and Whitehead, M. (2013) *Changing Behaviours: On the Rise of Psychological State*. Cheltenham, Edward Elgar.

Jones, R., Pykett, J. and Whitehead, M. (2014) 'The geographies of policy translation: how nudge became the default policy option', *Geoforum* 32(1): 54–69.

Kahneman, D. (2011) *Thinking, Fast and Slow*. London, Penguin.

Kahneman, D. Slavic, P. and Tversky, A. (eds) (1982) *Judgment under Uncertainty: Heuristics and Biases*. Cambridge, Cambridge University Press.

Karelaia, N. and Reb, J. (2014) 'Improving decision making through mindfulness', SSRN Scholarly Paper ID 2443808. Rochester, NY, Social Science Research Network, http://papers.ssrn.com/abstract=2443808 [accessed 24 February 2017].

Kelman, S. (2005) *Unleashing Change: A Study of Organizational Renewal in Government*. Washington, DC, Brookings Institution.

Keynes, J. M. (1936). *The General Theory of Employment, Interest and Money*. London, Macmillan.

Klein, N. (2007) *The Shock Doctrine: The Rise of Disaster Capitalism*. London, Penguin.

Kings Fund (2008) *Commissioning and Behaviour Change: Kicking Bad Habits, Final Report*. London, Kings Fund.

Kotler, P. and Zaltman, G. (1971) 'Social marketing: an approach to planned social change', *Journal of Marketing* 35(3): 3–12.

Latour, B. (1993) *We Have Never Been Modern*, transl. C. Porter. Cambridge, MA, Harvard University Press.

Latour, B. (2005). *Reassembling the Social: An Introduction to Actor-Network-Theory*. Oxford. Oxford University Press.

Le Grand, J. and New, B. (2015) *Government Paternalism. Nanny State or Helpful Friend?* Oxford, Princeton University Press.

Lee, B. (2016) 'A mindful path to a compassionate cultural diversity', Chapter 11 in M. Chapman Clarke, *Mindfulness in the Workplace: An Evidence Based Approach to Improving Well Being and Maximising Performance*. London, Kogan Page.

Leggett, W. (2014) 'The politics of behaviour change: nudge, neoliberalism, and the state', *Policy and Politics* 42(1): 3–19.

Levitt, S. D. and Dubner, S. J. (2007) *Freakonomics: A Rogue Economist Explores the Hidden Side of Everything*. London, Penguin.

Lewis, M. (2016) *The Undoing Project*. London, Penguin.

Lezaun, J. and Calvillo, N. (2013) 'In the political laboratory: Kurt Lewin's Atmospheres', *Journal of Cultural Economy* 7(4): 434–57.

Lilley, R., Whitehead, M., Howell, R., Jones, R. and Pykett, J. (2016) *Mindfulness, Behaviour Change and Engagement in Public Policy – Evaluation Report 2*. Aberystwyth, Aberystwyth University.

Lindstrom, M. (2005) *Brand Sense: Sensory Secrets behind the Stuff We Buy*. New York, Free Press.

Lindstrom, M. (2008) *Buy-ology: How Everything We Believe about Why We Buy Is Wrong*. New York, Random House.

Lockton, D. (2017) 'Design with intent: the book', http://designwithintent.co.uk/the-book/ [accessed 23 January 2017].

London Collaborative (2009) *Incentive Cards and Behaviour Change in London*. London, London Collaborative.

Low, D. (Ed.) (2011) *Behavioural Economics. Policy Design: Examples from Singapore*. Singapore, World Scientific Publishing.

Lueke, A. and Gibson, B. (2015) 'Mindfulness meditation reduces implicit age and race bias the role of reduced automaticity of responding', *Social Psychological and Personality Science* 6(3): 284–91. doi:10.1177/1948550614559651.

Lunn, P. (2014) *Regulatory Policy and Behavioural Economics*. Paris, OECD Publishing.

MacLeod, R. (ed) (1988) *Government and Expertise: Specialists, Administrators and Professionals, 1860–1919*. Cambridge, Cambridge University Press.

McClure, S. M., Laibson, D. I., Loewenstein, G. and Cohen, J. D. (2004) 'Separate neural system value immediate and delayed monetary rewards', *Science* 306 : 503–7.

McConnell, F. (2016) *Rehearsing the State: The Political Practices of the Tibetan Government-in-Exile*. Oxford, Blackwell.

McGann, J. G. (2016) 'Special report on top think tanks in Asia by country', TTCSP Global Go To Think Tank Index Reports. Paper 11, http://repository.upenn.edu/think_tanks/11 [accessed 31 March 2017].

Mcgee, R. (n.d.) 'Unconscious bias and mindfulness', http://greatergood.berkeley.edu/article/item/how_mindfulness_can_defeat_racial_bias [accessed 31 March 2017].

Marshall, G. (2014) *Don't Even Think about It: Why Are Brains Are Wired to Ignore Climate Change*. New York, Bloomsbury.

Mettler, S. (2011) *The Submerged State: How Invisible Government Policies Undermine American Democracy*. Chicago, IL, University of Chicago Press.

Mill, J. S. (1985 [1859]) *On Liberty*. Penguin Books, London.

Minton, A. (2009) *Ground Control: Fear and Happiness in the Twenty-First Century*. London, Penguin.

Mirowski, P. and Plehwe, D. (2009) *The Road from Mont Pèlerin: The Making of the Neoliberal Thought Collective*. Cambridge, MA, Harvard University Press.

Mitchell, T. (2006) [1999] 'Society, economy and the state effect', in A. Sharma and A. Gupta (eds) *The Anthropology of the State: A Reader*. Oxford, Blackwell, pp. 169–86.

Molotch, H. (1976) 'The city as a growth machine: toward a political economy of place', *American Journal of Sociology*, 82(2): 309–32.

Monbiot, G. (2016) 'Neoliberalism: the ideology at the root of our problems', *The Guardian*, 15 April.

Mukerji, C. (2015) *Impossible Engineering: Technology and Territoriality on the Canal du Midi*. Princeton, NJ, Princeton University Press.

Mullainathan, S. and Shafir, E. (2013) *Scarcity: Why Having Too Little Means so Much*. New York, Times Books.

Muschamp, H. (1998) 'Student Center as mall and visionary jukebox', *New York Times*, February.

National Consumer Council (with the National Social Marketing Centre) (2006) *It's Our Health: Realizing the Potential of Effective Social Marketing*. London, National Social Marketing Centre.

NEF (2005) *Behavioural Economics: Seven Principles for Policy-makers*. London, New Economics Foundation.

Nolan, J. L. Jnr (1998) *The Therapeutic State: Justifying Government at Century's End*. New York University Press, New York.

Nooteboom, B. (2000) *Learning and Innovation in Organizations and Economies*. Oxford University Press, Oxford.

Norman, D. (2002) *The Design of Everyday Things*. New York, Basic Books.

Olson, P. (2015) 'A massive social experiment on you is underway, and you will love it', *Forbes*, www.forbes.com/sites/parmyolson/2015/01/21/jawbone-guinea-pig-economy/#79a281655831 [accessed 31 March 2017].

Osman, M. (2014) *Future-Minded: The Psychology of Agency and Control*, Basingstoke, Palgrave Macmillan.

Packard, V. (1957) *The Hidden Persuaders*. London, Longmans.

Painter, J. (2006) 'Prosaic geographies of stateness', *Political Geography* 25(7): 752–74.

Pallet, H. (2012) 'The (re)publics of science: changing policy and participation', 3S Working Paper, Norwich, Science, Society and Sustainability Research Group.

Peck, J. (2010) *Constructions of Neoliberal Reason*. Oxford, Oxford University Press.

Pittick, R., Baeck, P. and Colligan, P. (2014) *iteams: The Teams and Funds Making Innovation Happen in Governments Around the World*. London, Nesta and Bloomberg Philanthropies.

Pykett, J., Lilley, R., Whitehead, M. and Howell, R. (2016) *Mindfulness, Behaviour Change, and Decision Making: An Experimental Trial*. Birmingham, University of Birmingham.

Pykett, J., Howell, R., Lilley, R., Jones, R. and Whitehead, M. (2017) 'Governing mindfully: shaping policy makers' emotional engagements with behaviour change', in E. Jupp, J. Pykett and F. Smith (eds) *Emotional States. Sites and Spaces of Affective Governance*. London, Routledge.

Quigley, M. (2014) 'Are health nudges coercive?' *Monash Bioethics Review*, 32:141–58.

Rhodes, R. (2011) *Everyday Life in British Government*. Oxford, Oxford University Press.

Rifkin, J. (2010) *The Empathic Civilization: The Race to Global Consciousness in a World in Crisis*. New York, J.P. Tarcher/Penguin.

Rip, A. and Kemp, R. (1998) 'Technological change', in S. Rayner and E. L. Malone (eds) *Human Choice and Climate Change: Resources and Technology*. Columbus, OH, Batelle Press.

RMO (2014) 'De verleiding weerstaan. Grenzen aan beïnvloeding van gedrag door de overheid' (Resisting temptation: limits to the government's attempts to change behaviour). The Hague, Raad voor Maatshappelijke Ontwikkeling.

Rose, N. (1998) *Inventing Ourselves: Psychology, Power and Personhood*. Cambridge University Press, Cambridge.

Rose, N. and Abi-Rached, J. M. (2013) *Neuro: The New Brain Sciences and the Management of the Brain*. Princeton, NJ, Princeton University Press.

Rowson, J. (2011) 'Transforming behaviour change: beyond nudge and neuromania', London, Royal Society for the Encouragement of Arts, Manufactures and Commerce.

Rowson, J. and Young, J. (2011) *Cabbies, Costs and Climate Change: An Engaged Approach to Fuel Efficient Behaviours*. London, RSA.

Runciman, D. (2014) '"Think like a freak", by Steven D. Levitt and Stephen J. Dubner: a review', The *Guardian*, https://www.theguardian.com/books/2014/may/15/think-like-a-freak-freakonomics-levitt-dubner-review [accessed 31 March 2017].

Sanders, M. (2014) quoted in Rutter, T. 'What next for the nudge unit?', *The Guardian*, 1 June, https://www.theguardian.com/public-leaders-network/2014/jun/01/nudge-unit-behavioural-insights-team-conference [accessed 19 July 2016].

SBST (2015) *Social and Behavioural Sciences Team: Annual Report*. Washington, DC, SBST, https://sbst.gov/download/2015%20SBST%20Annual%20Report.pdf [accessed 25 April 2017].

SBST (2016) *Social and Behavioural Sciences Team Annual Report*, Washington, DC, SBST, https://sbst.gov/download/2016%20SBST%20Annual%20Report.pdf [accessed 25 April 2017].

Schrauwers, A. (2011) 'A genealogy of corporate governmentality in the realm of the "merchant-king": the Netherlands Trading Company and the management of Dutch paupers', *Economy and Society* 40(3): 373–98.

Sen, A. (1993) 'Capability and well-being', in M. Nussbaum and A. Sen (eds) *The Quality of Life*. Oxford, Oxford University Press, pp. 30–53.

Sennett, R. (1998) *The Corrosion of Character: The Personal Consequences of Work in the New Capitalism*. New York, W.W. Norton.

Sent, E.-M. (2004) 'Behavioural economics: how psychology made its (limited) way back into economics', *History of Political Economy* 36(4): 735–60.

Service, O., Hallsworth, M., Halpern, D., Algate, F., Gallagher, R., Nguyen, S., Ruda, S., Sanders, M., Pelenur, M., Gyani, A., Harper, H., Reinhard, J. and Kirkman, E. (2014) *EAST: Four Simple Ways to Apply Behavioural Insights*. London, Cabinet Office and Nesta.

Shafir, E. ed. (2013) *The Behavioural Foundations of Public Policy*. Princeton, NJ, Princeton University Press.

Shove, E. (2003) *Comfort, Cleanliness and Convenience: The Social Organization of Normality*. Oxford, Berg.

Shove, E. (2010) 'Beyond the ABC: climate change policy and theories of social change', *Environment and Planning A* 42(6): 1273–85.

Sifry, M. L. (2014) 'Why Facebook's "voter megaphone" is the real manipulation to worry about', *Techpresident*, 3 July, http://techpresident.com/news/25165/why-facebooks-voter-megaphone-real-manipulation-worry-about [accessed 31 March 2017].

Simon, H. A. (1957) *Models of Man: Social and Rational*. London, John Wiley & Sons.

Simon, H. A. (1991) *Models of My Life*. New York, Basic Books.

Stone, D. (1996) *Capturing the Political Imagination. Think Tanks and the Policy Process*. London, Frank Cass.

Stone, D. and Denham, A. (eds) (2004) *Think Tank Traditions: Policy Research and the Politics of Ideas*. Manchester, Manchester University Press.

Sunder-Rajan, K. (2007) 'Experimental values: Indian clinical trials and surplus health', *New Left Review* 45(May–June): 67–88.

Sunder-Rajan, K. (2010) 'The experimental machinery of global clinical trials: case studies from India', in A. Ong and N. Chen (eds) *Asian Biotech: Ethics and Communities of Fate*. Durham, NC, Duke University Press, pp. 55–80.

Sunder-Rajan, K. (2011) 'Two tales of genomics: capital, epistemology, and global constitutions of the biomedical subject', in S. Jasanoff (ed) *Reframing Rights: Bioconstitutionalism in the Genetic Age*. Boston, MA, MIT Press, pp. 193–216.

Sunstein, C. (2013) *Simpler: The Future of Government*. New York, Simon & Schuster.

Sunstein, C. (2014) *Why Nudge: The Politics of Libertarian Paternalism*. New Haven, CT, Yale University Press.

Sunstein, C. (2015) *Choosing Not to Choose: Understanding the Value of Choice*. Oxford, Oxford University Press.

Sunstein, C. (2016) *The Ethics of Influence: Government in the Age of Behavioural Science*. Cambridge, Cambridge University Press.

SuslabNWE (2014) *SuslabNWE: Open Innovation Integration Co-Creation Living and Testing*. SuslabNWE, http://docplayer.net/12473782-Open-innovation-integration-co-creation-living-and-testing-sustainable-labs-north-west-europe.html [accessed 15 April 2015].

Tallis, R. (2011) *Aping Mankind: Neuromania, Darwinitis and the Misrepresentation of Humanity*. Durham, Acuman.

Taussig, M. (1997) *The Magic of the State*. New York, Routledge.

Taylor, M. (2009) 'Left brain, right brain', *Prospect*, 23 September.

Thaler, R. (2015) *Misbehaving: The Making of Behavioural Economics*. London, Penguin.

Thaler, R. H. and Sunstein, C. R. (2008) *Nudge: Improving Decisions about Health, Wealth and Happiness*. London, Yale University Press.

Thrift, N. J. (2004) 'Intensities of feeling: towards the spatial politics of affect', *Geografiska Annaler* 86B: 57–78.

Tufekci, Z. (2014) 'Facebook and engineering the public: it's not what's published (or not), but what's done', *The Message*, 29 June, https://medium.com/message/engineering-the-public-289c91390225 [accessed 31 March 2017].

Unilever (n.d.) *Project Sunlight: Inspiring Sustainable Living*. Unilever, https://www.unilever.com/Images/unileverprojectsunlight-inspiringsustainablelivingreport_tcm244-417252_en.pdf [accessed 26 April 2017].

Van Bavel, R., Herrmann, B., Esposito, G. and Proestakis, G. (2013) *Applying Behavioural Sciences to EU Policy-making*. Luxemburg, European Commission.

Weber, M. (1947) *The Theory of Economic and Social Organization*. London, Free Press.

Weber, M. (1991) *From Max Weber: Essays in Sociology*, edited by H. H. Gerth and C. W. Mills. London, Routledge.

Wendel, S. (2013) *Design for Behaviour Change: Applying Psychology and Behavioural Economics*. Sebastopol, CA, O'Reilly Media.

What Works Network (2014) *What Works? Evidence for Decision Makers*. London, What Works Network.

White, M. D. (2013) *The Manipulation of Choice*. New York, Palgrave Macmillan.

Whitehead, M. 2003. '"In the shadow of hierarchy": meta-governance, policy reform and urban regeneration in the West Midlands', *Area* 35(1): 6–14.

Whitehead, M., Jones, R. and Pykett, J. (2011) 'Governing irrationality, or a more-than-rational government: reflections on the re-scientization of decision-making in British public policy', *Environment and Planning A* 43(12): 2819–37.

Whitehead, M., Howell, R., Jones, R., Lilley, R. and Pykett, J. (2014) *Nudging All Over the World: Assessing the Global Impact of the Behavioural Sciences on Public Policy*, http://changingbehaviours.wordpress.com/2014/09/05/nudging-all-over-the-world-the-final-report/ [accessed 11 November 2014].

Whitehead, M., Howell, R., Jones, R., Lilley, R. and Pykett, J. (2014) *Nudging All Over the World: Assessing the Impacts of the Behavioural Sciences on Public Policy*. Aberystwyth, ESRC.

Whitehead, M., Lilley, R., Howell, R., Jones, R. and Pykett, J. (2016) '(Re)Inhabiting awareness: geography and mindfulness', *Social and Cultural Geography* 17(4): 553–73.

White House (2015) Executive Order – Using Behavioral Science Insights to Better Serve the American People, https://obamawhitehouse.archives.gov/the-press-office/2015/09/15/executive-order-using-behavioral-science-insights-better-serve-american [accessed 25 April 2017].

Wilby, P. (2010) 'The kindly words of Nudge are Cameron's ideal veneer', *The Guardian*, https://www.theguardian.com/commentisfree/2010/aug/15/nudge-cameron-veneer-thaler-dogma [accessed 2 February 2017].

Williams, M. G. and Kabat-Zinn, J. (eds) (2013) *Mindfulness: Diverse Perspectices on Its Meaning, Origins and Application*. Abingdon, Routledge.

Williams, M. and Penman, D. (2011) *Mindfulness: A Practical Guide to Finding Peace in a Frantic World*. London, Piatkus.

Williams, M., Teasdale, J., Segal, Z. and Kabat-Zinn, J. (2007) *The Mindful Way Through Depression: Freeing Yourself from Chronic Unhappiness*. New York, Guildford Press.

World Bank (2015) *World Development Report 2015: Mind, Society and Behaviour*. Washington, DC, World Bank.

METHODOLOGICAL APPENDIX

The research recounted in this project was based upon three inter-related research projects. The first was funded by the Leverhulme Trust (*The Time-Spaces of Soft Paternalism in the UK:* F/00 424/L) and ran between 2008 and 2011. This project focused upon the impacts of the behavioural and psychological sciences on public policy in the UK (with a particular focus on environmental, financial and health-related policies). The second grant was funded by the UK Government's Economic and Social Research Council (*Negotiating Neuroliberalism: Changing Behaviours, Values, and Beliefs*: ES/L003082/1) and ran from 2013 to 2015. This project explored critically the emerging impacts of the behavioural sciences on public policy in governments and organizations around the world. The third grant was an Economic and Social Research Council Impact Accelerator Award (*Mindfulness, Behaviour Change and Psychological Capital*), which ran between 2014 and 2016.

We also received small amounts of funding support from the Welsh Government, Global Action Plan and Ogilvy Change, which supported the delivery of the mindfulness and behaviour change interventions described in Chapter 9. The funding we received from these organizations did not impact upon the way in which we interpreted the data that emerged from the trials. Each organization was interested in discovering the impact of the trials we ran, but in no instance was funding dependent upon the nature of the results that emerged.

The main methodology deployed in the gathering of the data on which this book is based was in-depth, informal interviews. These interviews were transcribed and shared with participants to ensure that they reflected their views and beliefs. Where necessary, we have sought to preserve the anonymity of participants. We are grateful to the following organizations/individuals for participating in our research interviews:

Action for Happiness
Action on Smoking and Health (UK)
AD Analysis
Adam Smith Institute
Association of Psychological Sciences
Behavioural Insights Team, Australia
Changelabs
COIN
Consensus
Corporate Culture
Dutch Council for Social Development (RMO)
Dutch Government ministries (Ministry of Internal Affairs; Ministry of
    Economic Affairs; Ministry of Infrastructure and Environment)
Financial Services Authority (UK)
Food and Drink Federation (UK)
Global Action Plan
GreeNudge (Norway)
Helen Hamlyn Centre for Design
Institute for Economic Affairs
Institute for Government
iNudgeyou
National Institute on Aging (USA)
National Science Council (USA)
New Economics Foundation
NHS Choices (UK)
NSOB (Netherlands)
Nutrition Network Wales
Ogilvy Change
Peter John
PIRC
Policy Exchange
School Food Trust (UK)
Self-Regulation Lab
Singapore Government (Ministry of Trade and Industry; Public Service
    Division)
Social Marketing Foundation
Sustrans
The Behavioural Architects
The Social Brain Centre (RSA)
The Social Marketing Centre
UK Government departments (Department of Energy and Climate Change;
    Department of Work and Pensions; Department of Environment, Food
    and Rural Affairs; Department of Health; Cabinet Office).
Welsh Government

World Economic Forum (Global Agenda Council on Neuroscience and
   Behaviour)
WRAP
Yolande Stengers
Young Foundation

For purposes of confidentiality, not all of the organizations that we interviewed are
listed here.

The mindfulness and behaviour change interventions we recount in Chapter 9
were based upon a series of in-depth interviews and online questionnaires. Further
details of the methods we deployed within these studies is available in the analysis
reports that were produced in association with these interventions: see https://
changingbehaviours.wordpress.com/2016/06/10/mindfulness-and-behaviour-
change-exploring-the-connections/ [accessed 31 March 2017].

Selected transcripts, questionnaire data, ethical procedure forms and interview
and questionnaire schedules related to this project have been deposited with the
UK Data Service. These files and data sets can be freely downloaded from http://
reshare.ukdataservice.ac.uk/851870/ [accessed 31 March 2017].

INDEX